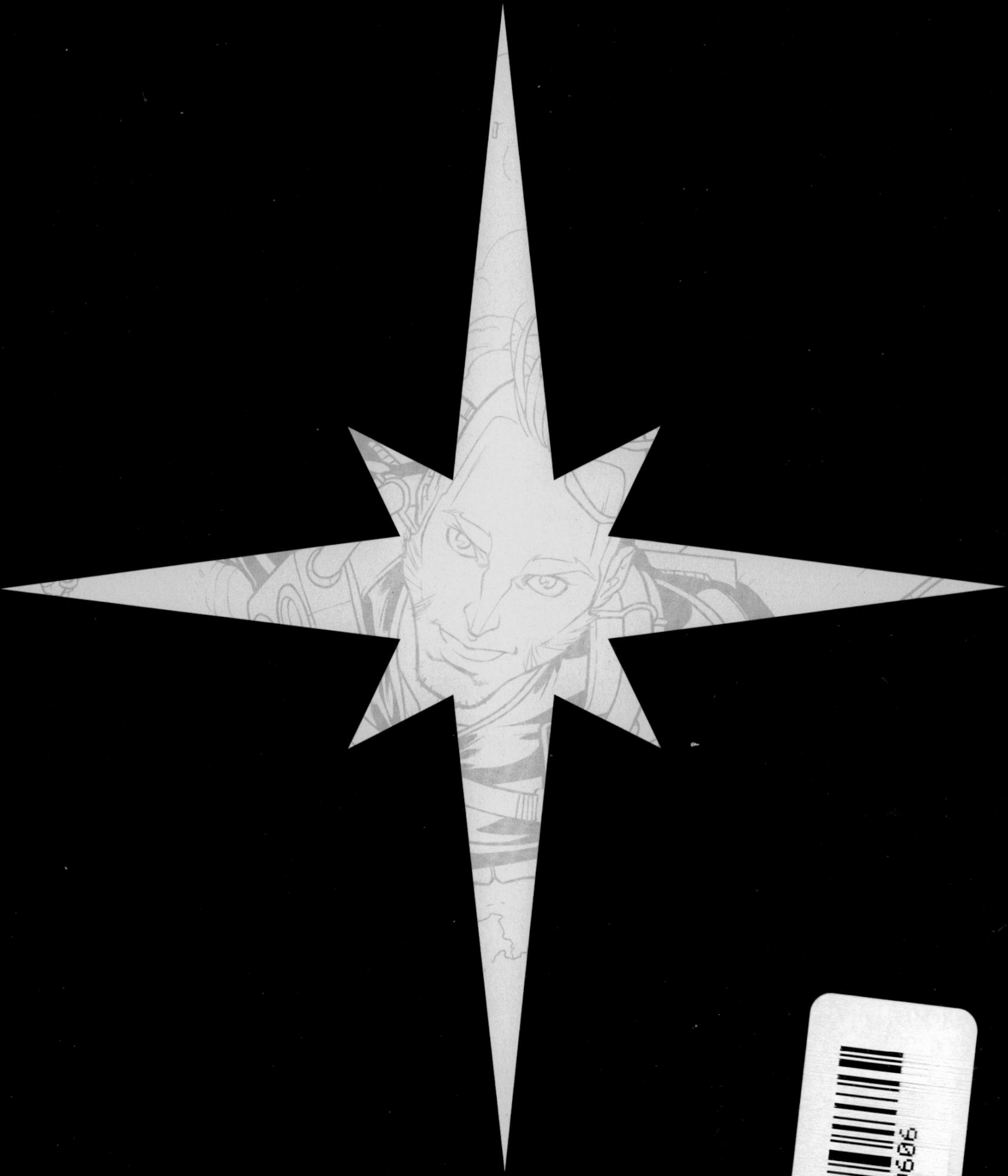

LONGSHOT SAVES the MARVEL UNIVERSE

WRITER
CHRISTOPHER HASTINGS

PENCILERS
JACOPO CAMAGNI (#1-4) WITH
VICTOR CALDERON-ZURITA (#3-4)

INKERS
JACOPO CAMAGNI (#1-4)
WITH **TERRY PALLOT** (#3-4)

COLORISTS
MATT MILLA (#1-4) WITH **JAMES CAMPBELL** (#3)

LETTERER
VC'S JOE CARAMAGNA

COVER ARTIST
DAVID NAKAYAMA

EDITOR
JORDAN D. WHITE

Collection Editor: Alex Starbuck Editors, Special Projects: Jennifer Grünwald & Mark D. Beazley
Senior Editor, Special Projects: Jeff Youngquist SVP Print, Sales & Marketing: David Gabriel Book Design: Jeff Powell
Editor in Chief: Axel Alonso Chief Creative Officer: Joe Quesada Publisher: Dan Buckley Executive Producer: Alan Fine

LONGSHOT SAVES THE MARVEL UNIVERSE. Contains material originally published in magazine form as LONGSHOT SAVES THE MARVEL UNIVERSE #1-4. First printing 2014. ISBN# 978-0-7851-9012-7. Published by MARVEL WORLDWIDE, INC., a subsidiary of MARVEL ENTERTAINMENT, LLC. OFFICE OF PUBLICATION: 135 West 50th Street, New York, NY 10020. **Printed in Canada.** ALAN FINE, EVP - Office of the President, Marvel Worldwide, Inc. and EVP & CMO Marvel Characters B.V.; DAN BUCKLEY, Publisher & President - Print, Animation & Digital Divisions; JOE QUESADA, Chief Creative Officer; TOM BREVOORT, SVP of Publishing; DAVID BOGART, SVP of Operations & Procurement, Publishing; C.B. CEBULSKI, SVP of Creator & Content Development; DAVID GABRIEL, SVP Print, Sales & Marketing; JIM O'KEEFE, VP of Operations & Logistics; DAN CARR, Executive Director of Publishing Technology; SUSAN CRESPI, Editorial Operations Manager; ALEX MORALES, Publishing Operations Manager; STAN LEE, Chairman Emeritus. For information regarding advertising in Marvel Comics or on Marvel.com, please contact Niza Disla, Director of Marvel Partnerships, at ndisla@marvel.com. For Marvel subscription inquiries, please call 800-217-9158. **Manufactured between 3/28/2014 and 5/5/2014 by SOLISCO PRINTERS, SCOTT, QC, CANADA.**

10 9 8 7 6 5 4 3 2 1

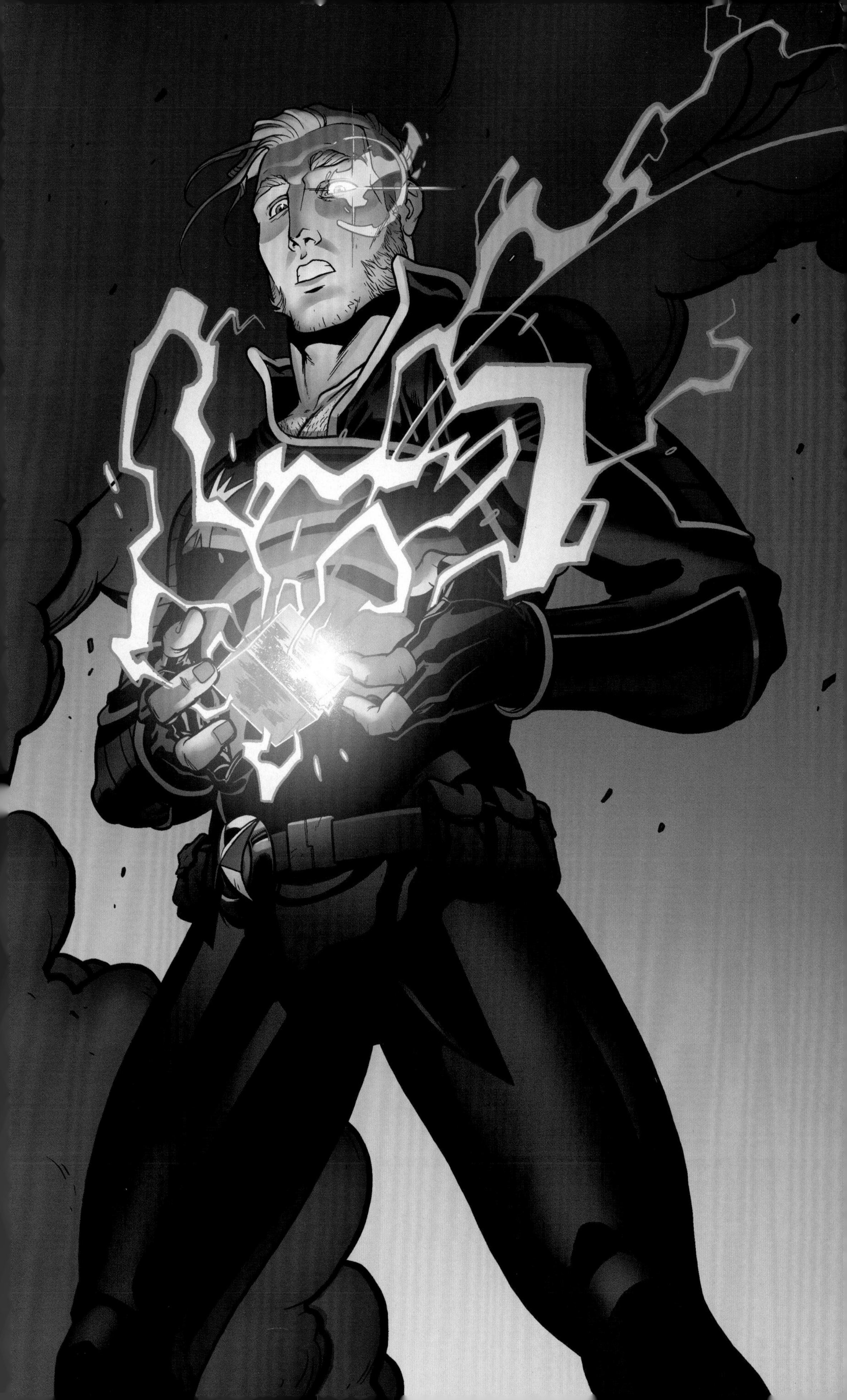

Former Mojoverse TV star, former Hollywood stuntman, former beau of pop princess Dazzler, former X-Man, former X-Factorian...Longshot is no stranger to the limelight, and he is only too ready to become your new favorite character!

Because of his long association with the X-Teams, many assume Longshot to be a mutant. Not so! He's a genetically created being from another universe. Be he sees how you might be confused by that and forgives you.

What are his powers, you ask? How does supernaturally good luck sound? That's right—so long as his motives are pure and good, things have a way of just working out for Longshot. Not enough? How about psychometry— the ability to mentally read past events from objects by touching them? Plus, he's unnaturally attractive. Seriously—it's a super-power. And he's GOT IT.

Oh, and his bones are hollow, so he weighs like...80 pounds.

Anyway, now that you've seen him, admit it—you love him. You love him with the mullet he's got here, and you'll love him with his new haircut. Know how I know?

Lucky guess.

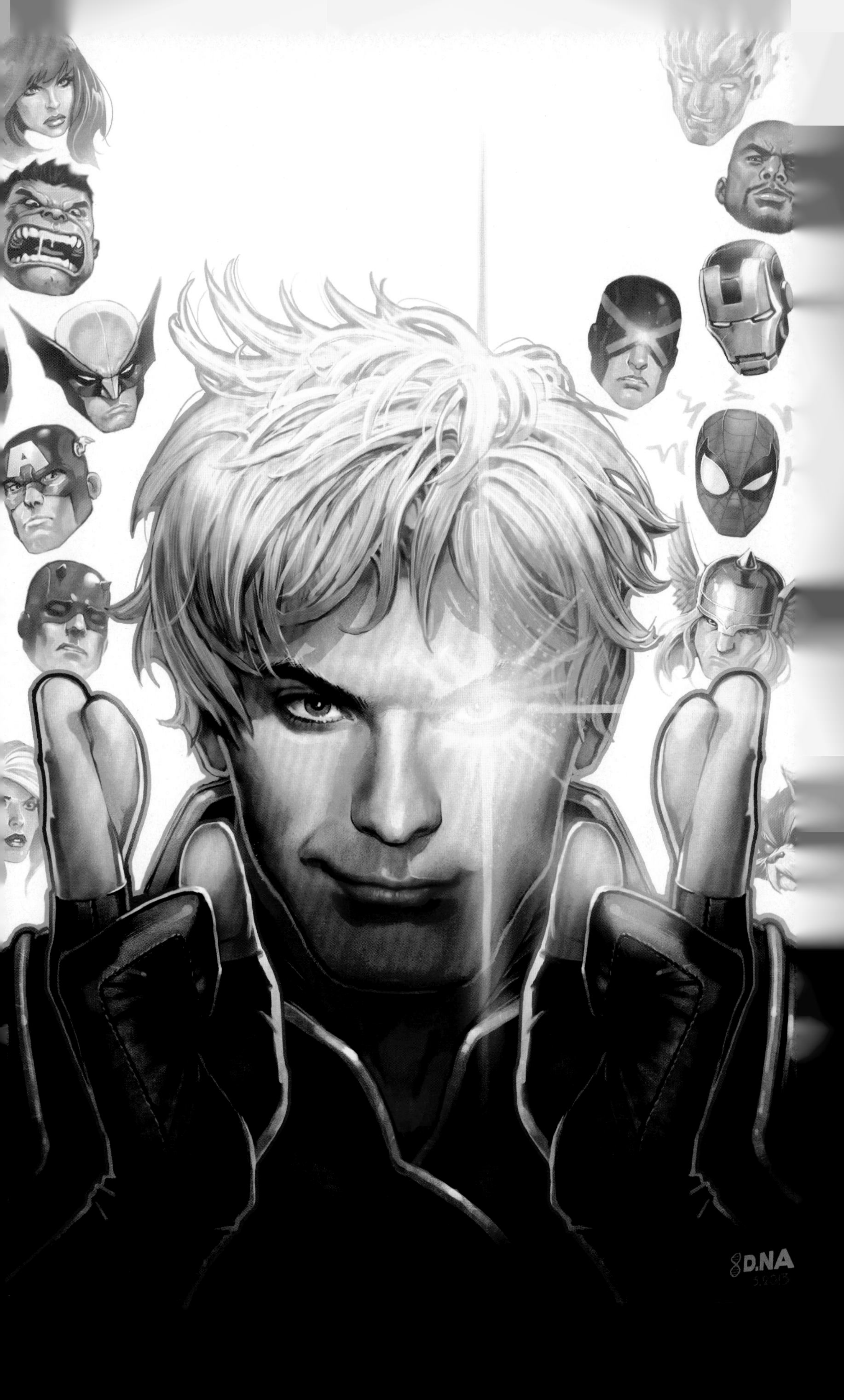
D.NA

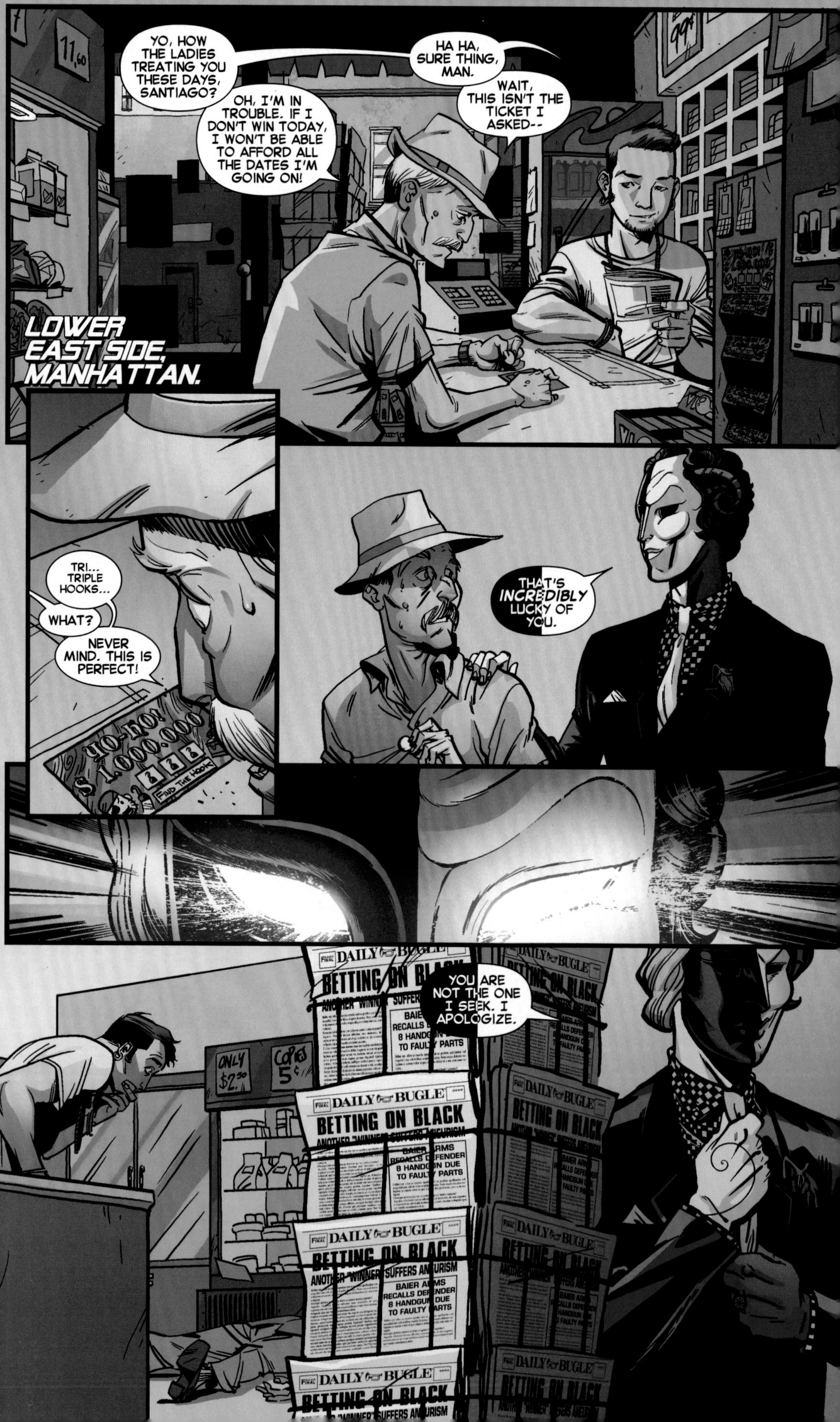
YO, HOW THE LADIES TREATING YOU THESE DAYS, SANTIAGO?
OH, I'M IN TROUBLE. IF I DON'T WIN TODAY, I WON'T BE ABLE TO AFFORD ALL THE DATES I'M GOING ON!
HA HA, SURE THING, MAN.
WAIT, THIS ISN'T THE TICKET I ASKED--
LOWER EAST SIDE, MANHATTAN.
TRI... TRIPLE HOOKS...
WHAT?
NEVER MIND. THIS IS PERFECT!
YO-HO! $1,000,000
FIND THE HOOK
THAT'S INCREDIBLY LUCKY OF YOU.
YOU ARE NOT THE ONE I SEEK. I APOLOGIZE.
ONLY $2.50
COPIES 5¢
DAILY BUGLE
BETTING ON BLACK
ANOTHER "WINNER" SUFFERS ANEURISM
BAIER ARMS RECALLS DEFENDER 8 HANDGUN DUE TO FAULTY PARTS

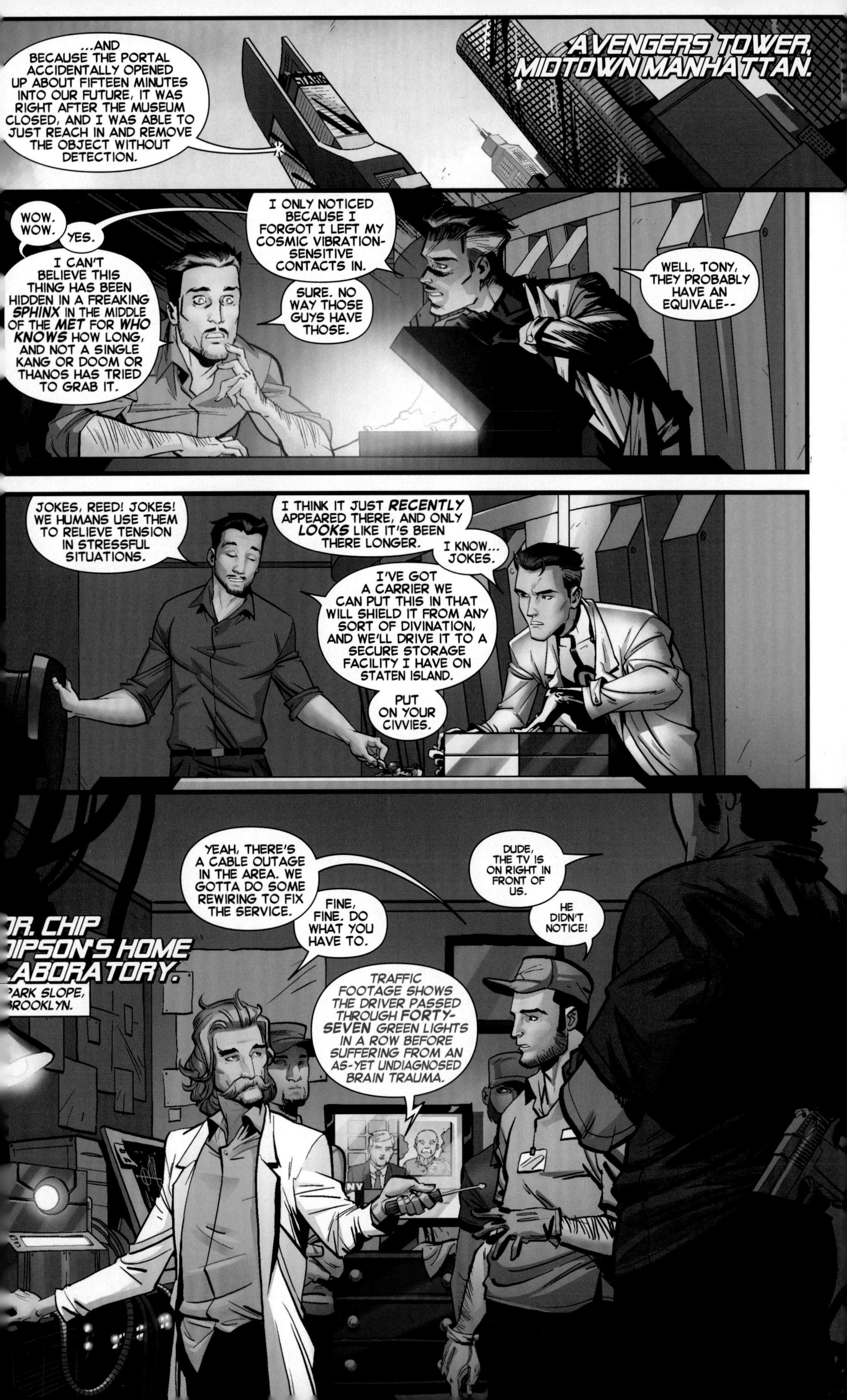
AVENGERS TOWER, MIDTOWN MANHATTAN.
...AND BECAUSE THE PORTAL ACCIDENTALLY OPENED UP ABOUT FIFTEEN MINUTES INTO OUR FUTURE, IT WAS RIGHT AFTER THE MUSEUM CLOSED, AND I WAS ABLE TO JUST REACH IN AND REMOVE THE OBJECT WITHOUT DETECTION.
WOW. WOW.
YES.
I CAN'T BELIEVE THIS THING HAS BEEN HIDDEN IN A FREAKING SPHINX IN THE MIDDLE OF THE MET FOR WHO KNOWS HOW LONG, AND NOT A SINGLE KANG OR DOOM OR THANOS HAS TRIED TO GRAB IT.
I ONLY NOTICED BECAUSE I FORGOT I LEFT MY COSMIC VIBRATION-SENSITIVE CONTACTS IN.
SURE. NO WAY THOSE GUYS HAVE THOSE.
WELL, TONY, THEY PROBABLY HAVE AN EQUIVALE--
JOKES, REED! JOKES! WE HUMANS USE THEM TO RELIEVE TENSION IN STRESSFUL SITUATIONS.
I THINK IT JUST RECENTLY APPEARED THERE, AND ONLY LOOKS LIKE IT'S BEEN THERE LONGER.
I KNOW... JOKES.
I'VE GOT A CARRIER WE CAN PUT THIS IN THAT WILL SHIELD IT FROM ANY SORT OF DIVINATION, AND WE'LL DRIVE IT TO A SECURE STORAGE FACILITY I HAVE ON STATEN ISLAND.
PUT ON YOUR CIVVIES.
R. CHIP IPSON'S HOME ABORATORY.
ARK SLOPE, ROOKLYN.
YEAH, THERE'S A CABLE OUTAGE IN THE AREA. WE GOTTA DO SOME REWIRING TO FIX THE SERVICE.
FINE, FINE. DO WHAT YOU HAVE TO.
DUDE, THE TV IS ON RIGHT IN FRONT OF US.
HE DIDN'T NOTICE!
TRAFFIC FOOTAGE SHOWS THE DRIVER PASSED THROUGH FORTY-SEVEN GREEN LIGHTS IN A ROW BEFORE SUFFERING FROM AN AS-YET UNDIAGNOSED BRAIN TRAUMA.

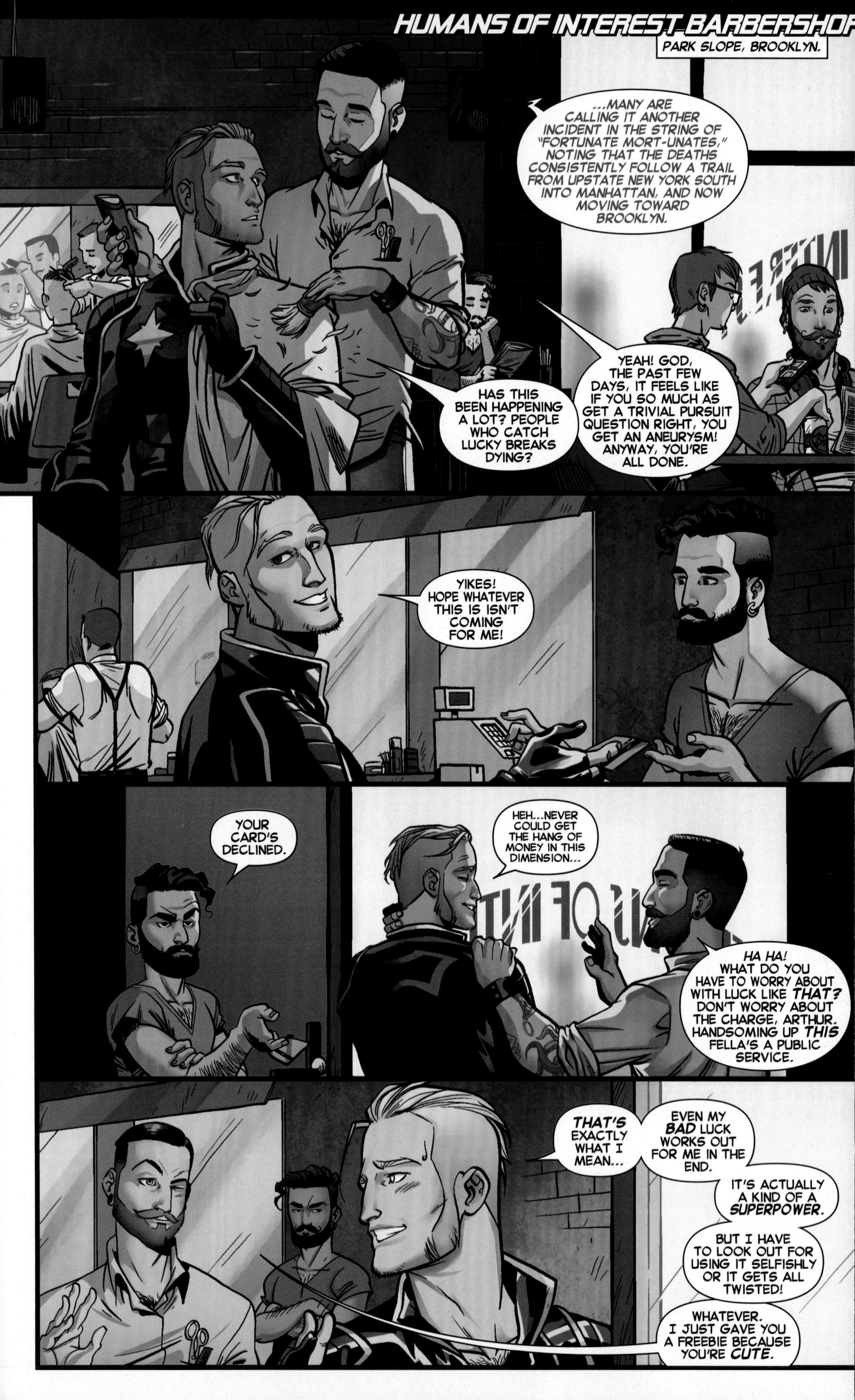

HUMANS OF INTEREST BARBERSHOP
PARK SLOPE, BROOKLYN.
...MANY ARE CALLING IT ANOTHER INCIDENT IN THE STRING OF "FORTUNATE MORT-UNATES," NOTING THAT THE DEATHS CONSISTENTLY FOLLOW A TRAIL FROM UPSTATE NEW YORK SOUTH INTO MANHATTAN, AND NOW MOVING TOWARD BROOKLYN.
HAS THIS BEEN HAPPENING A LOT? PEOPLE WHO CATCH LUCKY BREAKS DYING?
YEAH! GOD, THE PAST FEW DAYS, IT FEELS LIKE IF YOU SO MUCH AS GET A TRIVIAL PURSUIT QUESTION RIGHT, YOU GET AN ANEURYSM! ANYWAY, YOU'RE ALL DONE.
YIKES! HOPE WHATEVER THIS IS ISN'T COMING FOR ME!
YOUR CARD'S DECLINED.
HEH...NEVER COULD GET THE HANG OF MONEY IN THIS DIMENSION...
HA HA! WHAT DO YOU HAVE TO WORRY ABOUT WITH LUCK LIKE THAT? DON'T WORRY ABOUT THE CHARGE, ARTHUR. HANDSOMING UP THIS FELLA'S A PUBLIC SERVICE.
THAT'S EXACTLY WHAT I MEAN...
EVEN MY BAD LUCK WORKS OUT FOR ME IN THE END.
IT'S ACTUALLY A KIND OF A SUPERPOWER.
BUT I HAVE TO LOOK OUT FOR USING IT SELFISHLY OR IT GETS ALL TWISTED!
WHATEVER. I JUST GAVE YOU A FREEBIE BECAUSE YOU'RE CUTE.

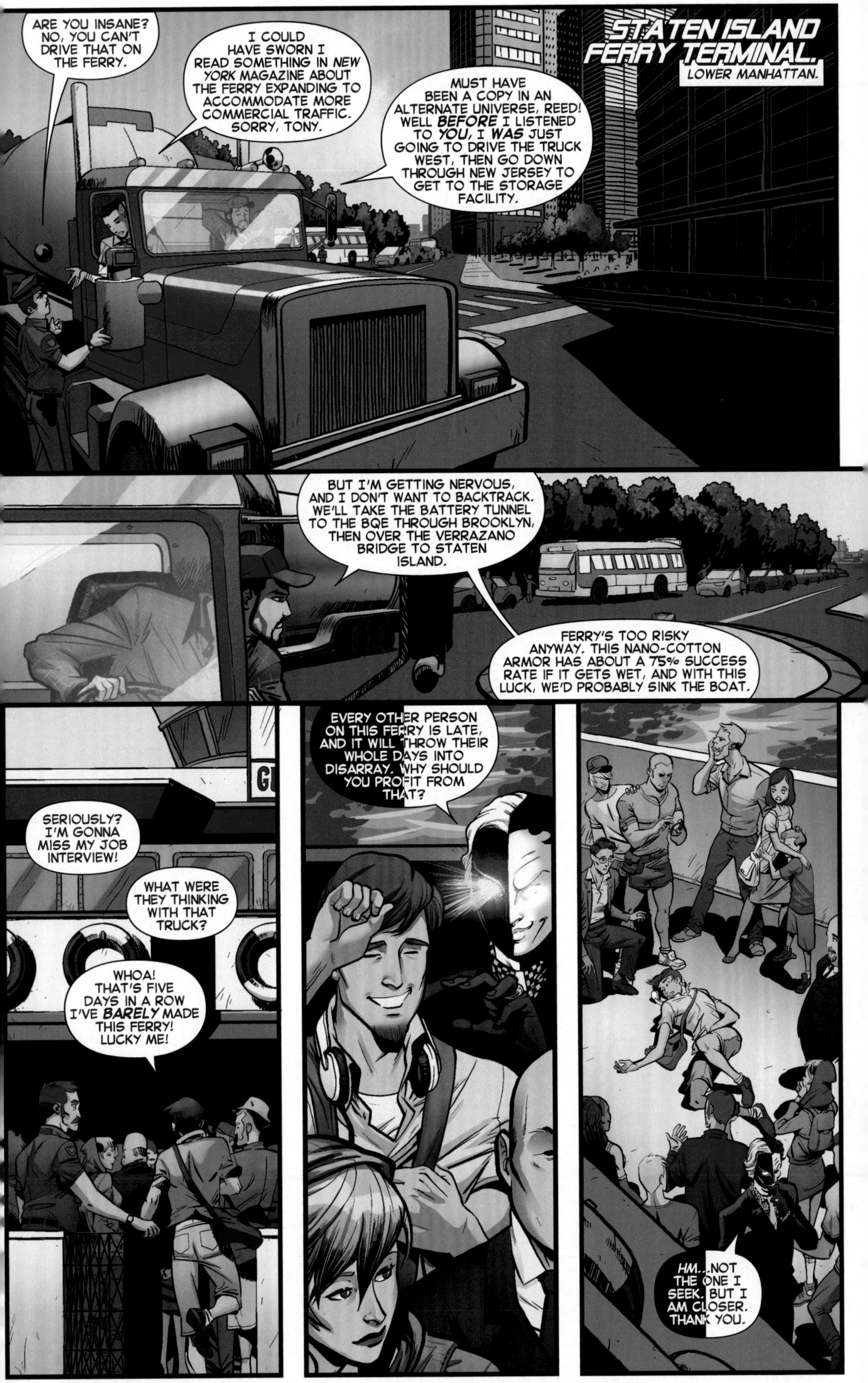
STATEN ISLAND FERRY TERMINAL.
LOWER MANHATTAN.
ARE YOU INSANE? NO, YOU CAN'T DRIVE THAT ON THE FERRY.
I COULD HAVE SWORN I READ SOMETHING IN NEW YORK MAGAZINE ABOUT THE FERRY EXPANDING TO ACCOMMODATE MORE COMMERCIAL TRAFFIC. SORRY, TONY.
MUST HAVE BEEN A COPY IN AN ALTERNATE UNIVERSE, REED! WELL BEFORE I LISTENED TO YOU, I WAS JUST GOING TO DRIVE THE TRUCK WEST, THEN GO DOWN THROUGH NEW JERSEY TO GET TO THE STORAGE FACILITY.
BUT I'M GETTING NERVOUS, AND I DON'T WANT TO BACKTRACK. WE'LL TAKE THE BATTERY TUNNEL TO THE BQE THROUGH BROOKLYN, THEN OVER THE VERRAZANO BRIDGE TO STATEN ISLAND.
FERRY'S TOO RISKY ANYWAY. THIS NANO-COTTON ARMOR HAS ABOUT A 75% SUCCESS RATE IF IT GETS WET, AND WITH THIS LUCK, WE'D PROBABLY SINK THE BOAT.
SERIOUSLY? I'M GONNA MISS MY JOB INTERVIEW!
WHAT WERE THEY THINKING WITH THAT TRUCK?
WHOA! THAT'S FIVE DAYS IN A ROW I'VE BARELY MADE THIS FERRY! LUCKY ME!
EVERY OTHER PERSON ON THIS FERRY IS LATE, AND IT WILL THROW THEIR WHOLE DAYS INTO DISARRAY. WHY SHOULD YOU PROFIT FROM THAT?
HM...NOT THE ONE I SEEK. BUT I AM CLOSER. THANK YOU.

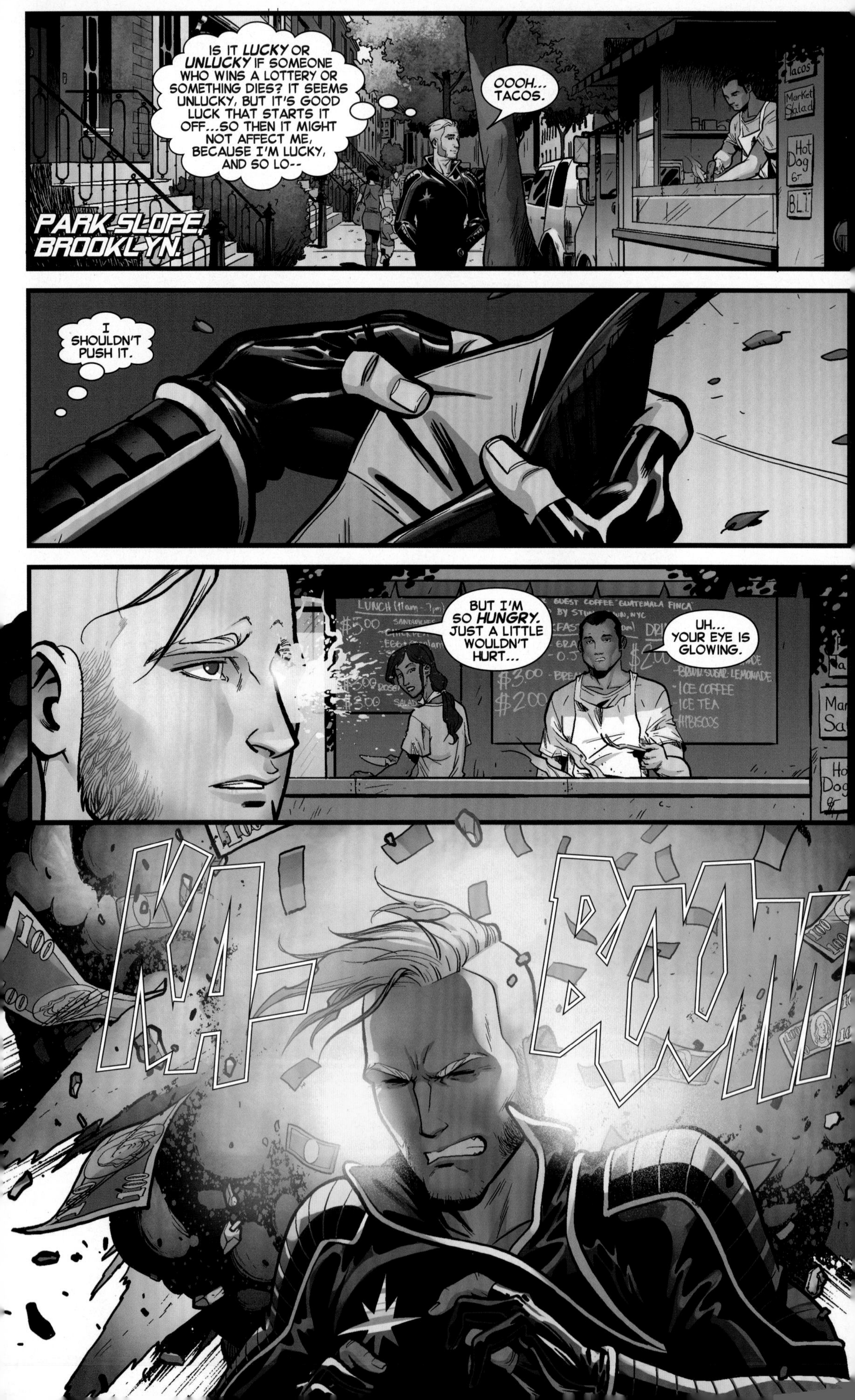
PARK SLOPE, BROOKLYN.
IS IT LUCKY OR UNLUCKY IF SOMEONE WHO WINS A LOTTERY OR SOMETHING DIES? IT SEEMS UNLUCKY, BUT IT'S GOOD LUCK THAT STARTS IT OFF...SO THEN IT MIGHT NOT AFFECT ME, BECAUSE I'M LUCKY, AND SO LO--
OOOH... TACOS.
Tacos
Market Salad
Hot Dog
BLT
I SHOULDN'T PUSH IT.
BUT I'M SO HUNGRY. JUST A LITTLE WOULDN'T HURT...
UH... YOUR EYE IS GLOWING.
KA-BOOM

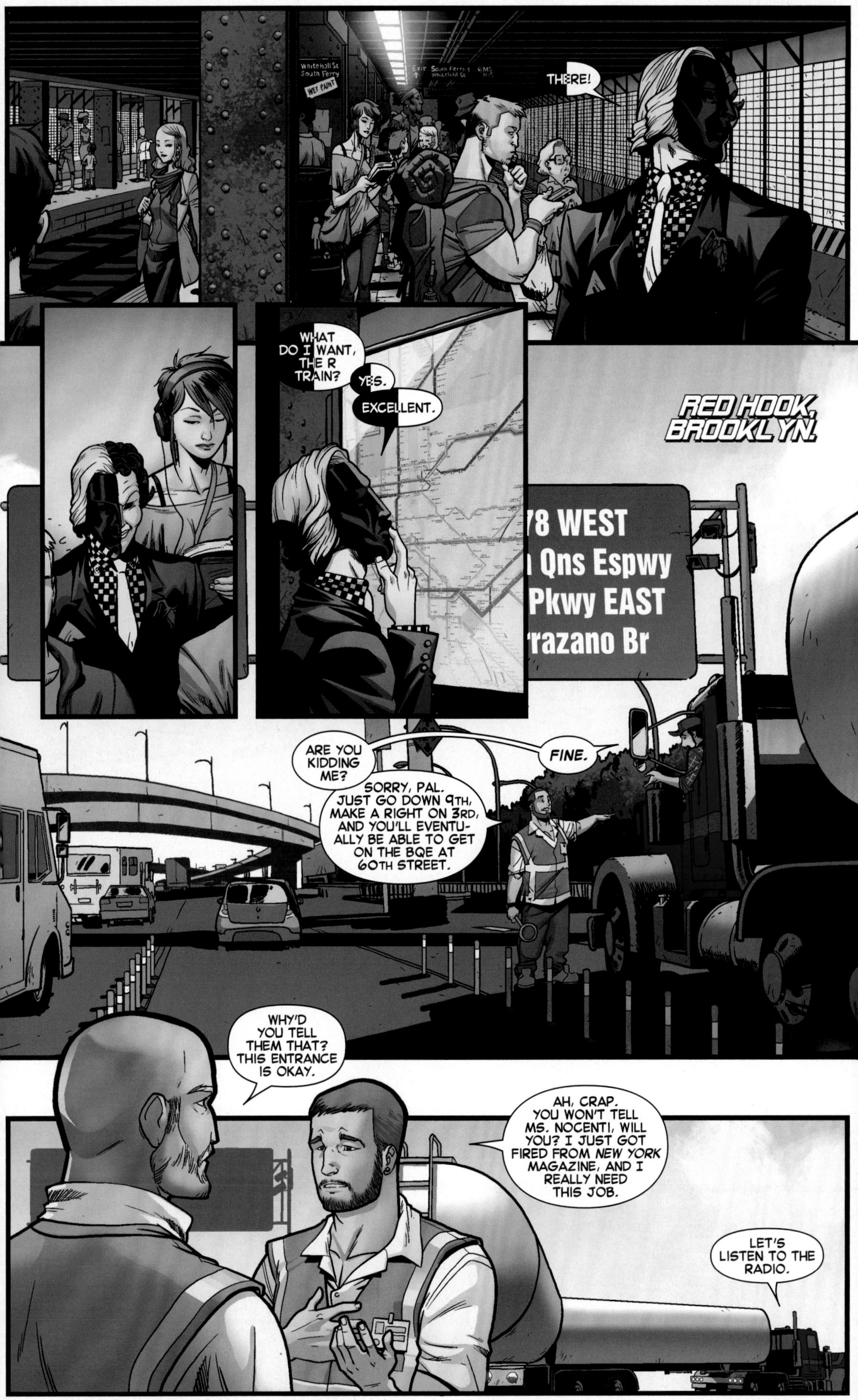
Whitehall St South Ferry
WET PAINT
Exit South Ferry Whitehall St
THERE!
WHAT DO I WANT, THE R TRAIN?
YES.
EXCELLENT.
RED HOOK, BROOKLYN.
78 WEST
n Qns Espwy
Pkwy EAST
rrazano Br
ARE YOU KIDDING ME?
FINE.
SORRY, PAL. JUST GO DOWN 9TH, MAKE A RIGHT ON 3RD, AND YOU'LL EVENTUALLY BE ABLE TO GET ON THE BQE AT 60TH STREET.
WHY'D YOU TELL THEM THAT? THIS ENTRANCE IS OKAY.
AH, CRAP. YOU WON'T TELL MS. NOCENTI, WILL YOU? I JUST GOT FIRED FROM *NEW YORK* MAGAZINE, AND I REALLY NEED THIS JOB.
LET'S LISTEN TO THE RADIO.

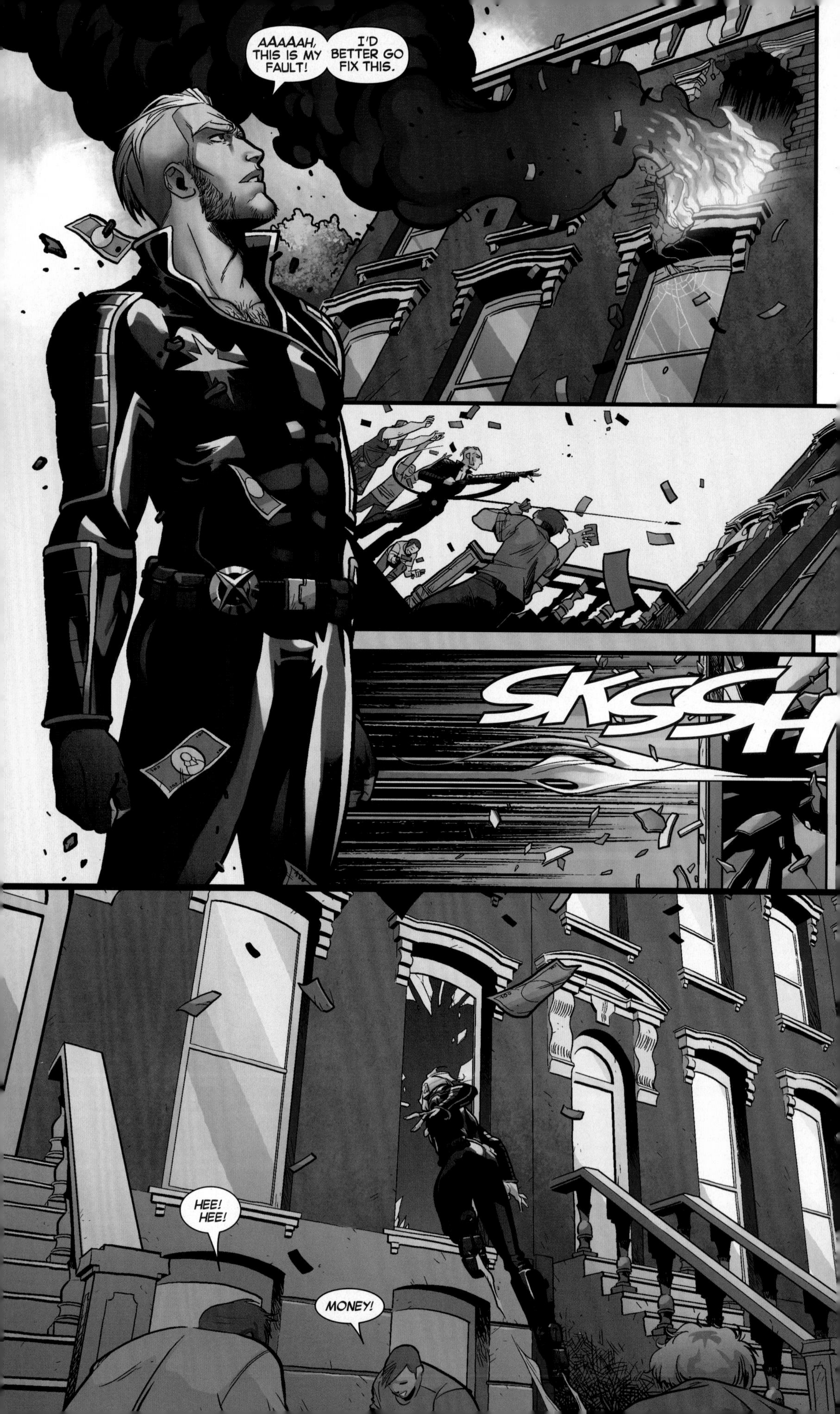
AAAAAH, THIS IS MY FAULT!
I'D BETTER GO FIX THIS.
SKSSH
HEE! HEE!
MONEY!

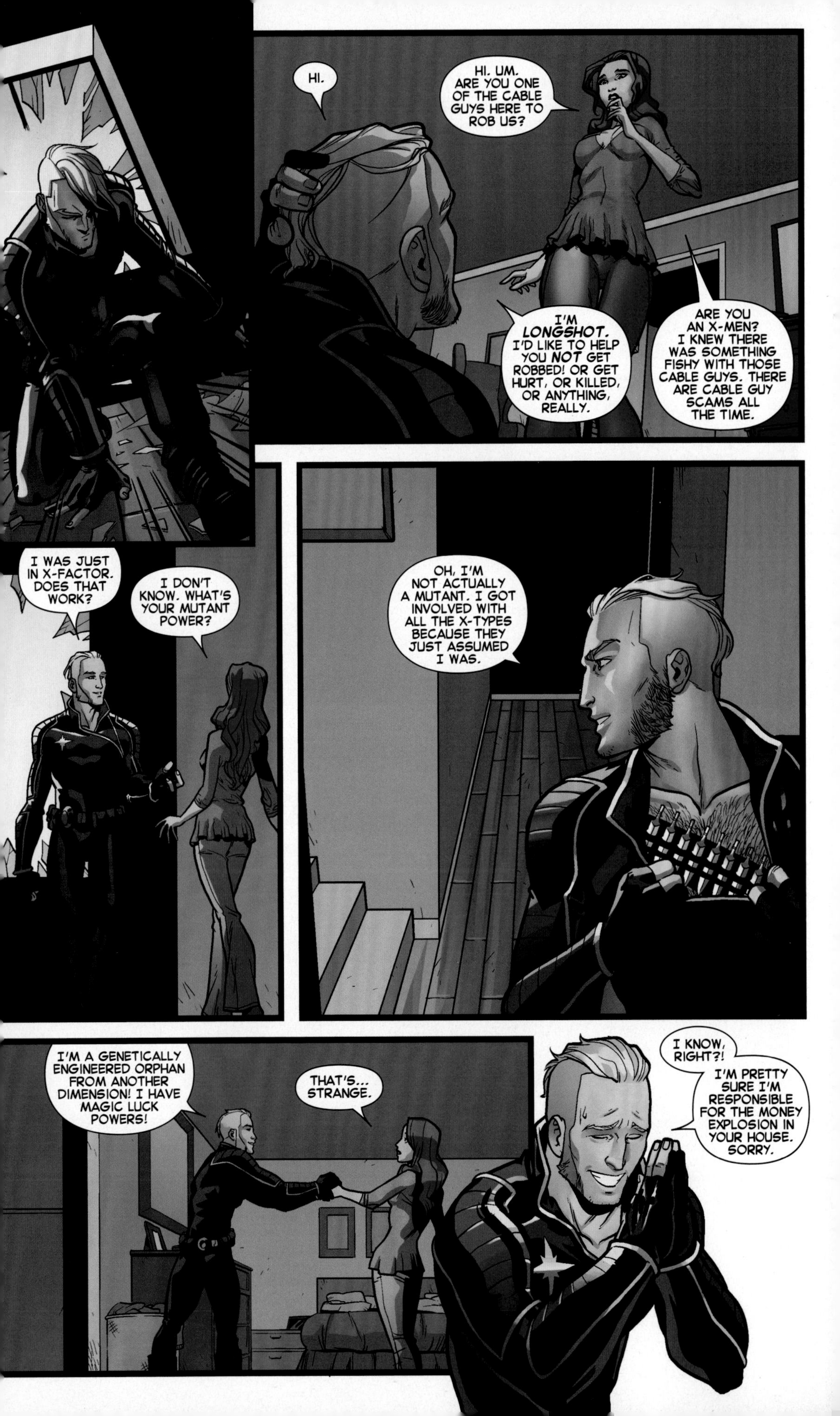
HI.
HI. UM. ARE YOU ONE OF THE CABLE GUYS HERE TO ROB US?
I'M LONGSHOT. I'D LIKE TO HELP YOU NOT GET ROBBED! OR GET HURT, OR KILLED, OR ANYTHING, REALLY.
ARE YOU AN X-MEN? I KNEW THERE WAS SOMETHING FISHY WITH THOSE CABLE GUYS. THERE ARE CABLE GUY SCAMS ALL THE TIME.
I WAS JUST IN X-FACTOR. DOES THAT WORK?
I DON'T KNOW. WHAT'S YOUR MUTANT POWER?
OH, I'M NOT ACTUALLY A MUTANT. I GOT INVOLVED WITH ALL THE X-TYPES BECAUSE THEY JUST ASSUMED I WAS.
I'M A GENETICALLY ENGINEERED ORPHAN FROM ANOTHER DIMENSION! I HAVE MAGIC LUCK POWERS!
THAT'S... STRANGE.
I KNOW, RIGHT?!
I'M PRETTY SURE I'M RESPONSIBLE FOR THE MONEY EXPLOSION IN YOUR HOUSE. SORRY.

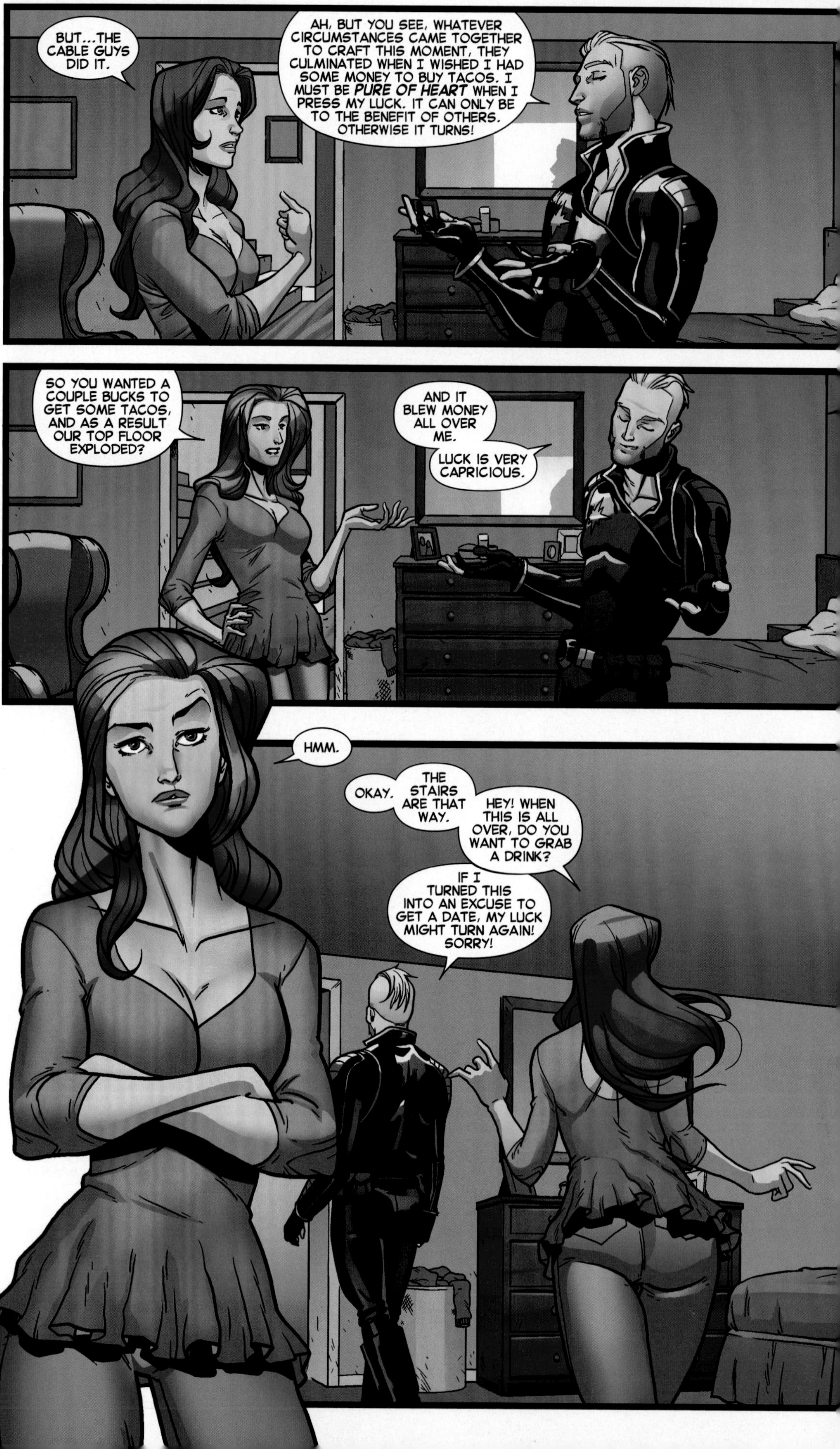
BUT...THE CABLE GUYS DID IT.
AH, BUT YOU SEE, WHATEVER CIRCUMSTANCES CAME TOGETHER TO CRAFT THIS MOMENT, THEY CULMINATED WHEN I WISHED I HAD SOME MONEY TO BUY TACOS. I MUST BE PURE OF HEART WHEN I PRESS MY LUCK. IT CAN ONLY BE TO THE BENEFIT OF OTHERS. OTHERWISE IT TURNS!
SO YOU WANTED A COUPLE BUCKS TO GET SOME TACOS, AND AS A RESULT OUR TOP FLOOR EXPLODED?
AND IT BLEW MONEY ALL OVER ME.
LUCK IS VERY CAPRICIOUS.
HMM.
OKAY.
THE STAIRS ARE THAT WAY.
HEY! WHEN THIS IS ALL OVER, DO YOU WANT TO GRAB A DRINK?
IF I TURNED THIS INTO AN EXCUSE TO GET A DATE, MY LUCK MIGHT TURN AGAIN! SORRY!

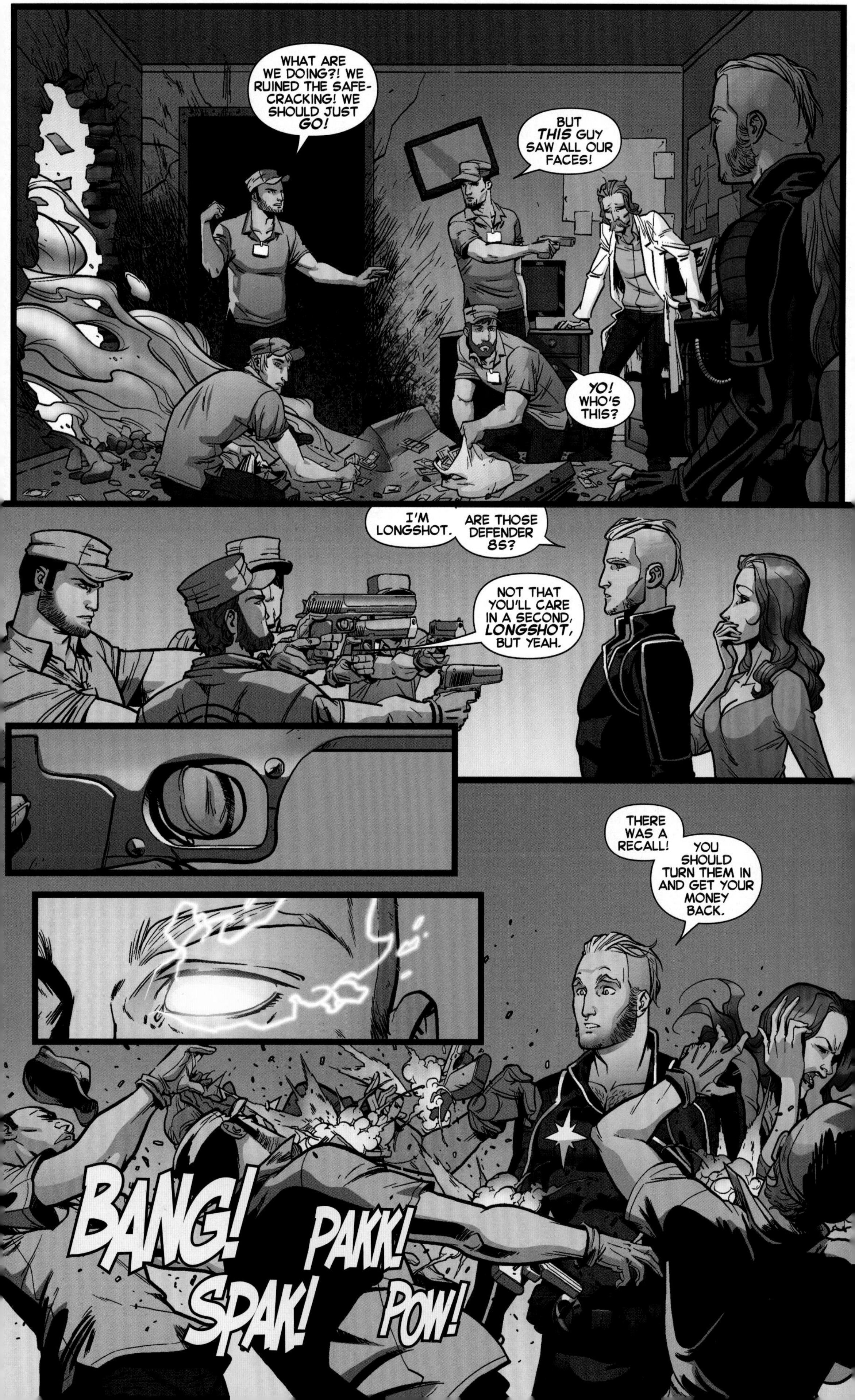

WHAT ARE WE DOING?! WE RUINED THE SAFE-CRACKING! WE SHOULD JUST GO!
BUT THIS GUY SAW ALL OUR FACES!
YO! WHO'S THIS?
I'M LONGSHOT.
ARE THOSE DEFENDER 8S?
NOT THAT YOU'LL CARE IN A SECOND, LONGSHOT, BUT YEAH.
THERE WAS A RECALL!
YOU SHOULD TURN THEM IN AND GET YOUR MONEY BACK.
BANG!
PAKK!
SPAK!
POW!

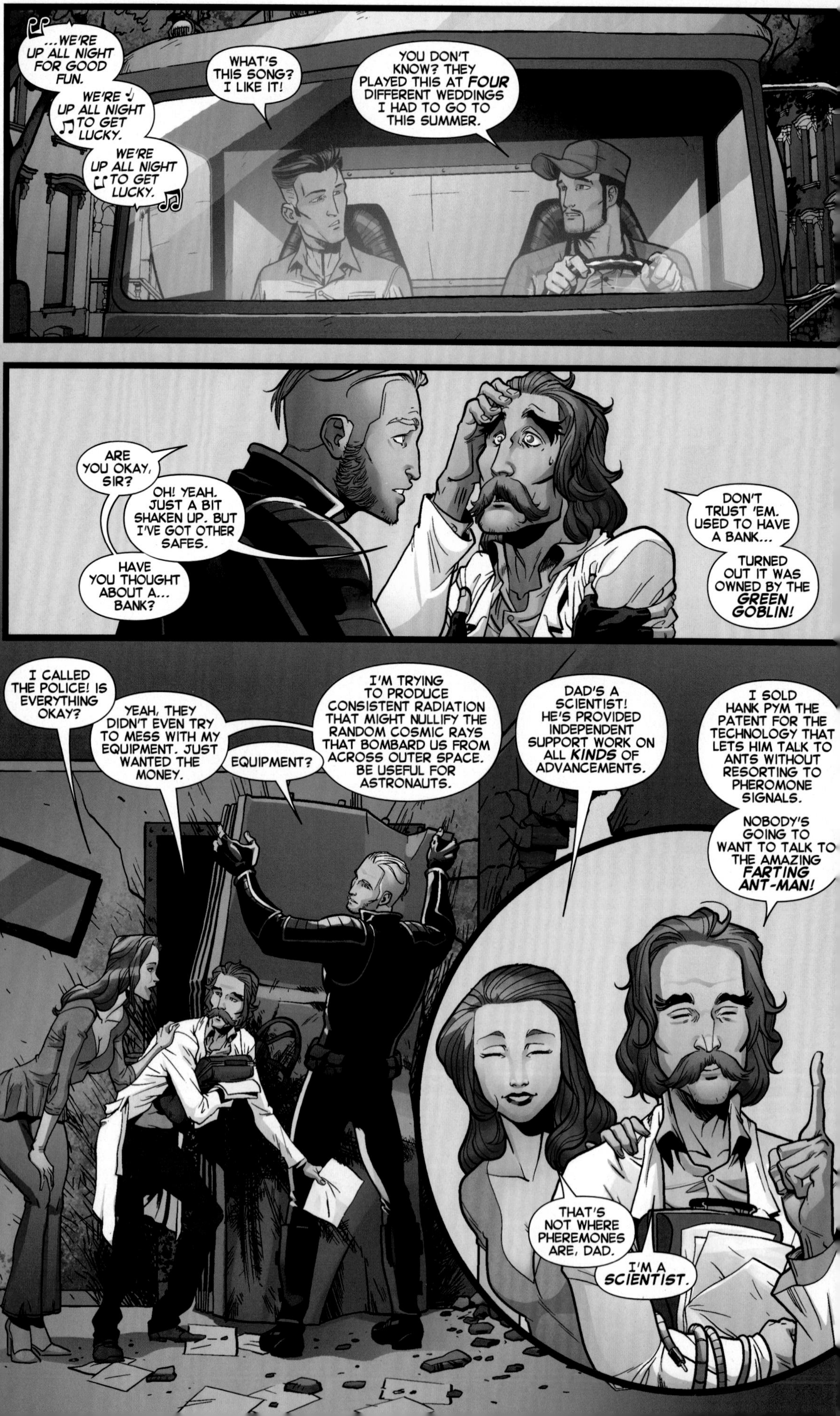

...WE'RE UP ALL NIGHT FOR GOOD FUN.
WE'RE UP ALL NIGHT TO GET LUCKY.
WE'RE UP ALL NIGHT TO GET LUCKY.
WHAT'S THIS SONG? I LIKE IT!
YOU DON'T KNOW? THEY PLAYED THIS AT FOUR DIFFERENT WEDDINGS I HAD TO GO TO THIS SUMMER.
ARE YOU OKAY, SIR?
OH! YEAH. JUST A BIT SHAKEN UP. BUT I'VE GOT OTHER SAFES.
HAVE YOU THOUGHT ABOUT A... BANK?
DON'T TRUST 'EM. USED TO HAVE A BANK...
TURNED OUT IT WAS OWNED BY THE GREEN GOBLIN!
I CALLED THE POLICE! IS EVERYTHING OKAY?
YEAH, THEY DIDN'T EVEN TRY TO MESS WITH MY EQUIPMENT. JUST WANTED THE MONEY.
EQUIPMENT?
I'M TRYING TO PRODUCE CONSISTENT RADIATION THAT MIGHT NULLIFY THE RANDOM COSMIC RAYS THAT BOMBARD US FROM ACROSS OUTER SPACE. BE USEFUL FOR ASTRONAUTS.
DAD'S A SCIENTIST! HE'S PROVIDED INDEPENDENT SUPPORT WORK ON ALL KINDS OF ADVANCEMENTS.
I SOLD HANK PYM THE PATENT FOR THE TECHNOLOGY THAT LETS HIM TALK TO ANTS WITHOUT RESORTING TO PHEROMONE SIGNALS.
NOBODY'S GOING TO WANT TO TALK TO THE AMAZING FARTING ANT-MAN!
THAT'S NOT WHERE PHEREMONES ARE, DAD.
I'M A SCIENTIST.

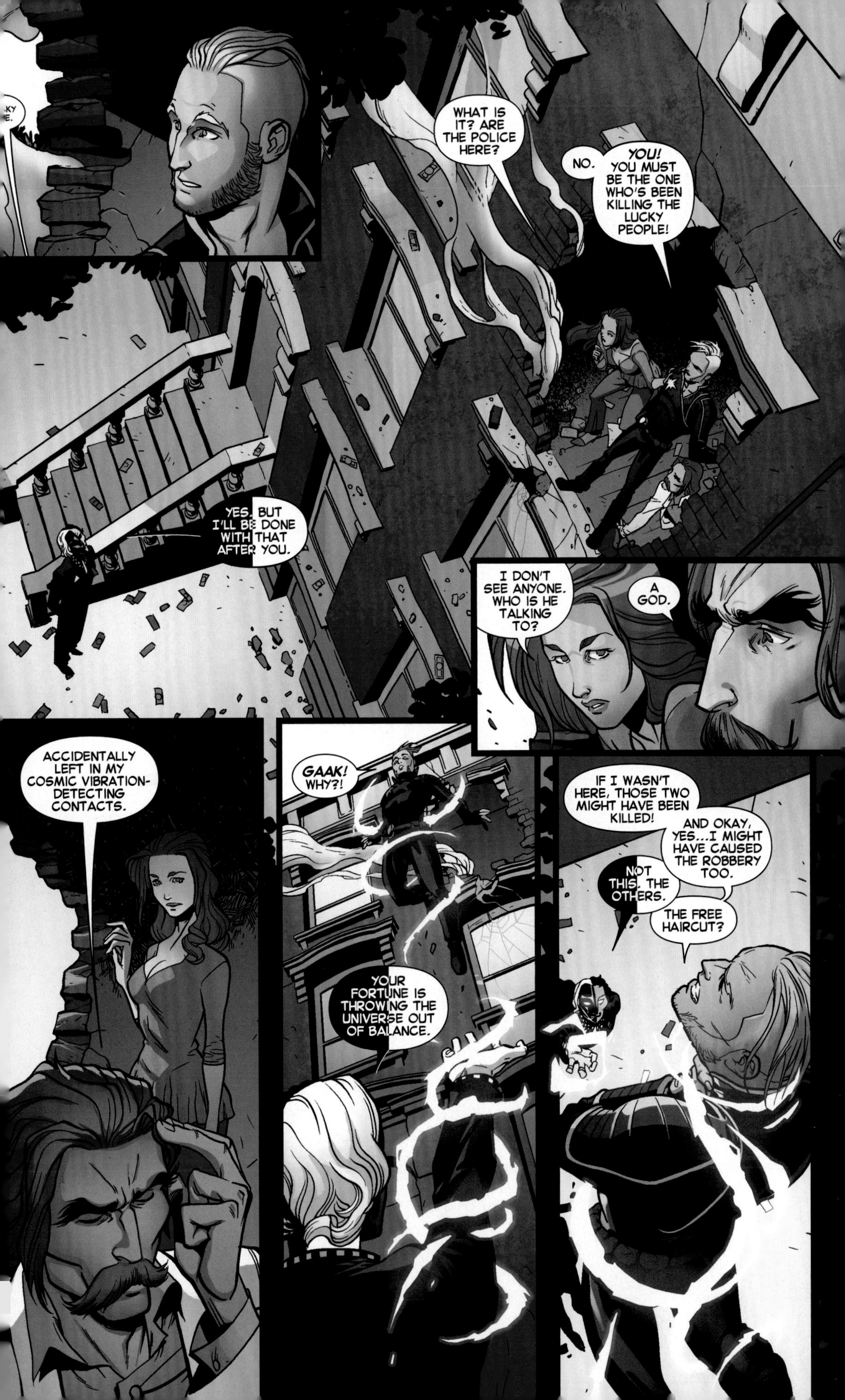

WHAT IS IT? ARE THE POLICE HERE?
NO.
YOU! YOU MUST BE THE ONE WHO'S BEEN KILLING THE LUCKY PEOPLE!
YES. BUT I'LL BE DONE WITH THAT AFTER YOU.
I DON'T SEE ANYONE. WHO IS HE TALKING TO?
A GOD.
ACCIDENTALLY LEFT IN MY COSMIC VIBRATION-DETECTING CONTACTS.
GAAK! WHY?!
YOUR FORTUNE IS THROWING THE UNIVERSE OUT OF BALANCE.
IF I WASN'T HERE, THOSE TWO MIGHT HAVE BEEN KILLED!
AND OKAY, YES...I MIGHT HAVE CAUSED THE ROBBERY TOO.
NOT THIS. THE OTHERS.
THE FREE HAIRCUT?

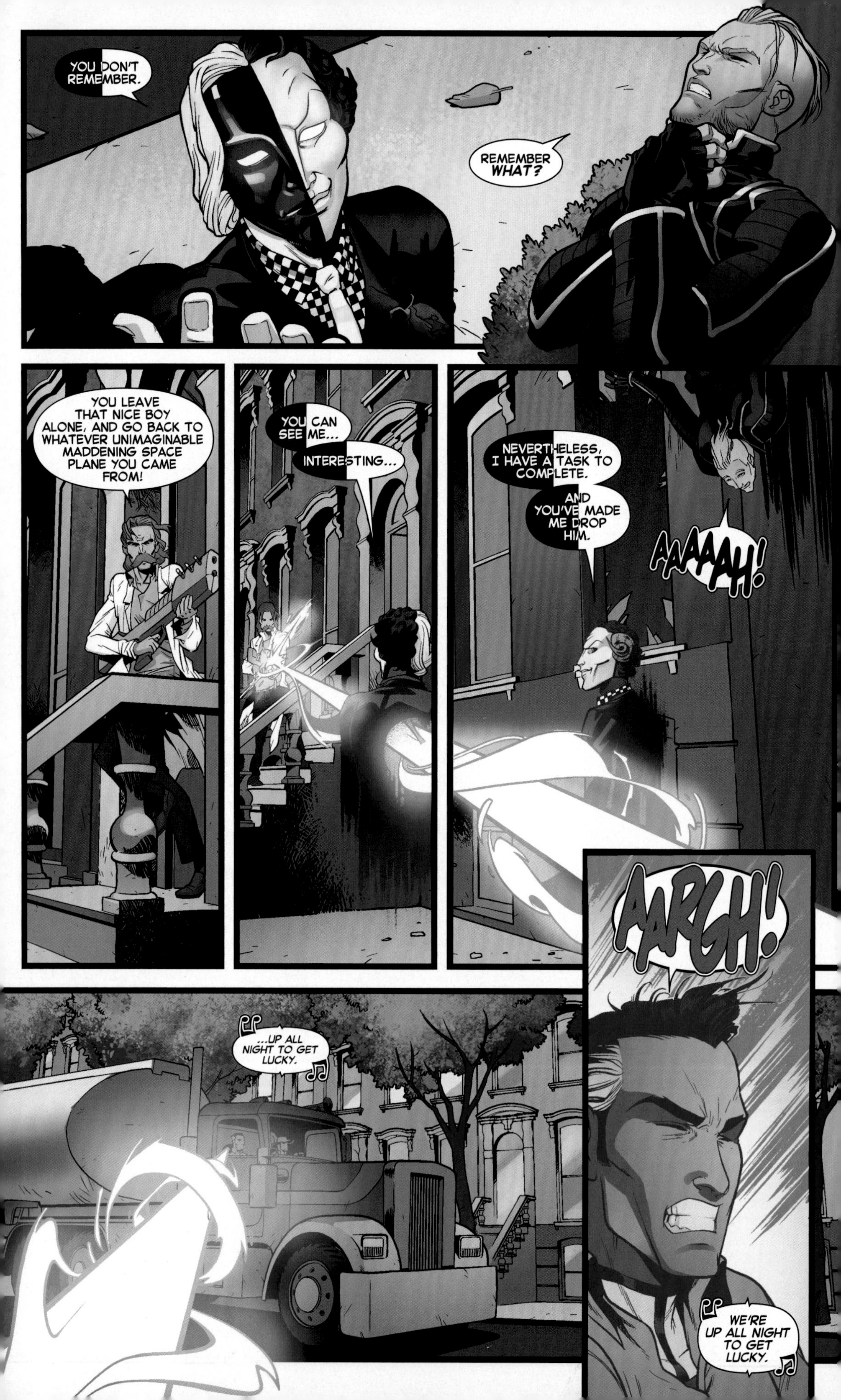
YOU DON'T REMEMBER.
REMEMBER WHAT?
YOU LEAVE THAT NICE BOY ALONE, AND GO BACK TO WHATEVER UNIMAGINABLE MADDENING SPACE PLANE YOU CAME FROM!
YOU CAN SEE ME...
INTERESTING...
NEVERTHELESS, I HAVE A TASK TO COMPLETE.
AND YOU'VE MADE ME DROP HIM.
AAAAAH!
AARGH!
...UP ALL NIGHT TO GET LUCKY.
WE'RE UP ALL NIGHT TO GET LUCKY.

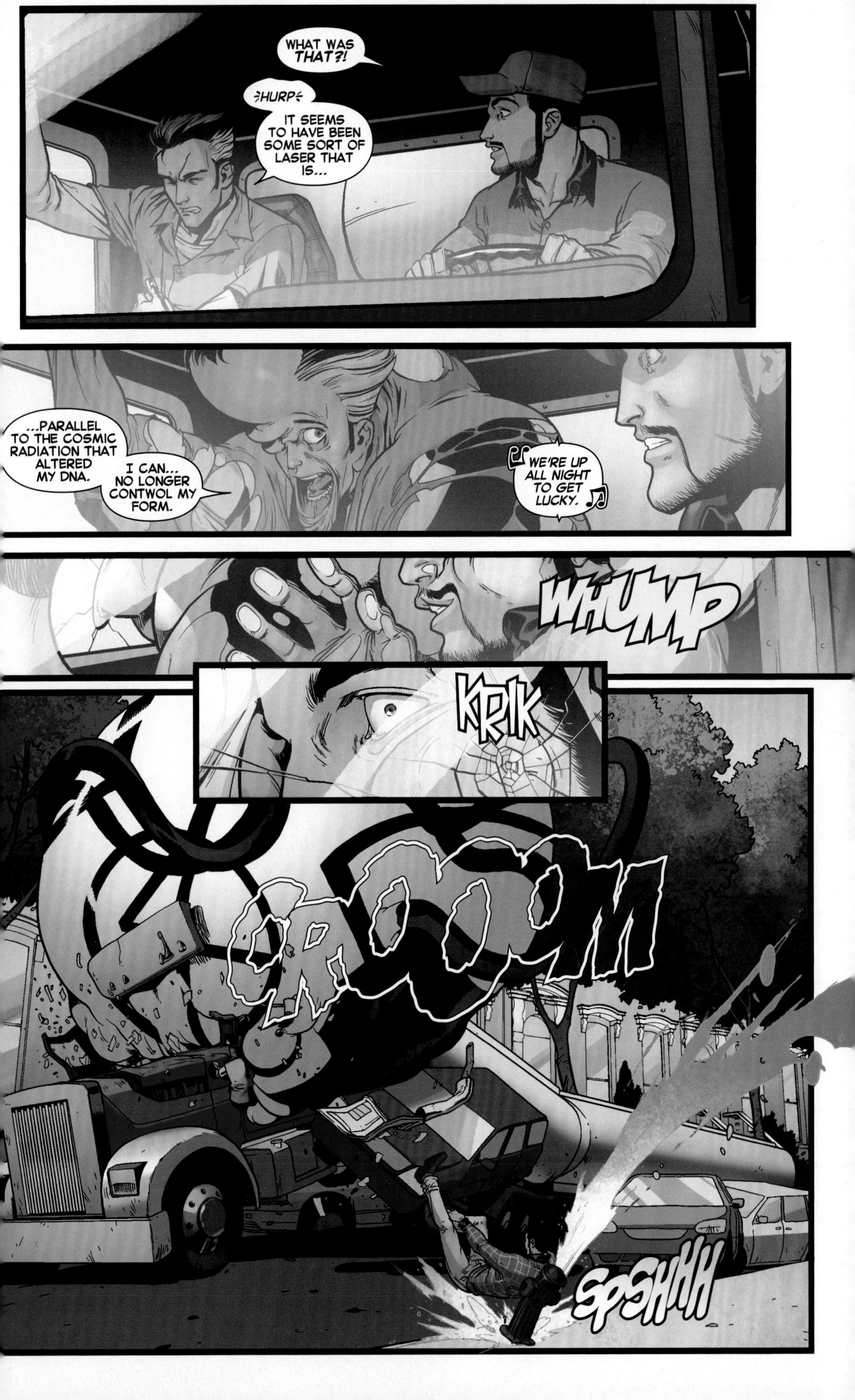
WHAT WAS THAT?!
HURP
IT SEEMS TO HAVE BEEN SOME SORT OF LASER THAT IS...
...PARALLEL TO THE COSMIC RADIATION THAT ALTERED MY DNA.
I CAN... NO LONGER CONTWOL MY FORM.
WE'RE UP ALL NIGHT TO GET LUCKY.
WHUMP
KRIK
KRAOOOM
SPSHHH

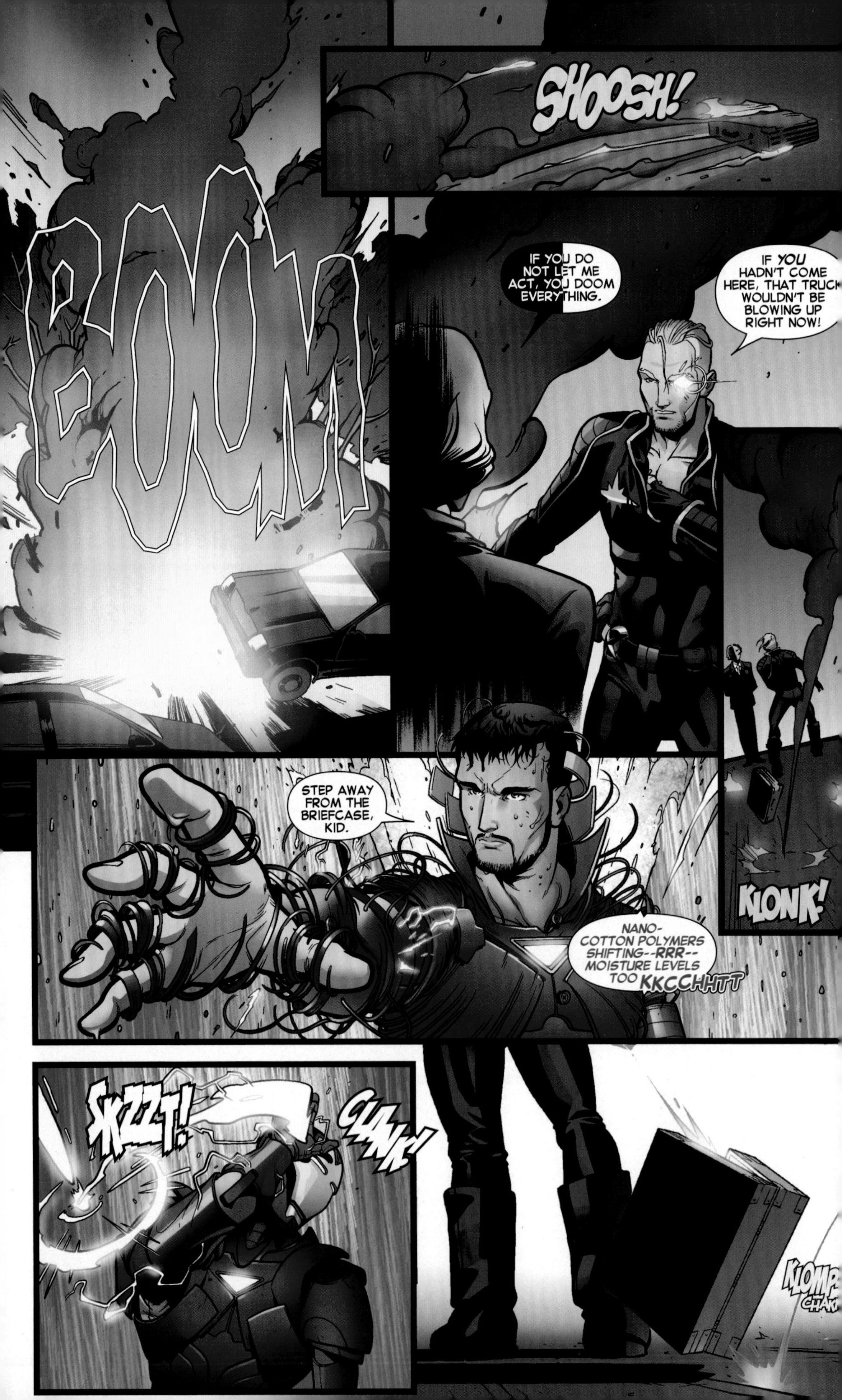
BOOM
SHOOSH!
IF YOU DO NOT LET ME ACT, YOU DOOM EVERYTHING.
IF YOU HADN'T COME HERE, THAT TRUCK WOULDN'T BE BLOWING UP RIGHT NOW!
KLONK!
STEP AWAY FROM THE BRIEFCASE, KID.
NANO-COTTON POLYMERS SHIFTING--RRR--MOISTURE LEVELS TOO KKCCHHTT
SKZZT!
CLANK!
KLOMP
CHAK

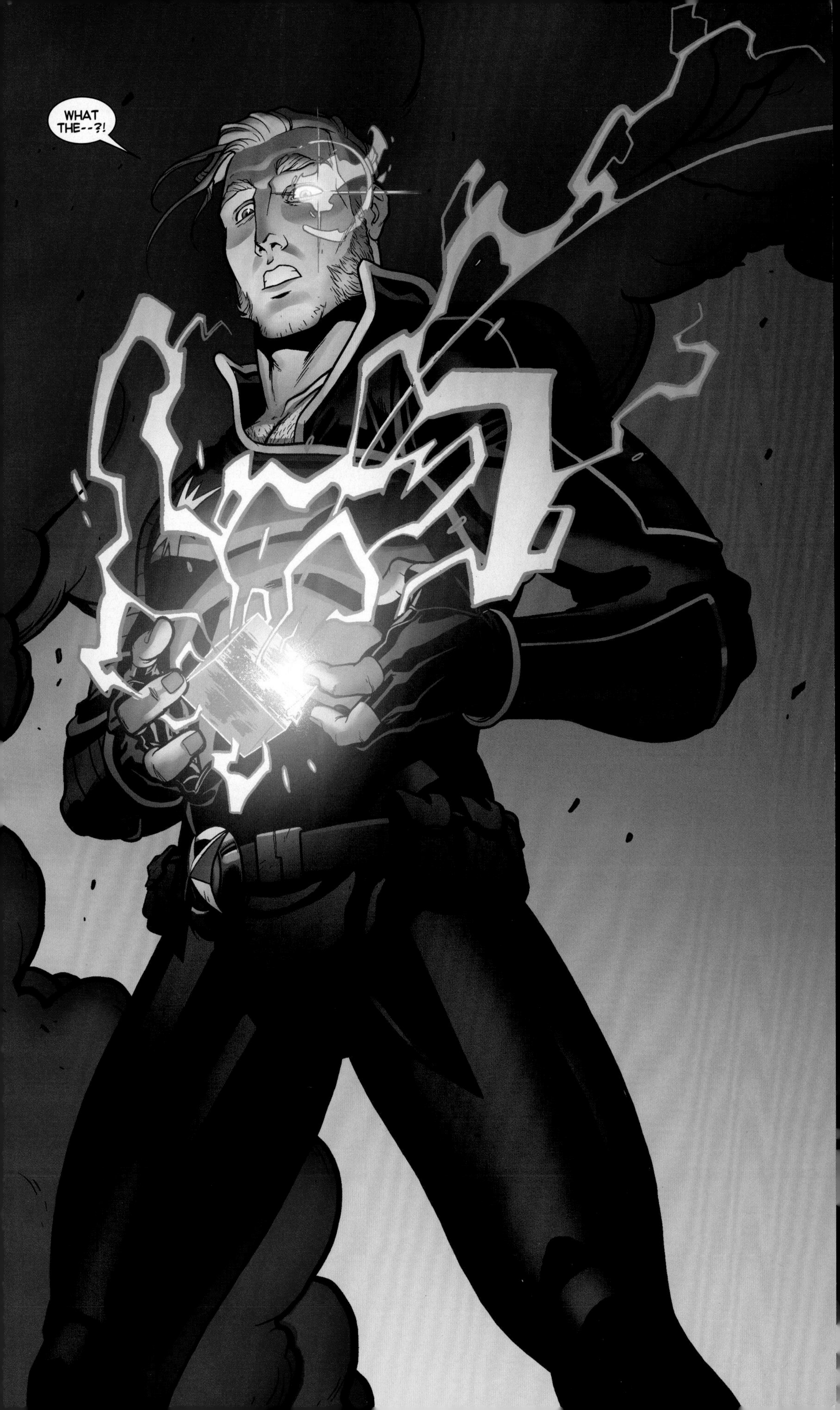
WHAT THE--?!

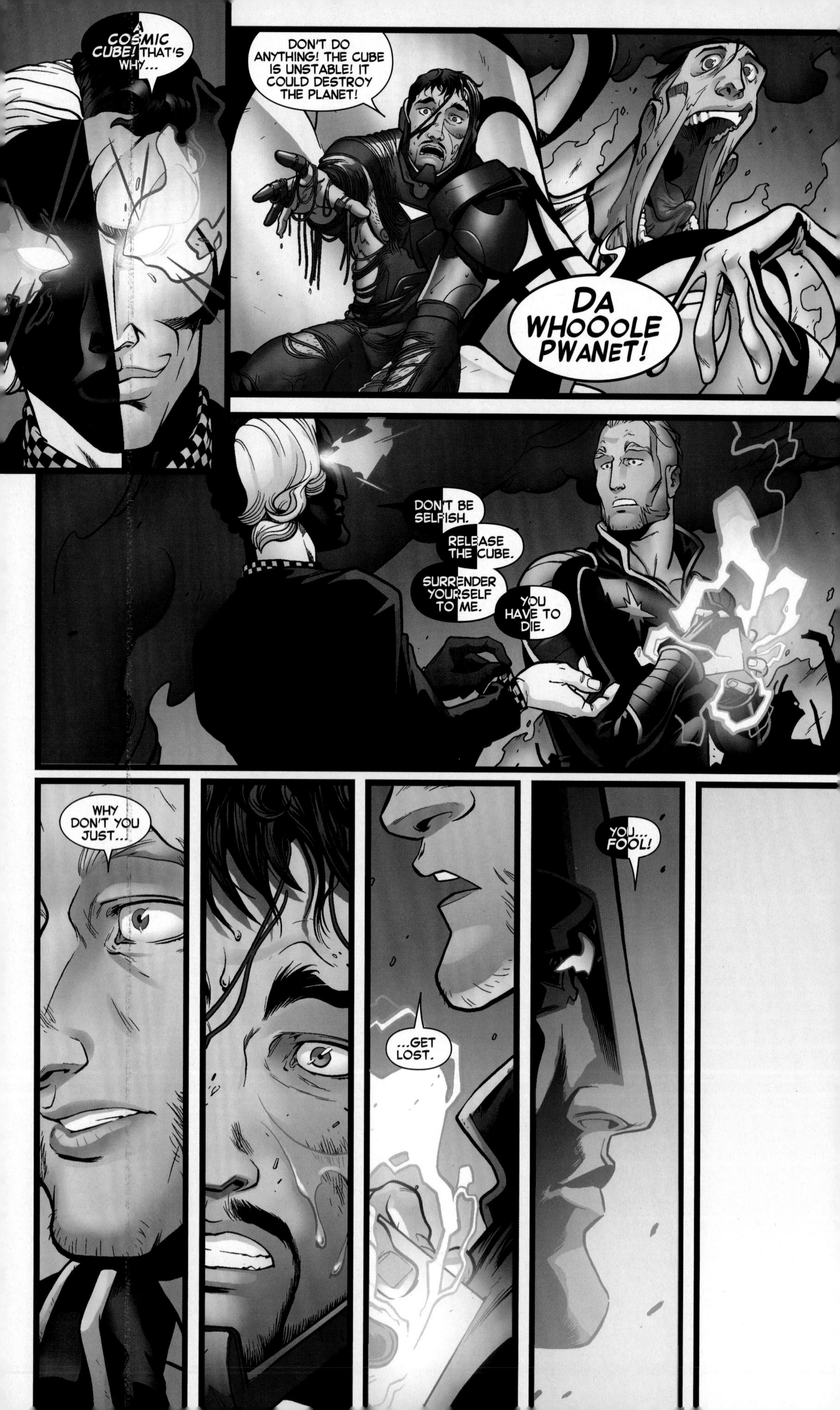
A COSMIC CUBE! THAT'S WHY...
DON'T DO ANYTHING! THE CUBE IS UNSTABLE! IT COULD DESTROY THE PLANET!
DA WHOOOLE PWANET!
DON'T BE SELFISH.
RELEASE THE CUBE.
SURRENDER YOURSELF TO ME.
YOU HAVE TO DIE.
WHY DON'T YOU JUST...
...GET LOST.
YOU... FOOL!

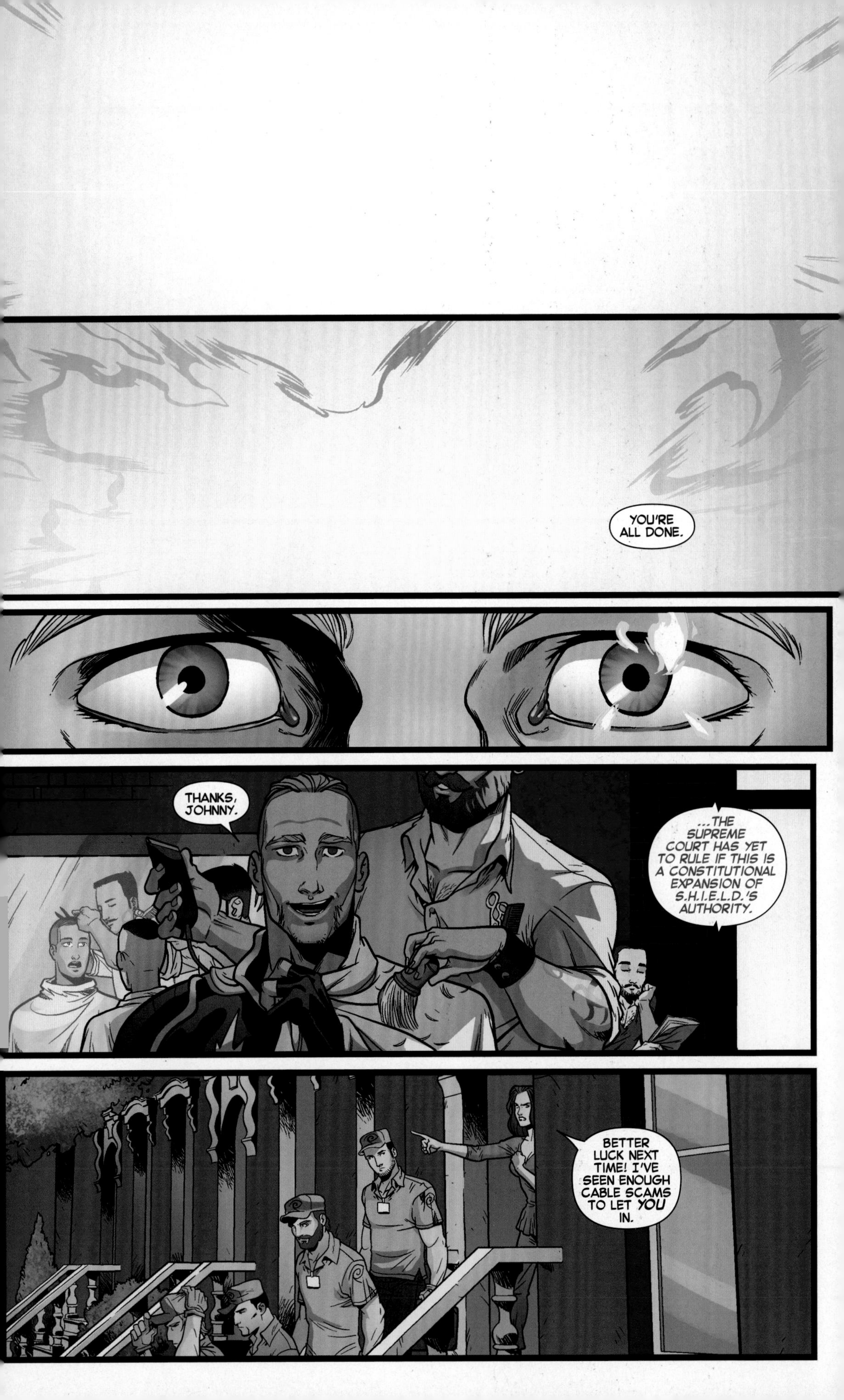
YOU'RE ALL DONE.
THANKS, JOHNNY.
...THE SUPREME COURT HAS YET TO RULE IF THIS IS A CONSTITUTIONAL EXPANSION OF S.H.I.E.L.D.'S AUTHORITY.
BETTER LUCK NEXT TIME! I'VE SEEN ENOUGH CABLE SCAMS TO LET YOU IN.

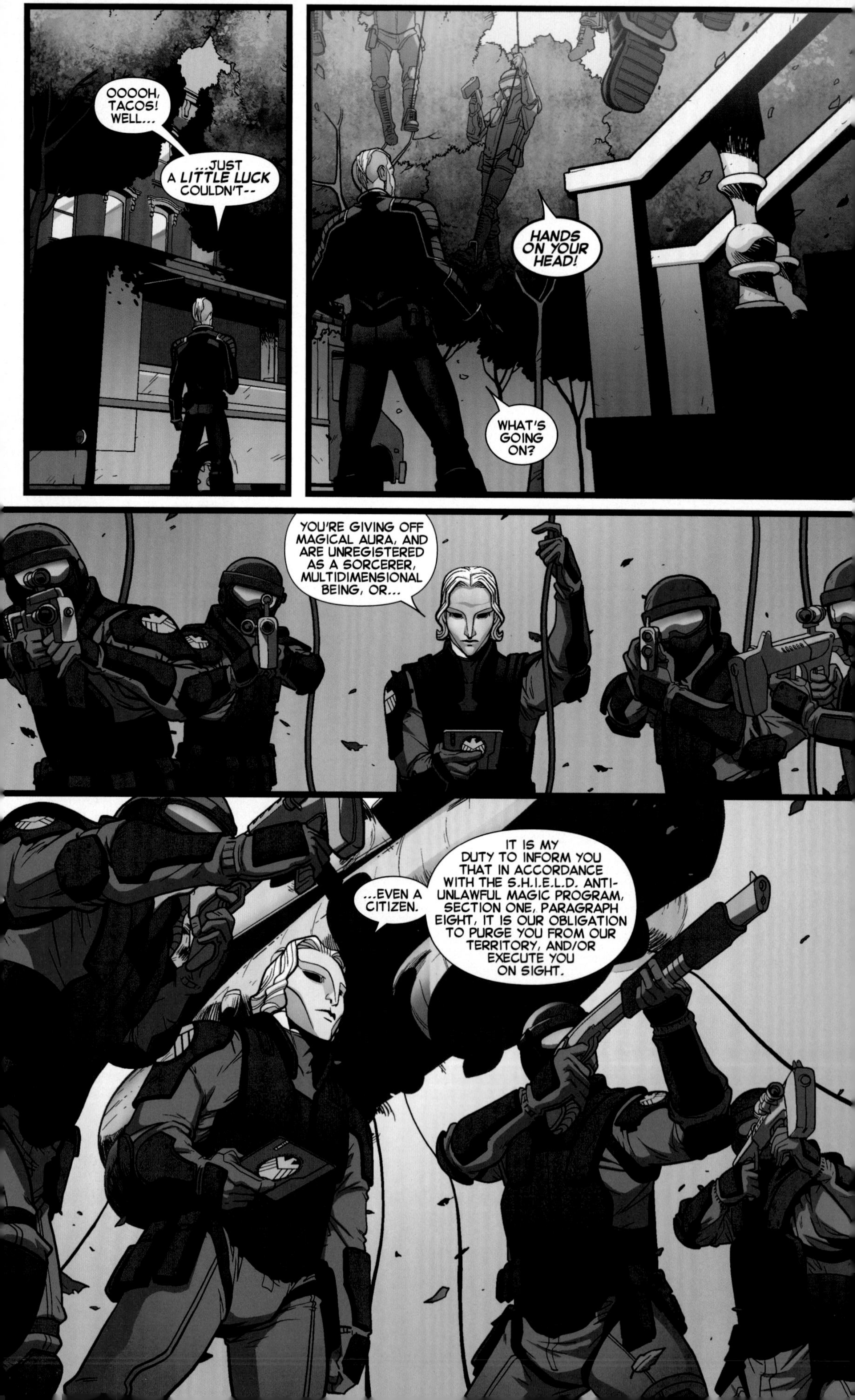
OOOOH, TACOS! WELL...
...JUST A LITTLE LUCK COULDN'T--
HANDS ON YOUR HEAD!
WHAT'S GOING ON?
YOU'RE GIVING OFF MAGICAL AURA, AND ARE UNREGISTERED AS A SORCERER, MULTIDIMENSIONAL BEING, OR...
...EVEN A CITIZEN.
IT IS MY DUTY TO INFORM YOU THAT IN ACCORDANCE WITH THE S.H.I.E.L.D. ANTI-UNLAWFUL MAGIC PROGRAM, SECTION ONE, PARAGRAPH EIGHT, IT IS OUR OBLIGATION TO PURGE YOU FROM OUR TERRITORY, AND/OR EXECUTE YOU ON SIGHT.

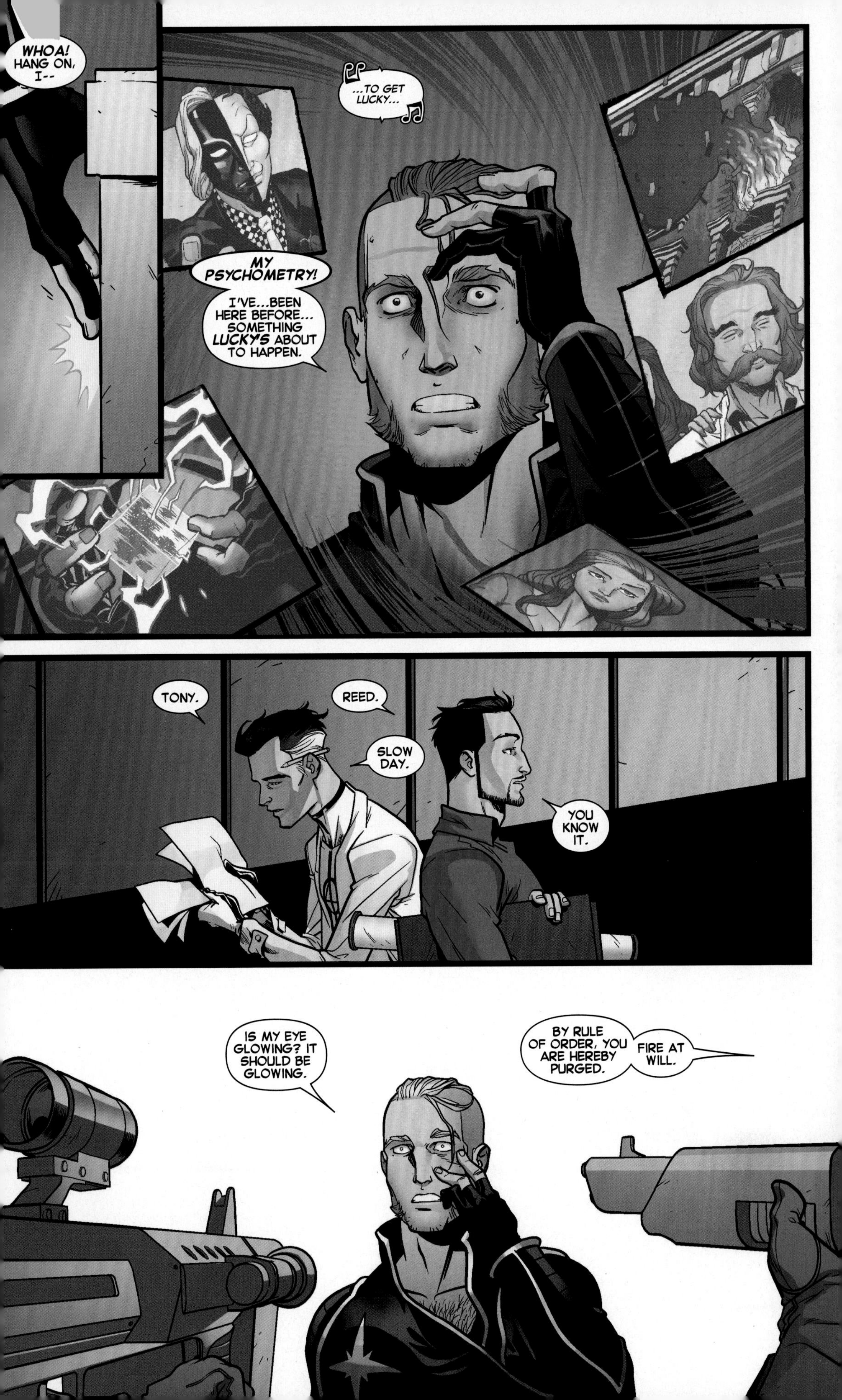
WHOA! HANG ON, I--
...TO GET LUCKY...
MY PSYCHOMETRY!
I'VE...BEEN HERE BEFORE... SOMETHING LUCKY'S ABOUT TO HAPPEN.
TONY.
REED.
SLOW DAY.
YOU KNOW IT.
IS MY EYE GLOWING? IT SHOULD BE GLOWING.
BY RULE OF ORDER, YOU ARE HEREBY PURGED.
FIRE AT WILL.

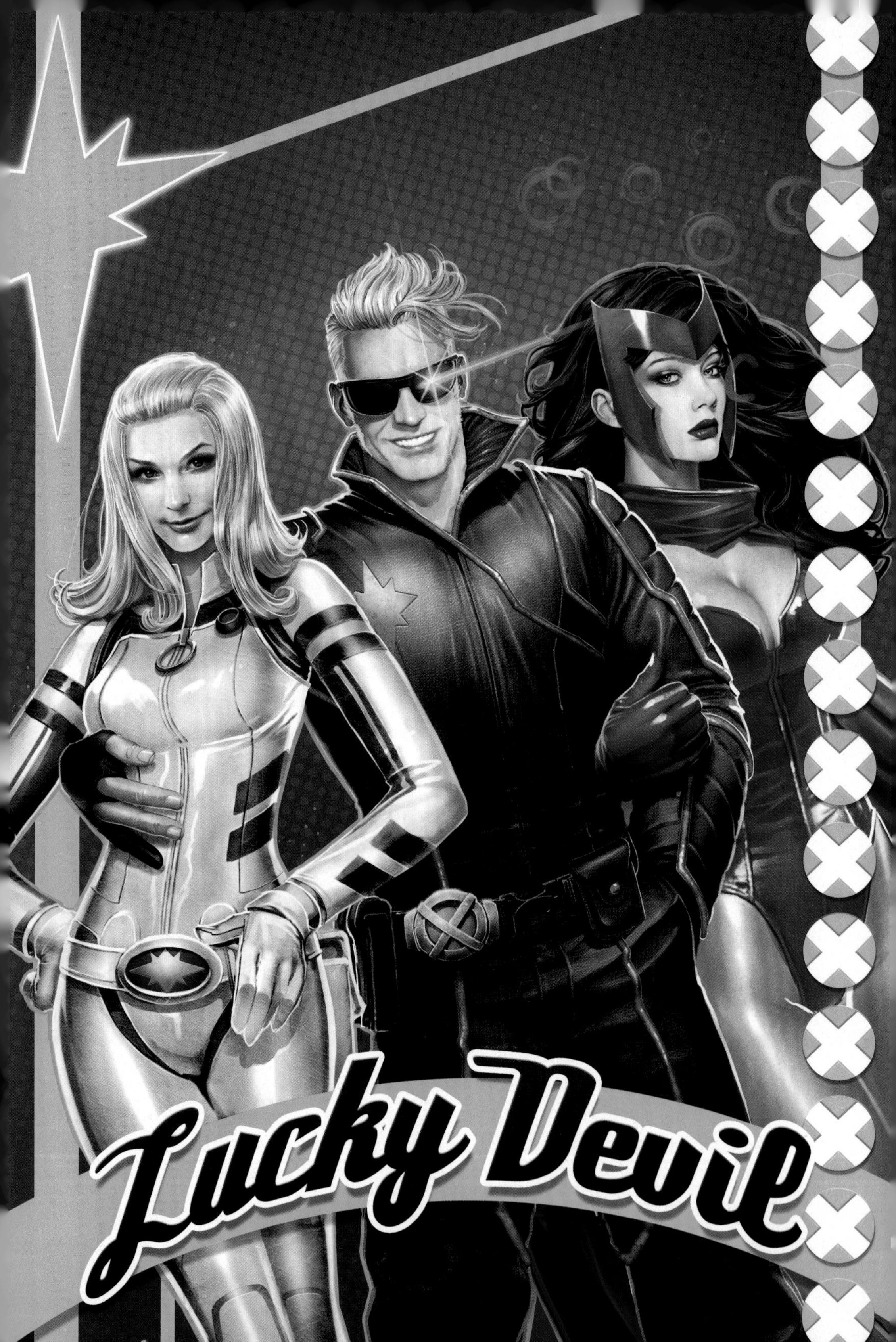
Lucky Devil
D.NA
9.2K13

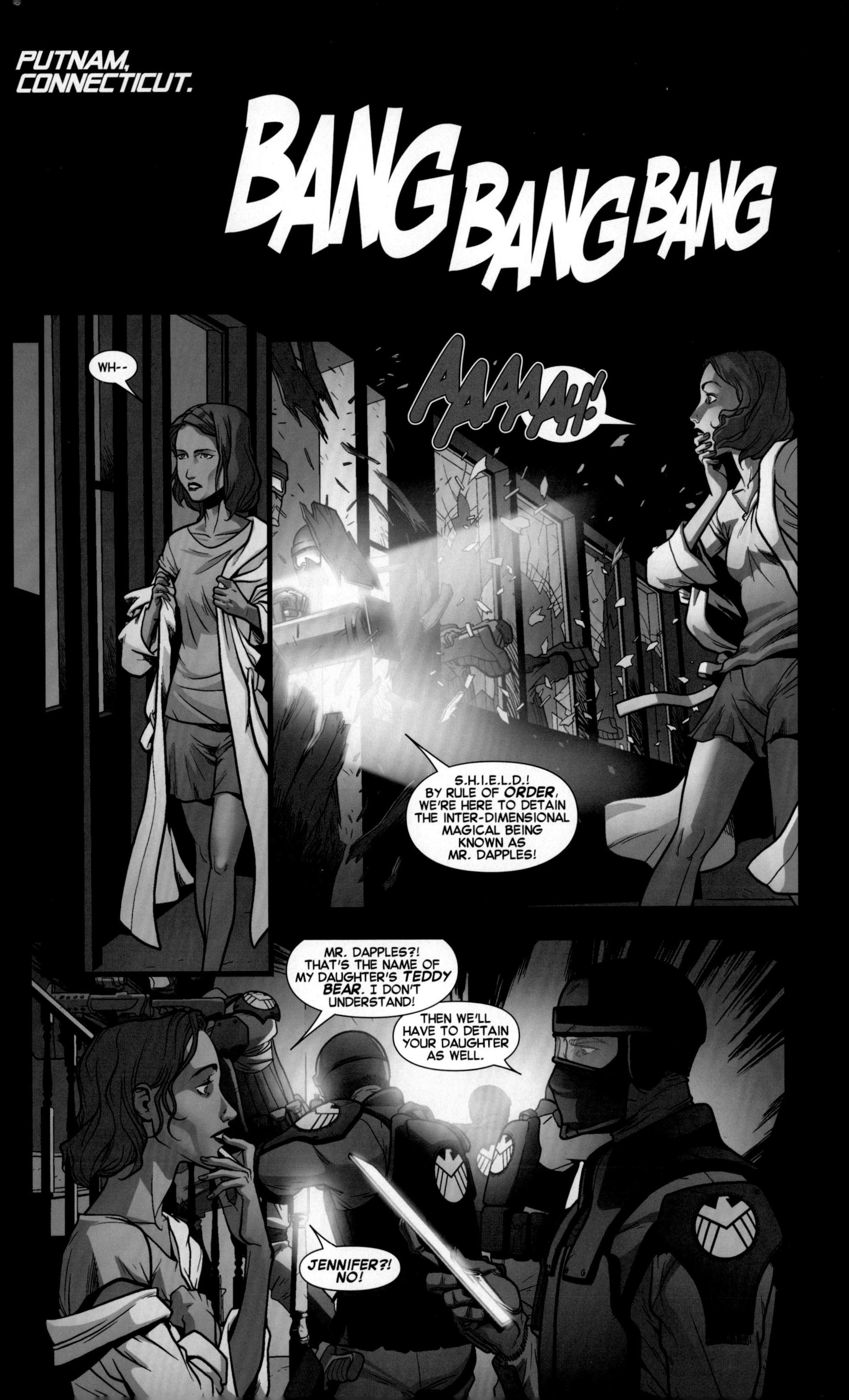
PUTNAM, CONNECTICUT.
BANG BANG BANG
WH--
AAAAAH!
S.H.I.E.L.D.! BY RULE OF ORDER, WE'RE HERE TO DETAIN THE INTER-DIMENSIONAL MAGICAL BEING KNOWN AS MR. DAPPLES!
MR. DAPPLES?! THAT'S THE NAME OF MY DAUGHTER'S TEDDY BEAR. I DON'T UNDERSTAND!
THEN WE'LL HAVE TO DETAIN YOUR DAUGHTER AS WELL.
JENNIFER?! NO!

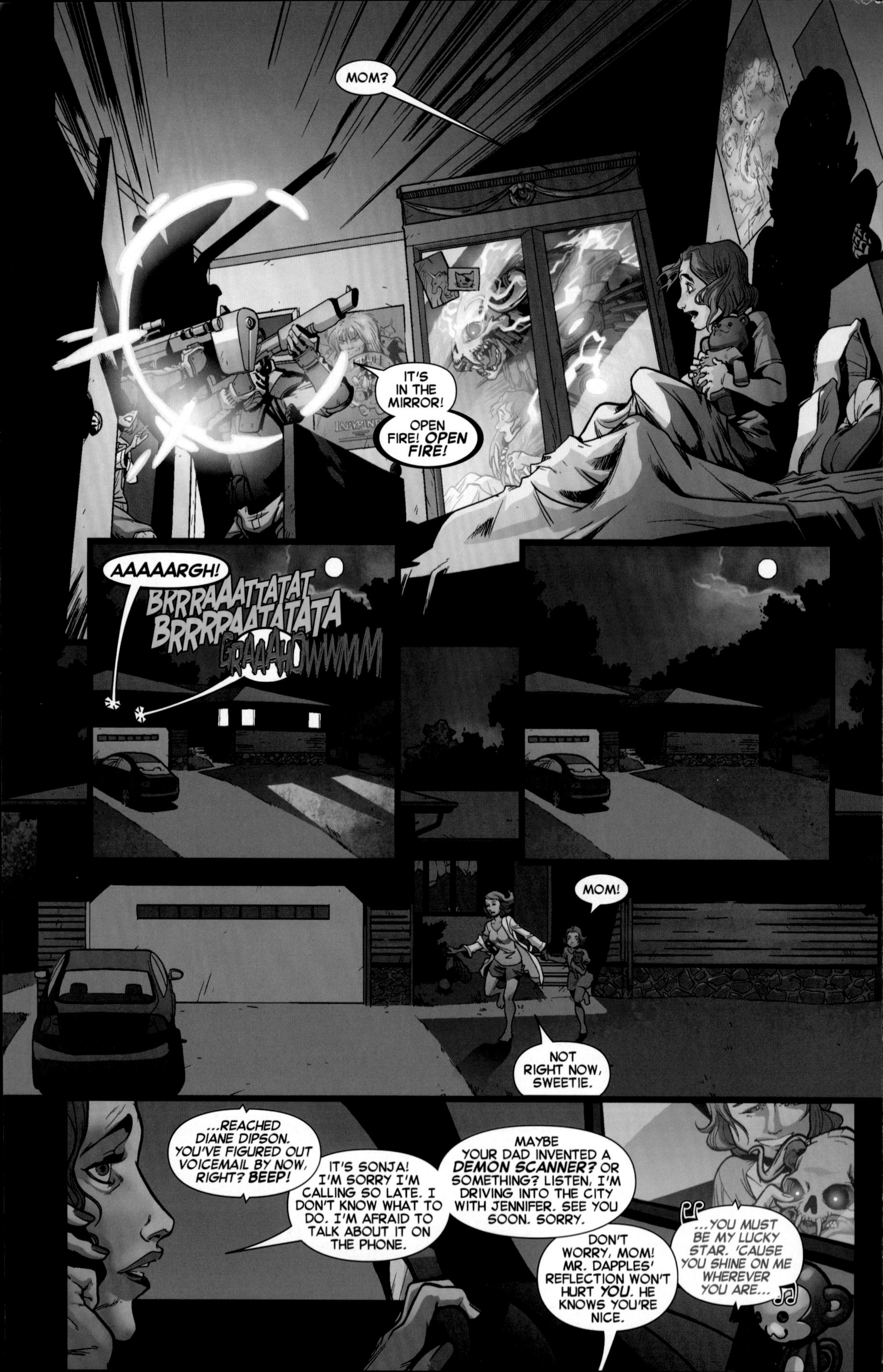
MOM?
IT'S IN THE MIRROR!
OPEN FIRE! OPEN FIRE!
LABYRINTH
AAAAARGH!
BRRRAAATTATAT
BRRRRAATATATA
GRAAAHOWWMM
MOM!
NOT RIGHT NOW, SWEETIE.
...REACHED DIANE DIPSON. YOU'VE FIGURED OUT VOICEMAIL BY NOW, RIGHT? BEEP!
IT'S SONJA! I'M SORRY I'M CALLING SO LATE. I DON'T KNOW WHAT TO DO. I'M AFRAID TO TALK ABOUT IT ON THE PHONE.
MAYBE YOUR DAD INVENTED A DEMON SCANNER? OR SOMETHING? LISTEN, I'M DRIVING INTO THE CITY WITH JENNIFER. SEE YOU SOON. SORRY.
DON'T WORRY, MOM! MR. DAPPLES' REFLECTION WON'T HURT YOU. HE KNOWS YOU'RE NICE.
...YOU MUST BE MY LUCKY STAR. 'CAUSE YOU SHINE ON ME WHEREVER YOU ARE...

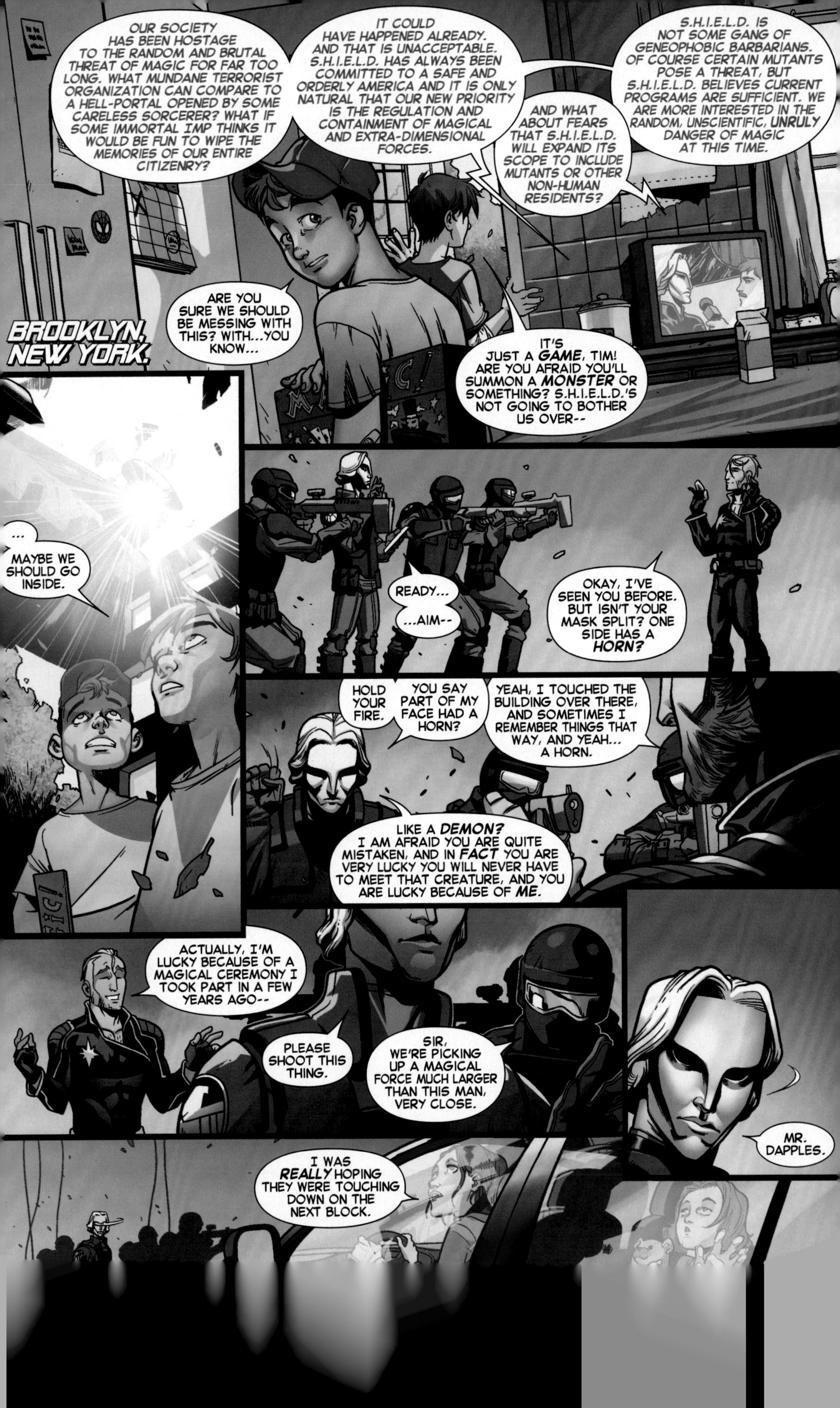

OUR SOCIETY HAS BEEN HOSTAGE TO THE RANDOM AND BRUTAL THREAT OF MAGIC FOR FAR TOO LONG. WHAT MUNDANE TERRORIST ORGANIZATION CAN COMPARE TO A HELL-PORTAL OPENED BY SOME CARELESS SORCERER? WHAT IF SOME IMMORTAL IMP THINKS IT WOULD BE FUN TO WIPE THE MEMORIES OF OUR ENTIRE CITIZENRY?
IT COULD HAVE HAPPENED ALREADY. AND THAT IS UNACCEPTABLE. S.H.I.E.L.D. HAS ALWAYS BEEN COMMITTED TO A SAFE AND ORDERLY AMERICA AND IT IS ONLY NATURAL THAT OUR NEW PRIORITY IS THE REGULATION AND CONTAINMENT OF MAGICAL AND EXTRA-DIMENSIONAL FORCES.
AND WHAT ABOUT FEARS THAT S.H.I.E.L.D. WILL EXPAND ITS SCOPE TO INCLUDE MUTANTS OR OTHER NON-HUMAN RESIDENTS?
S.H.I.E.L.D. IS NOT SOME GANG OF GENEOPHOBIC BARBARIANS. OF COURSE CERTAIN MUTANTS POSE A THREAT, BUT S.H.I.E.L.D. BELIEVES CURRENT PROGRAMS ARE SUFFICIENT. WE ARE MORE INTERESTED IN THE RANDOM, UNSCIENTIFIC, UNRULY DANGER OF MAGIC AT THIS TIME.
BROOKLYN, NEW YORK.
ARE YOU SURE WE SHOULD BE MESSING WITH THIS? WITH...YOU KNOW...
IT'S JUST A GAME, TIM! ARE YOU AFRAID YOU'LL SUMMON A MONSTER OR SOMETHING? S.H.I.E.L.D.'S NOT GOING TO BOTHER US OVER--
...
MAYBE WE SHOULD GO INSIDE.
READY...
...AIM--
OKAY, I'VE SEEN YOU BEFORE. BUT ISN'T YOUR MASK SPLIT? ONE SIDE HAS A HORN?
HOLD YOUR FIRE.
YOU SAY PART OF MY FACE HAD A HORN?
YEAH, I TOUCHED THE BUILDING OVER THERE, AND SOMETIMES I REMEMBER THINGS THAT WAY, AND YEAH... A HORN.
LIKE A DEMON? I AM AFRAID YOU ARE QUITE MISTAKEN, AND IN FACT YOU ARE VERY LUCKY YOU WILL NEVER HAVE TO MEET THAT CREATURE, AND YOU ARE LUCKY BECAUSE OF ME.
ACTUALLY, I'M LUCKY BECAUSE OF A MAGICAL CEREMONY I TOOK PART IN A FEW YEARS AGO--
PLEASE SHOOT THIS THING.
SIR, WE'RE PICKING UP A MAGICAL FORCE MUCH LARGER THAN THIS MAN, VERY CLOSE.
MR. DAPPLES.
I WAS REALLY HOPING THEY WERE TOUCHING DOWN ON THE NEXT BLOCK.

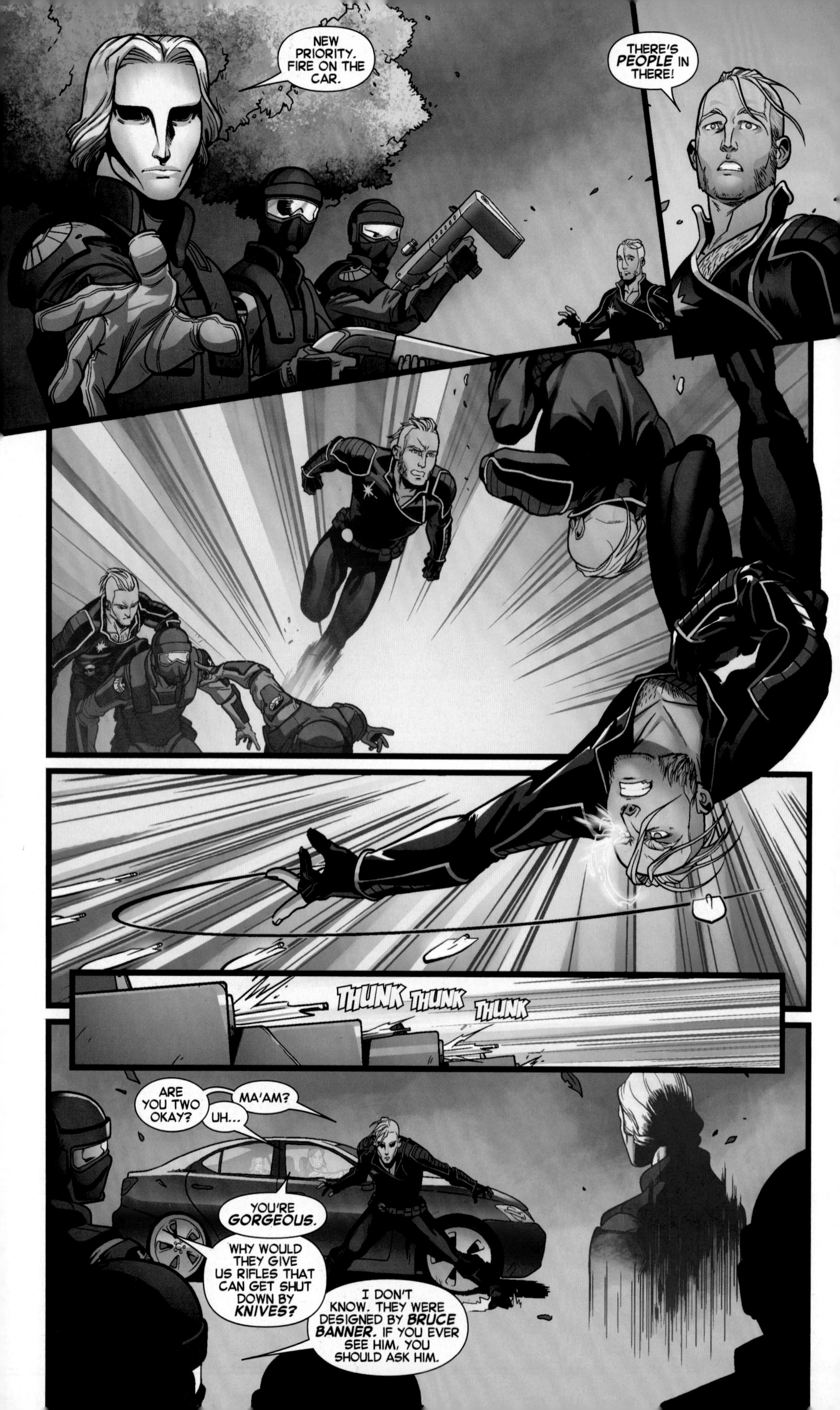
NEW PRIORITY. FIRE ON THE CAR.
THERE'S *PEOPLE* IN THERE!
THUNK THUNK THUNK
ARE YOU TWO OKAY?
MA'AM?
UH...
YOU'RE *GORGEOUS.*
WHY WOULD THEY GIVE US RIFLES THAT CAN GET SHUT DOWN BY *KNIVES?*
I DON'T KNOW. THEY WERE DESIGNED BY *BRUCE BANNER.* IF YOU EVER SEE HIM, YOU SHOULD ASK HIM.

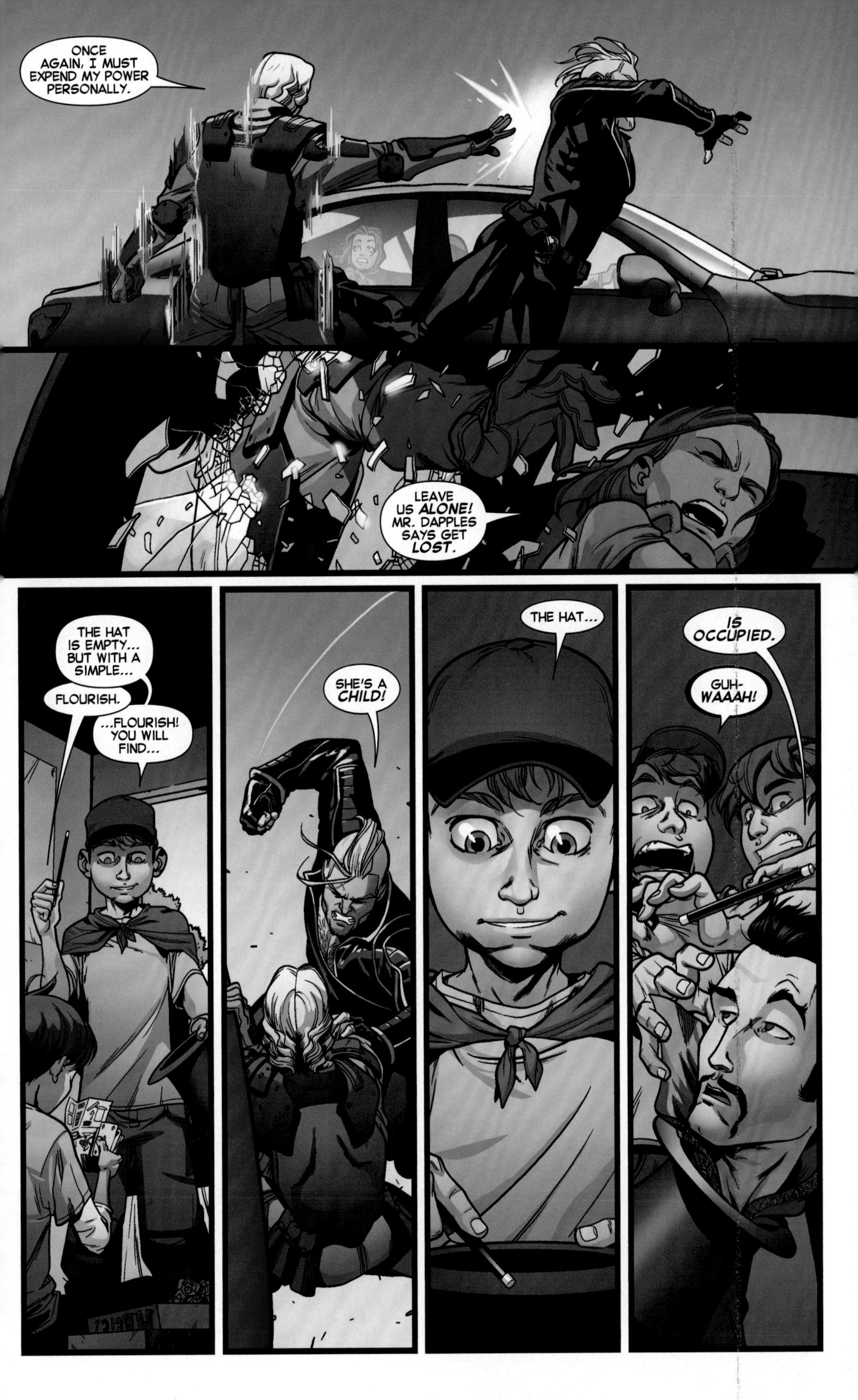
ONCE AGAIN, I MUST EXPEND MY POWER PERSONALLY.
LEAVE US ALONE! MR. DAPPLES SAYS GET LOST.
THE HAT IS EMPTY... BUT WITH A SIMPLE...
FLOURISH.
...FLOURISH! YOU WILL FIND...
SHE'S A CHILD!
THE HAT...
IS OCCUPIED.
GUH-WAAAH!

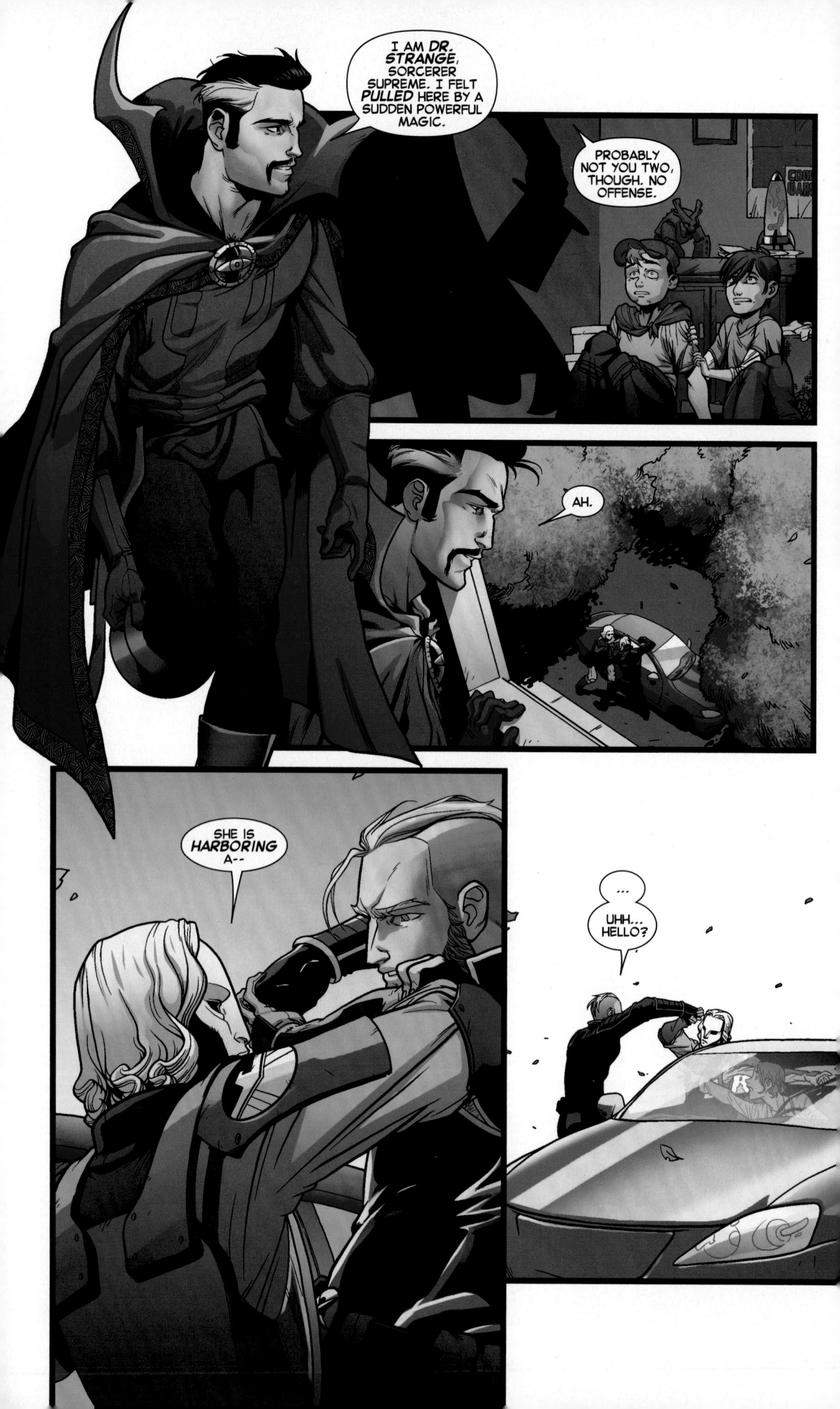
I AM DR. STRANGE, SORCERER SUPREME. I FELT PULLED HERE BY A SUDDEN POWERFUL MAGIC.
PROBABLY NOT YOU TWO, THOUGH. NO OFFENSE.
AH.
SHE IS HARBORING A--
...
UHH... HELLO?

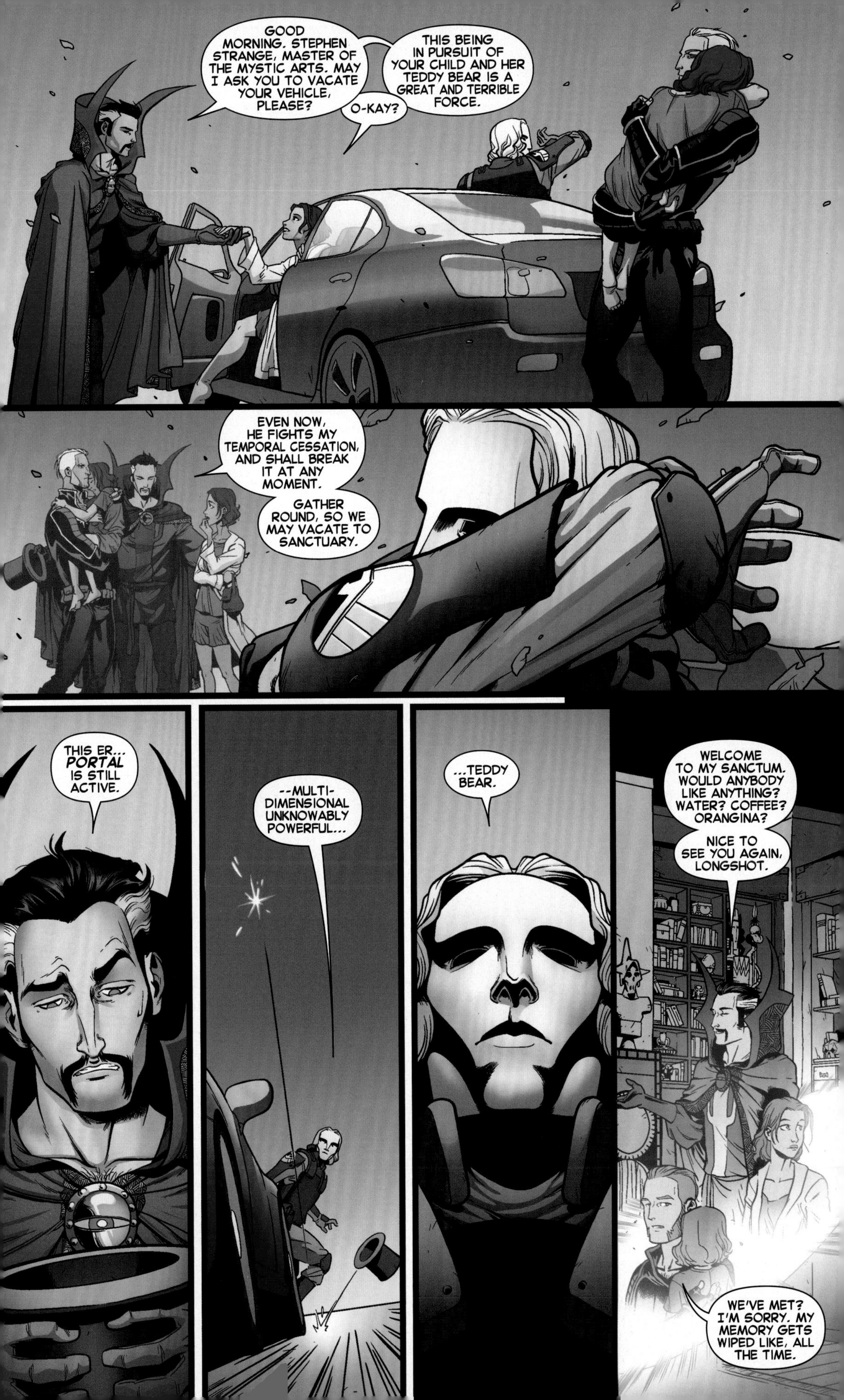
GOOD MORNING. STEPHEN STRANGE, MASTER OF THE MYSTIC ARTS. MAY I ASK YOU TO VACATE YOUR VEHICLE, PLEASE?
O-KAY?
THIS BEING IN PURSUIT OF YOUR CHILD AND HER TEDDY BEAR IS A GREAT AND TERRIBLE FORCE.
EVEN NOW, HE FIGHTS MY TEMPORAL CESSATION, AND SHALL BREAK IT AT ANY MOMENT.
GATHER ROUND, SO WE MAY VACATE TO SANCTUARY.
THIS ER... *PORTAL* IS STILL ACTIVE.
--MULTI-DIMENSIONAL UNKNOWABLY POWERFUL...
...TEDDY BEAR.
WELCOME TO MY SANCTUM. WOULD ANYBODY LIKE ANYTHING? WATER? COFFEE? ORANGINA?
NICE TO SEE YOU AGAIN, LONGSHOT.
WE'VE MET? I'M SORRY. MY MEMORY GETS WIPED LIKE, ALL THE TIME.

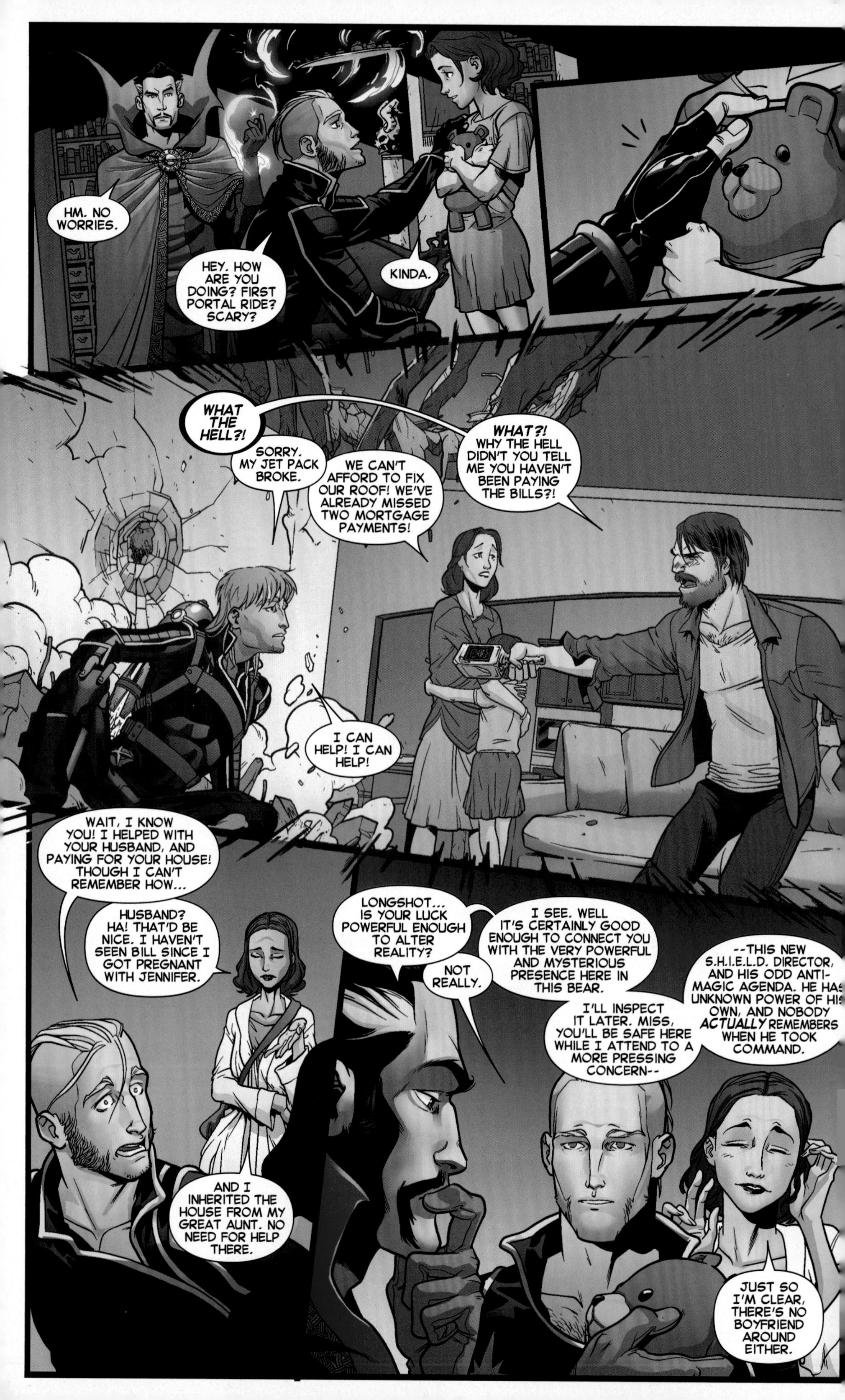
HM. NO WORRIES.
HEY. HOW ARE YOU DOING? FIRST PORTAL RIDE? SCARY?
KINDA.
WHAT THE HELL?!
SORRY. MY JET PACK BROKE.
WE CAN'T AFFORD TO FIX OUR ROOF! WE'VE ALREADY MISSED TWO MORTGAGE PAYMENTS!
WHAT?! WHY THE HELL DIDN'T YOU TELL ME YOU HAVEN'T BEEN PAYING THE BILLS?!
I CAN HELP! I CAN HELP!
WAIT, I KNOW YOU! I HELPED WITH YOUR HUSBAND, AND PAYING FOR YOUR HOUSE! THOUGH I CAN'T REMEMBER HOW...
HUSBAND? HA! THAT'D BE NICE. I HAVEN'T SEEN BILL SINCE I GOT PREGNANT WITH JENNIFER.
AND I INHERITED THE HOUSE FROM MY GREAT AUNT. NO NEED FOR HELP THERE.
LONGSHOT... IS YOUR LUCK POWERFUL ENOUGH TO ALTER REALITY?
NOT REALLY.
I SEE. WELL IT'S CERTAINLY GOOD ENOUGH TO CONNECT YOU WITH THE VERY POWERFUL AND MYSTERIOUS PRESENCE HERE IN THIS BEAR.
I'LL INSPECT IT LATER. MISS, YOU'LL BE SAFE HERE WHILE I ATTEND TO A MORE PRESSING CONCERN--
--THIS NEW S.H.I.E.L.D. DIRECTOR, AND HIS ODD ANTI-MAGIC AGENDA. HE HAS UNKNOWN POWER OF HIS OWN, AND NOBODY ACTUALLY REMEMBERS WHEN HE TOOK COMMAND.
JUST SO I'M CLEAR, THERE'S NO BOYFRIEND AROUND EITHER.

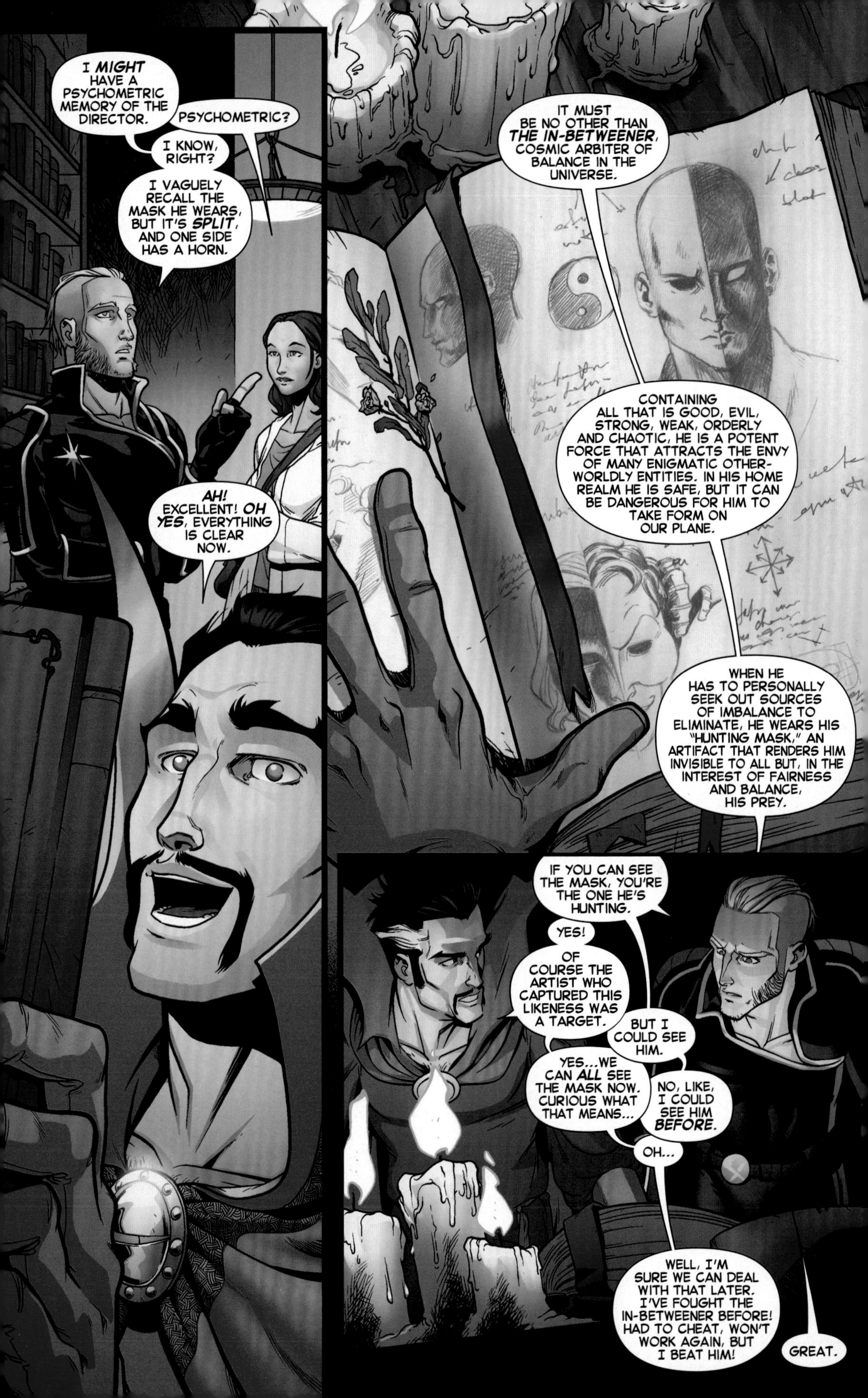
I MIGHT HAVE A PSYCHOMETRIC MEMORY OF THE DIRECTOR.
PSYCHOMETRIC?
I KNOW, RIGHT?
I VAGUELY RECALL THE MASK HE WEARS, BUT IT'S SPLIT, AND ONE SIDE HAS A HORN.
AH! EXCELLENT! OH YES, EVERYTHING IS CLEAR NOW.
IT MUST BE NO OTHER THAN THE IN-BETWEENER, COSMIC ARBITER OF BALANCE IN THE UNIVERSE.
CONTAINING ALL THAT IS GOOD, EVIL, STRONG, WEAK, ORDERLY AND CHAOTIC, HE IS A POTENT FORCE THAT ATTRACTS THE ENVY OF MANY ENIGMATIC OTHER-WORLDLY ENTITIES. IN HIS HOME REALM HE IS SAFE, BUT IT CAN BE DANGEROUS FOR HIM TO TAKE FORM ON OUR PLANE.
WHEN HE HAS TO PERSONALLY SEEK OUT SOURCES OF IMBALANCE TO ELIMINATE, HE WEARS HIS "HUNTING MASK," AN ARTIFACT THAT RENDERS HIM INVISIBLE TO ALL BUT, IN THE INTEREST OF FAIRNESS AND BALANCE, HIS PREY.
IF YOU CAN SEE THE MASK, YOU'RE THE ONE HE'S HUNTING.
YES!
OF COURSE THE ARTIST WHO CAPTURED THIS LIKENESS WAS A TARGET.
BUT I COULD SEE HIM.
YES...WE CAN ALL SEE THE MASK NOW. CURIOUS WHAT THAT MEANS...
NO, LIKE, I COULD SEE HIM BEFORE.
OH...
WELL, I'M SURE WE CAN DEAL WITH THAT LATER. I'VE FOUGHT THE IN-BETWEENER BEFORE! HAD TO CHEAT, WON'T WORK AGAIN, BUT I BEAT HIM!
GREAT.

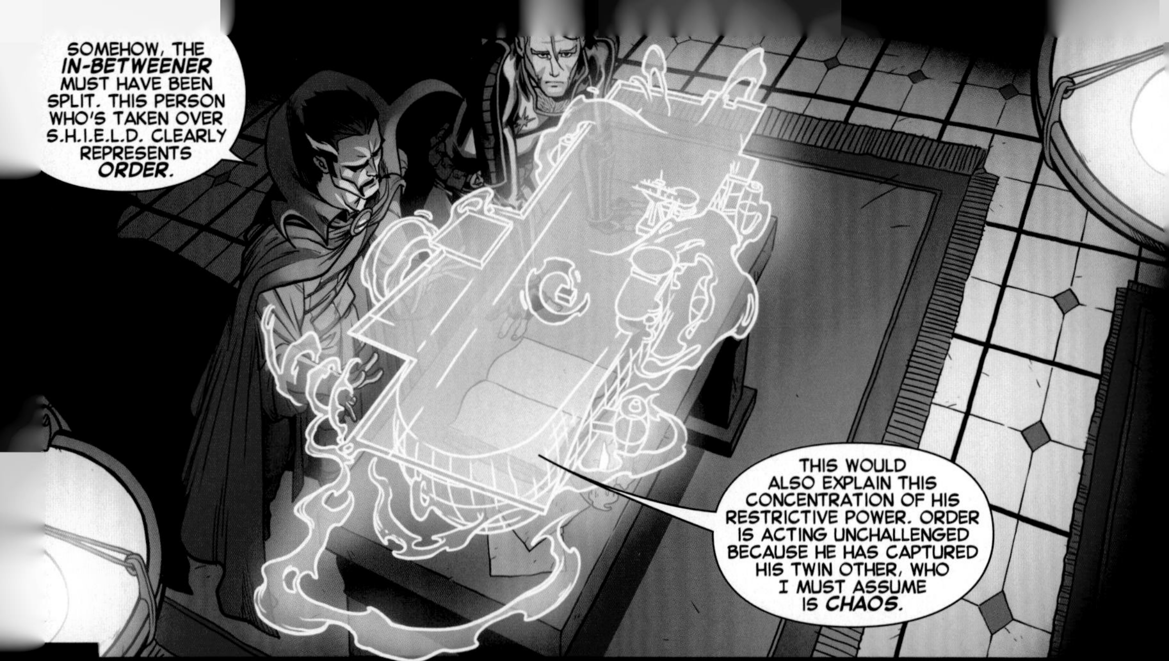
SOMEHOW, THE IN-BETWEENER MUST HAVE BEEN SPLIT. THIS PERSON WHO'S TAKEN OVER S.H.I.E.L.D. CLEARLY REPRESENTS ORDER.
THIS WOULD ALSO EXPLAIN THIS CONCENTRATION OF HIS RESTRICTIVE POWER. ORDER IS ACTING UNCHALLENGED BECAUSE HE HAS CAPTURED HIS TWIN OTHER, WHO I MUST ASSUME IS CHAOS.

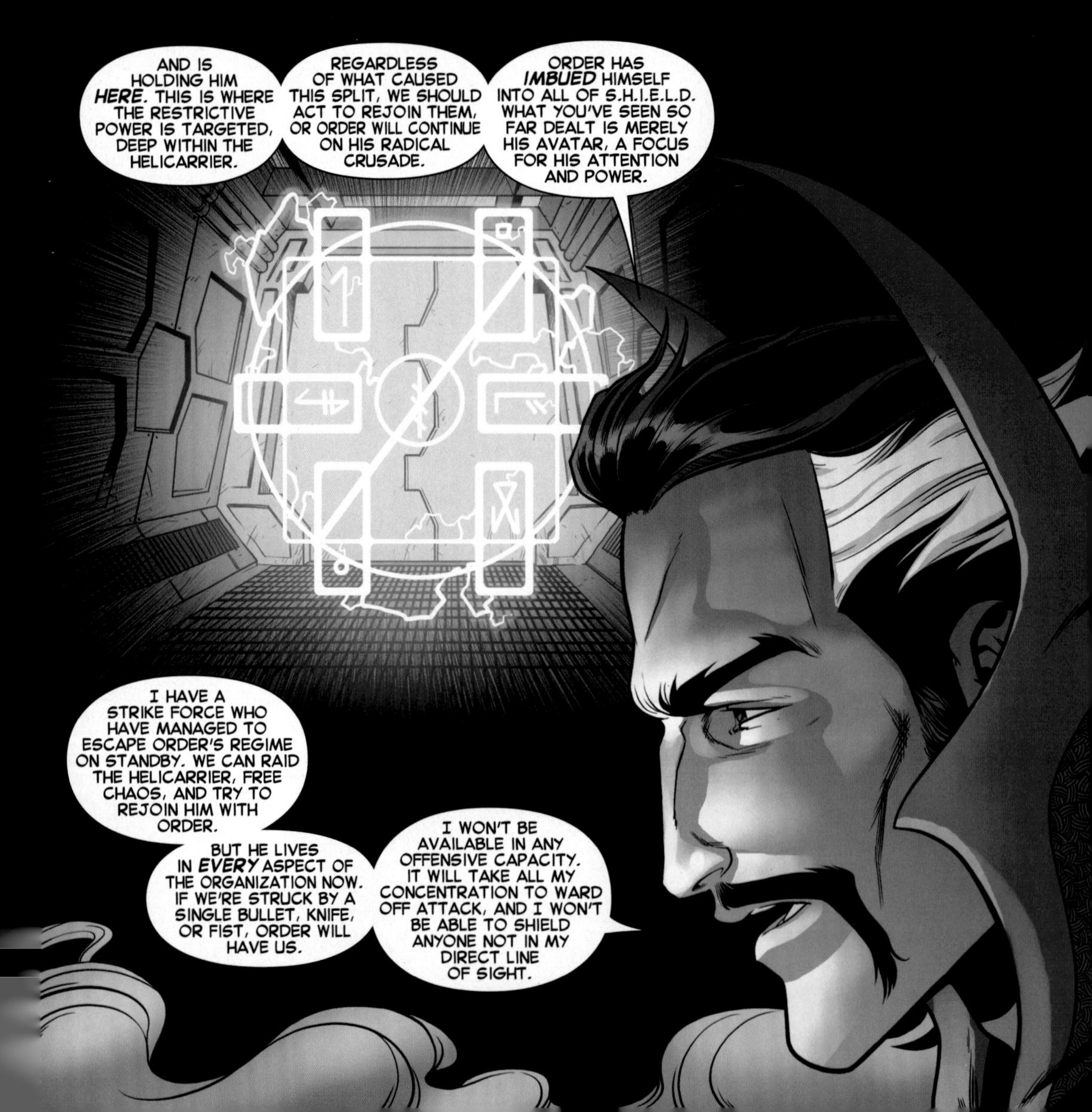
AND IS HOLDING HIM HERE. THIS IS WHERE THE RESTRICTIVE POWER IS TARGETED, DEEP WITHIN THE HELICARRIER.
REGARDLESS OF WHAT CAUSED THIS SPLIT, WE SHOULD ACT TO REJOIN THEM, OR ORDER WILL CONTINUE ON HIS RADICAL CRUSADE.
ORDER HAS IMBUED HIMSELF INTO ALL OF S.H.I.E.L.D. WHAT YOU'VE SEEN SO FAR DEALT IS MERELY HIS AVATAR, A FOCUS FOR HIS ATTENTION AND POWER.
I HAVE A STRIKE FORCE WHO HAVE MANAGED TO ESCAPE ORDER'S REGIME ON STANDBY. WE CAN RAID THE HELICARRIER, FREE CHAOS, AND TRY TO REJOIN HIM WITH ORDER.
BUT HE LIVES IN EVERY ASPECT OF THE ORGANIZATION NOW. IF WE'RE STRUCK BY A SINGLE BULLET, KNIFE, OR FIST, ORDER WILL HAVE US.
I WON'T BE AVAILABLE IN ANY OFFENSIVE CAPACITY. IT WILL TAKE ALL MY CONCENTRATION TO WARD OFF ATTACK, AND I WON'T BE ABLE TO SHIELD ANYONE NOT IN MY DIRECT LINE OF SIGHT.

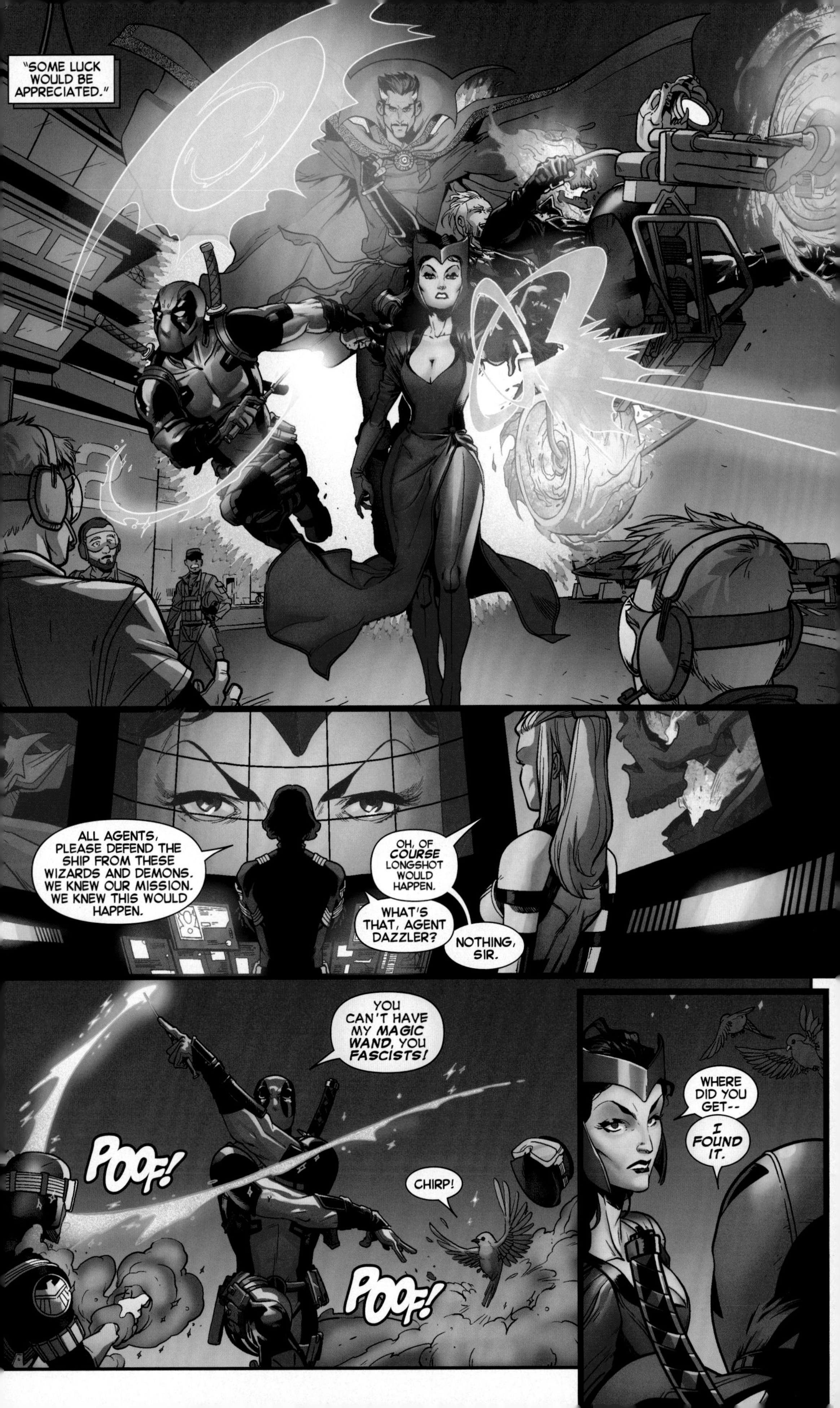

"SOME LUCK WOULD BE APPRECIATED."
ALL AGENTS, PLEASE DEFEND THE SHIP FROM THESE WIZARDS AND DEMONS. WE KNEW OUR MISSION. WE KNEW THIS WOULD HAPPEN.
OH, OF COURSE LONGSHOT WOULD HAPPEN.
WHAT'S THAT, AGENT DAZZLER?
NOTHING, SIR.
YOU CAN'T HAVE MY MAGIC WAND, YOU FASCISTS!
POOF!
CHIRP!
POOF!
WHERE DID YOU GET--
I FOUND IT.

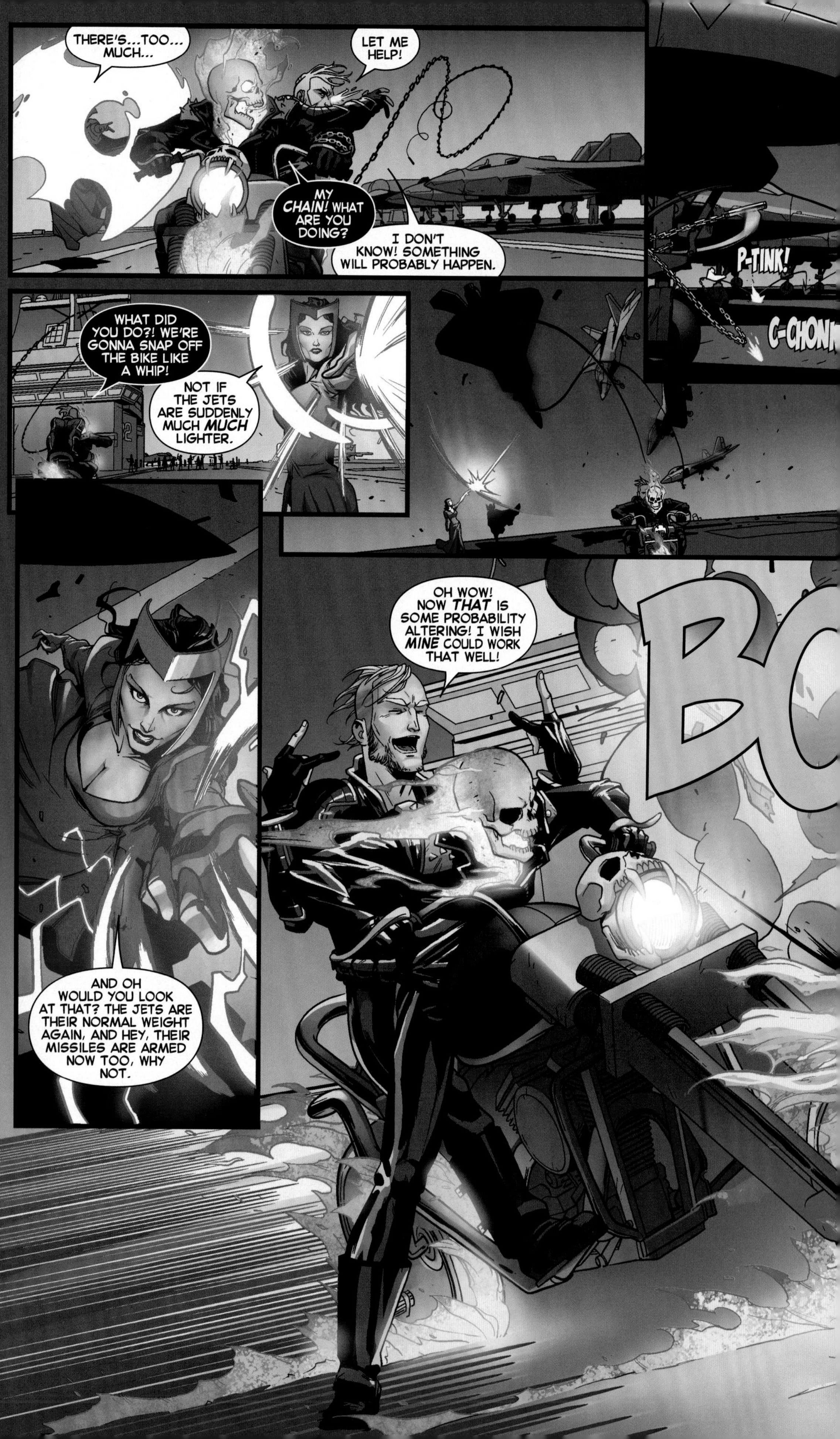

THERE'S...TOO... MUCH...
LET ME HELP!
MY CHAIN! WHAT ARE YOU DOING?
I DON'T KNOW! SOMETHING WILL PROBABLY HAPPEN.
P-TINK!
C-CHONK
WHAT DID YOU DO?! WE'RE GONNA SNAP OFF THE BIKE LIKE A WHIP!
NOT IF THE JETS ARE SUDDENLY MUCH *MUCH* LIGHTER.
OH WOW! NOW *THAT* IS SOME PROBABILITY ALTERING! I WISH *MINE* COULD WORK THAT WELL!
BO
AND OH WOULD YOU LOOK AT THAT? THE JETS ARE THEIR NORMAL WEIGHT AGAIN, AND HEY, THEIR MISSILES ARE ARMED NOW TOO, WHY NOT.

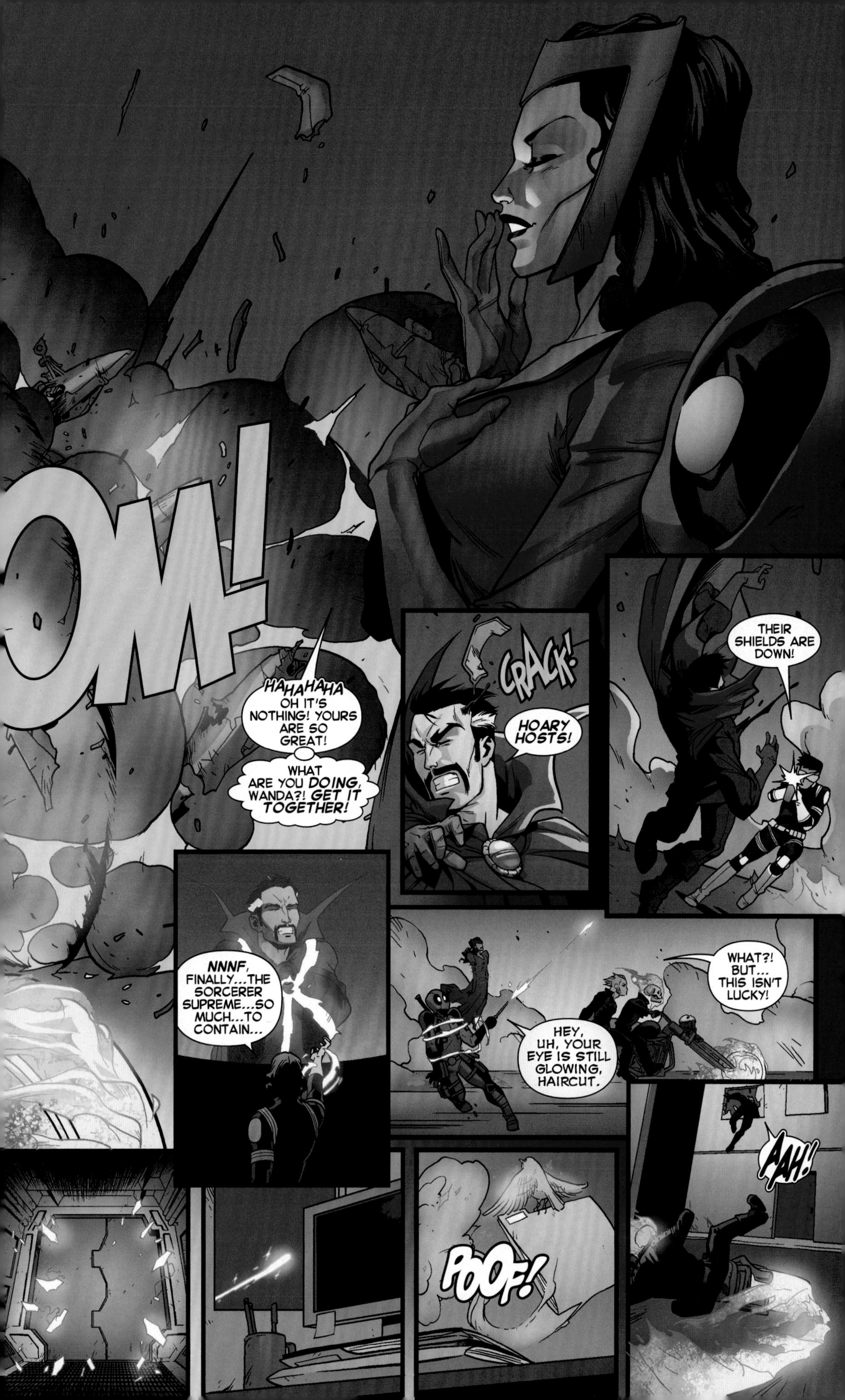
OM!
HAHAHAHA OH IT'S NOTHING! YOURS ARE SO GREAT!
WHAT ARE YOU DOING, WANDA?! GET IT TOGETHER!
CRACK!
HOARY HOSTS!
THEIR SHIELDS ARE DOWN!
NNNF, FINALLY...THE SORCERER SUPREME...SO MUCH...TO CONTAIN...
WHAT?! BUT... THIS ISN'T LUCKY!
HEY, UH, YOUR EYE IS STILL GLOWING, HAIRCUT.
AAH!
POOF!

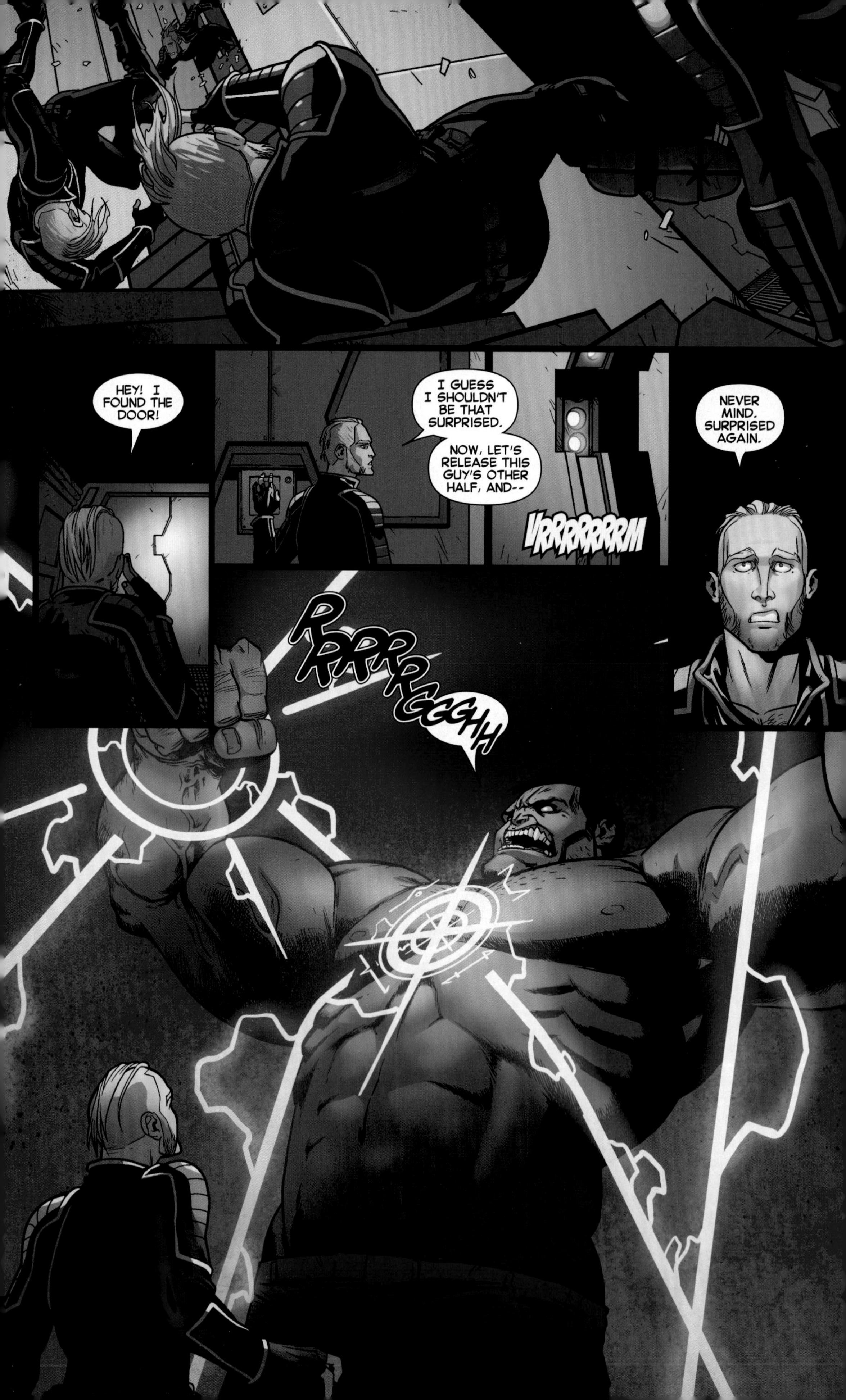
HEY! I FOUND THE DOOR!
I GUESS I SHOULDN'T BE THAT SURPRISED.
NOW, LET'S RELEASE THIS GUY'S OTHER HALF, AND--
VRRRRRRRM
NEVER MIND. SURPRISED AGAIN.
RRRRRGGGHH

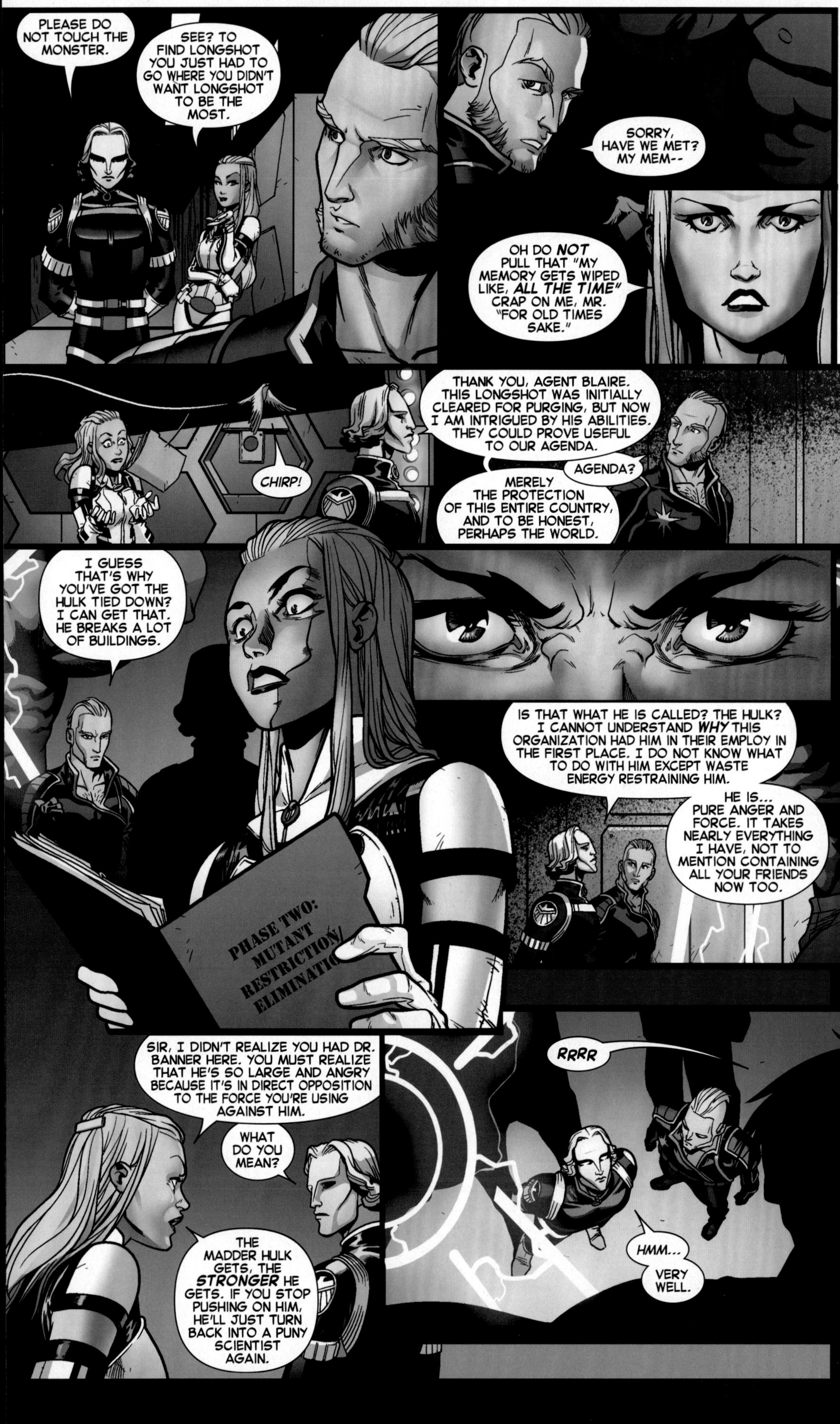

PLEASE DO NOT TOUCH THE MONSTER.
SEE? TO FIND LONGSHOT YOU JUST HAD TO GO WHERE YOU DIDN'T WANT LONGSHOT TO BE THE MOST.
SORRY, HAVE WE MET? MY MEM--
OH DO NOT PULL THAT "MY MEMORY GETS WIPED LIKE, ALL THE TIME" CRAP ON ME, MR. "FOR OLD TIMES SAKE."
CHIRP!
THANK YOU, AGENT BLAIRE. THIS LONGSHOT WAS INITIALLY CLEARED FOR PURGING, BUT NOW I AM INTRIGUED BY HIS ABILITIES. THEY COULD PROVE USEFUL TO OUR AGENDA.
AGENDA?
MERELY THE PROTECTION OF THIS ENTIRE COUNTRY, AND TO BE HONEST, PERHAPS THE WORLD.
I GUESS THAT'S WHY YOU'VE GOT THE HULK TIED DOWN? I CAN GET THAT. HE BREAKS A LOT OF BUILDINGS.
PHASE TWO: MUTANT RESTRICTION/ ELIMINATIO
IS THAT WHAT HE IS CALLED? THE HULK? I CANNOT UNDERSTAND WHY THIS ORGANIZATION HAD HIM IN THEIR EMPLOY IN THE FIRST PLACE. I DO NOT KNOW WHAT TO DO WITH HIM EXCEPT WASTE ENERGY RESTRAINING HIM.
HE IS... PURE ANGER AND FORCE. IT TAKES NEARLY EVERYTHING I HAVE, NOT TO MENTION CONTAINING ALL YOUR FRIENDS NOW TOO.
SIR, I DIDN'T REALIZE YOU HAD DR. BANNER HERE. YOU MUST REALIZE THAT HE'S SO LARGE AND ANGRY BECAUSE IT'S IN DIRECT OPPOSITION TO THE FORCE YOU'RE USING AGAINST HIM.
WHAT DO YOU MEAN?
THE MADDER HULK GETS, THE STRONGER HE GETS. IF YOU STOP PUSHING ON HIM, HE'LL JUST TURN BACK INTO A PUNY SCIENTIST AGAIN.
RRRR
HMM...
VERY WELL.

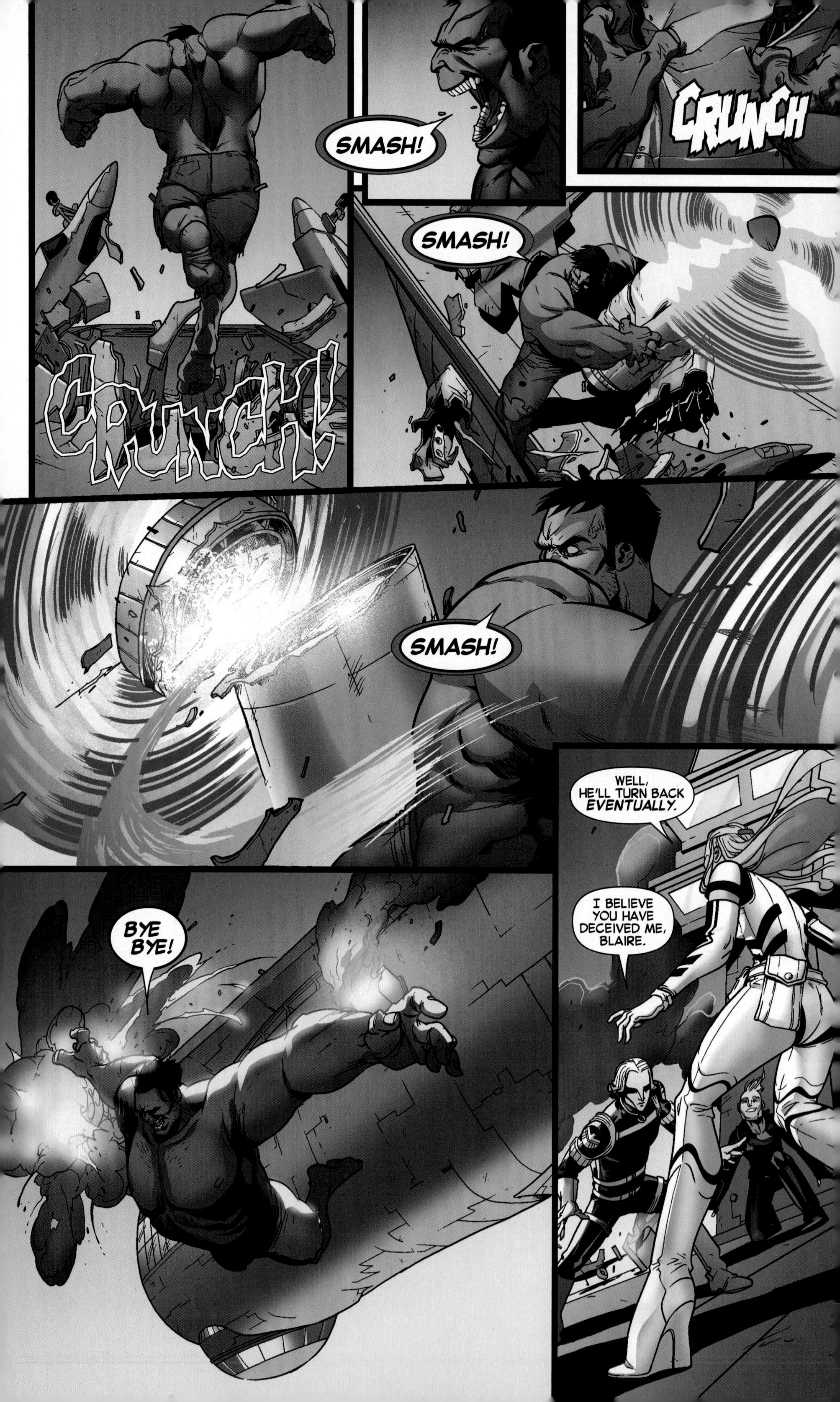
CRUNCH!
SMASH!
CRUNCH
SMASH!
SMASH!
WELL, HE'LL TURN BACK EVENTUALLY.
BYE BYE!
I BELIEVE YOU HAVE DECEIVED ME, BLAIRE.

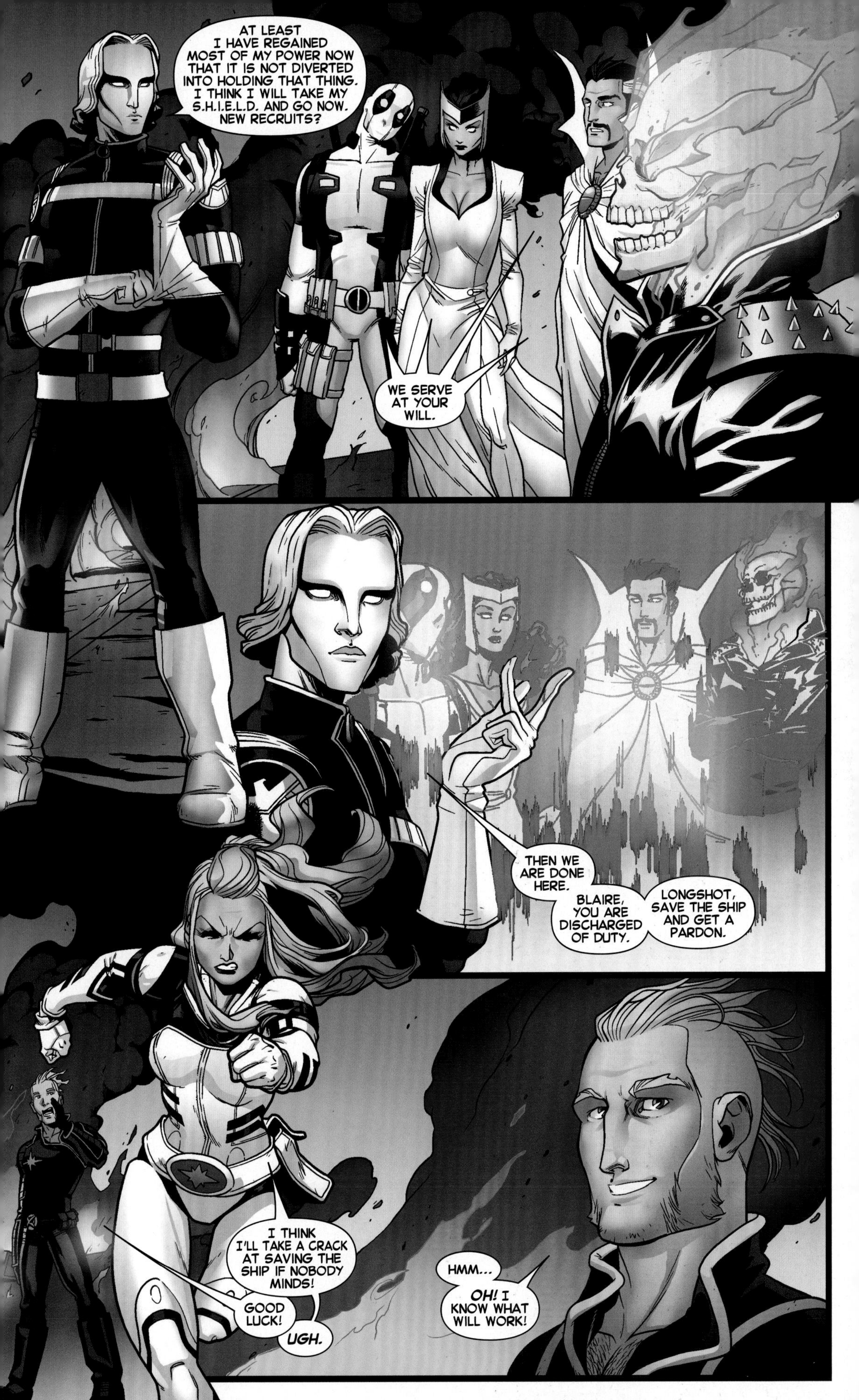
AT LEAST I HAVE REGAINED MOST OF MY POWER NOW THAT IT IS NOT DIVERTED INTO HOLDING THAT THING. I THINK I WILL TAKE MY S.H.I.E.L.D. AND GO NOW. NEW RECRUITS?
WE SERVE AT YOUR WILL.
THEN WE ARE DONE HERE.
BLAIRE, YOU ARE DISCHARGED OF DUTY.
LONGSHOT, SAVE THE SHIP AND GET A PARDON.
I THINK I'LL TAKE A CRACK AT SAVING THE SHIP IF NOBODY MINDS!
GOOD LUCK!
UGH.
HMM...
OH! I KNOW WHAT WILL WORK!

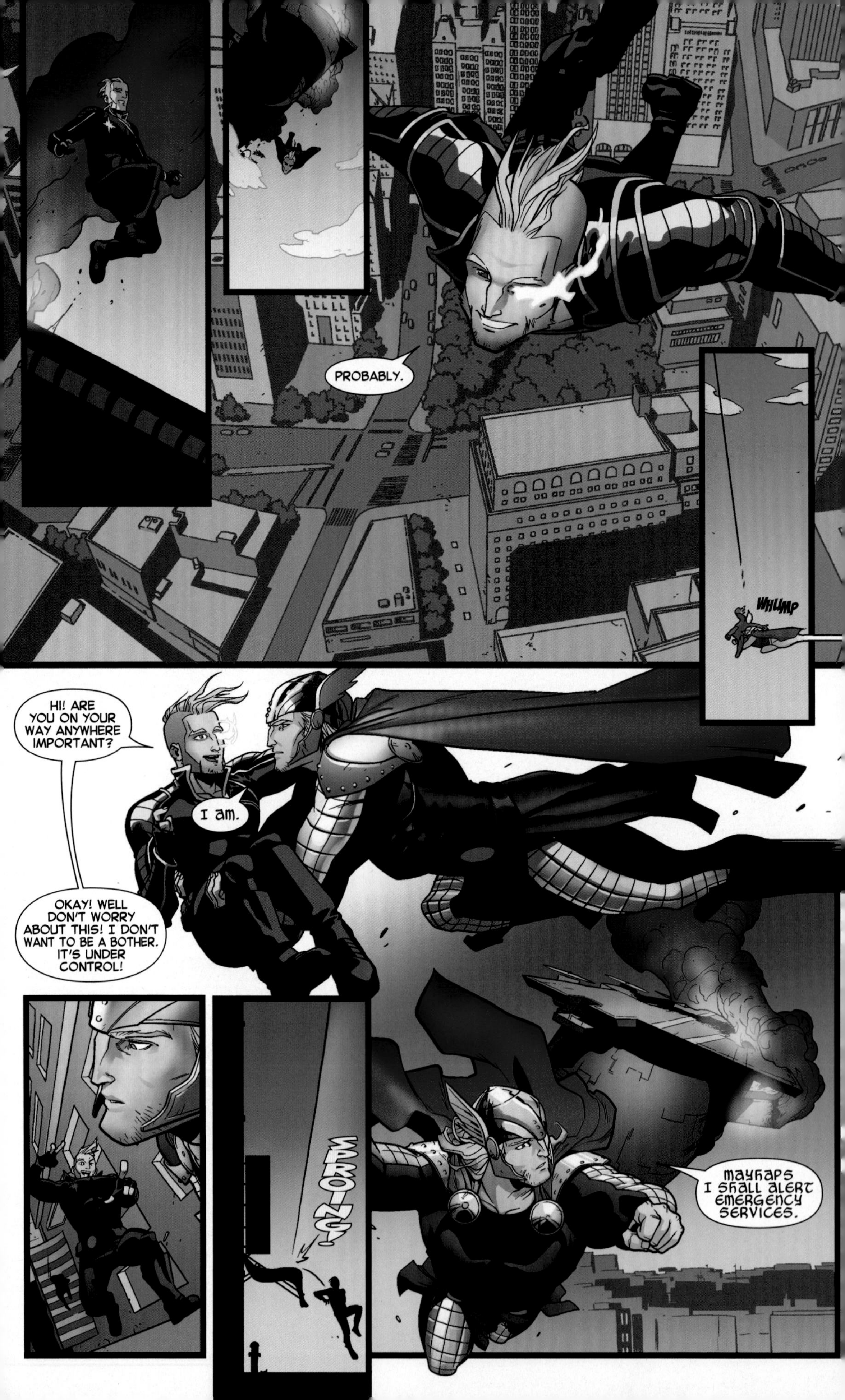
PROBABLY.
WHUMP
HI! ARE YOU ON YOUR WAY ANYWHERE IMPORTANT?
I am.
OKAY! WELL DON'T WORRY ABOUT THIS! I DON'T WANT TO BE A BOTHER. IT'S UNDER CONTROL!
SPROING!
MAYHAPS I SHALL ALERT EMERGENCY SERVICES.

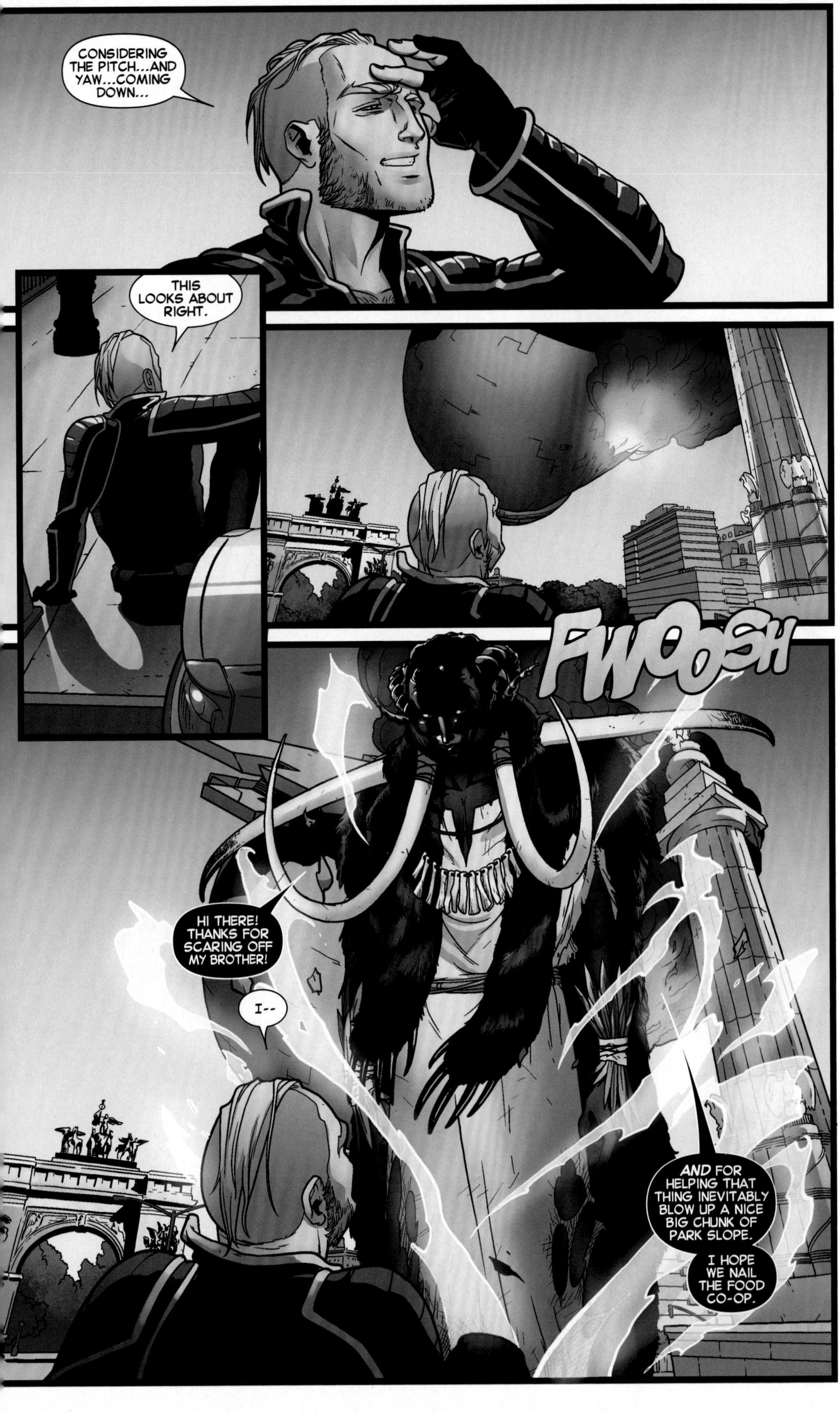
CONSIDERING THE PITCH...AND YAW...COMING DOWN...
THIS LOOKS ABOUT RIGHT.
FWOOSH
HI THERE! THANKS FOR SCARING OFF MY BROTHER!
I--
AND FOR HELPING THAT THING INEVITABLY BLOW UP A NICE BIG CHUNK OF PARK SLOPE.
I HOPE WE NAIL THE FOOD CO-OP.

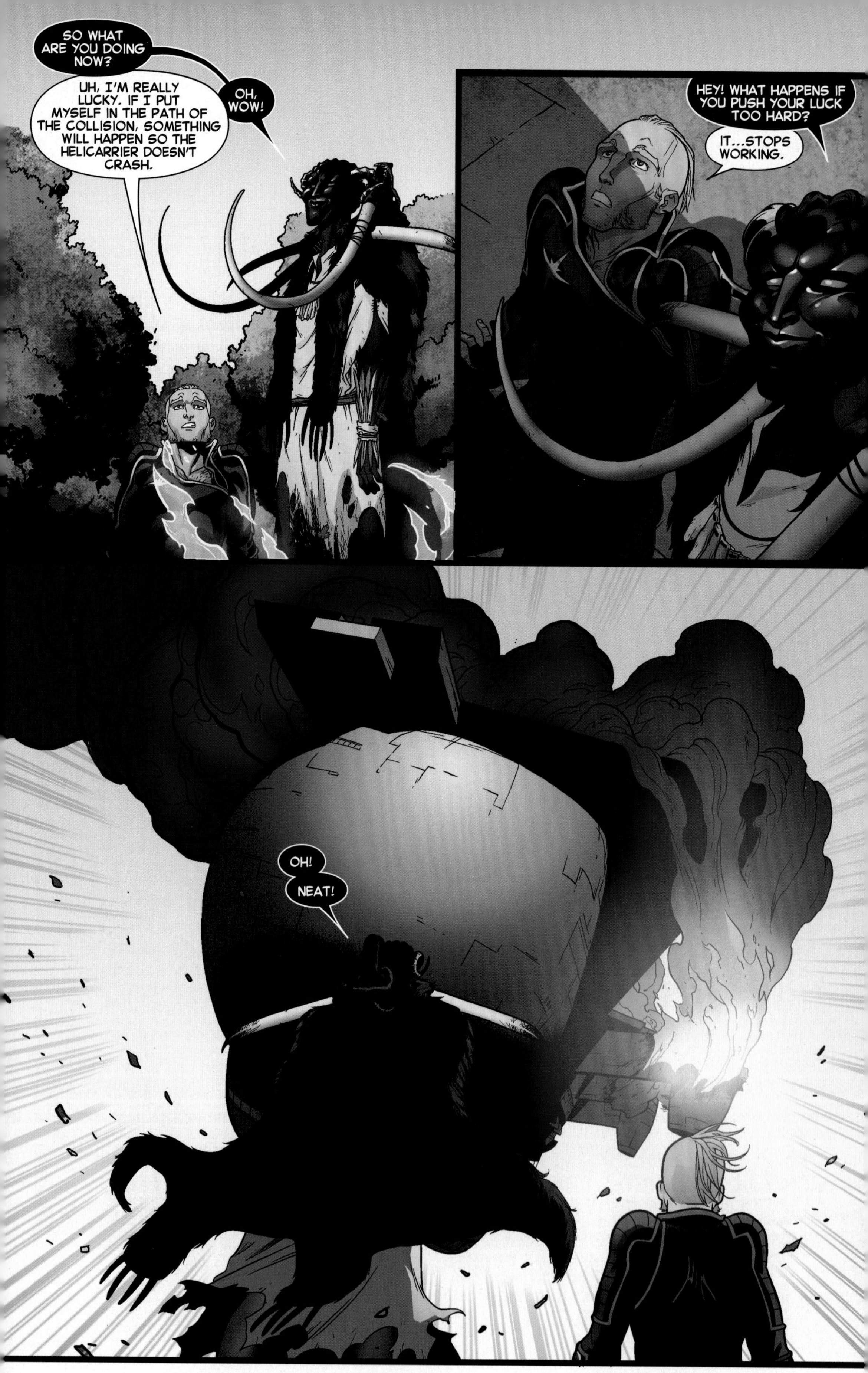
SO WHAT ARE YOU DOING NOW?
UH, I'M REALLY LUCKY. IF I PUT MYSELF IN THE PATH OF THE COLLISION, SOMETHING WILL HAPPEN SO THE HELICARRIER DOESN'T CRASH.
OH, WOW!
HEY! WHAT HAPPENS IF YOU PUSH YOUR LUCK TOO HARD?
IT...STOPS WORKING.
OH!
NEAT!

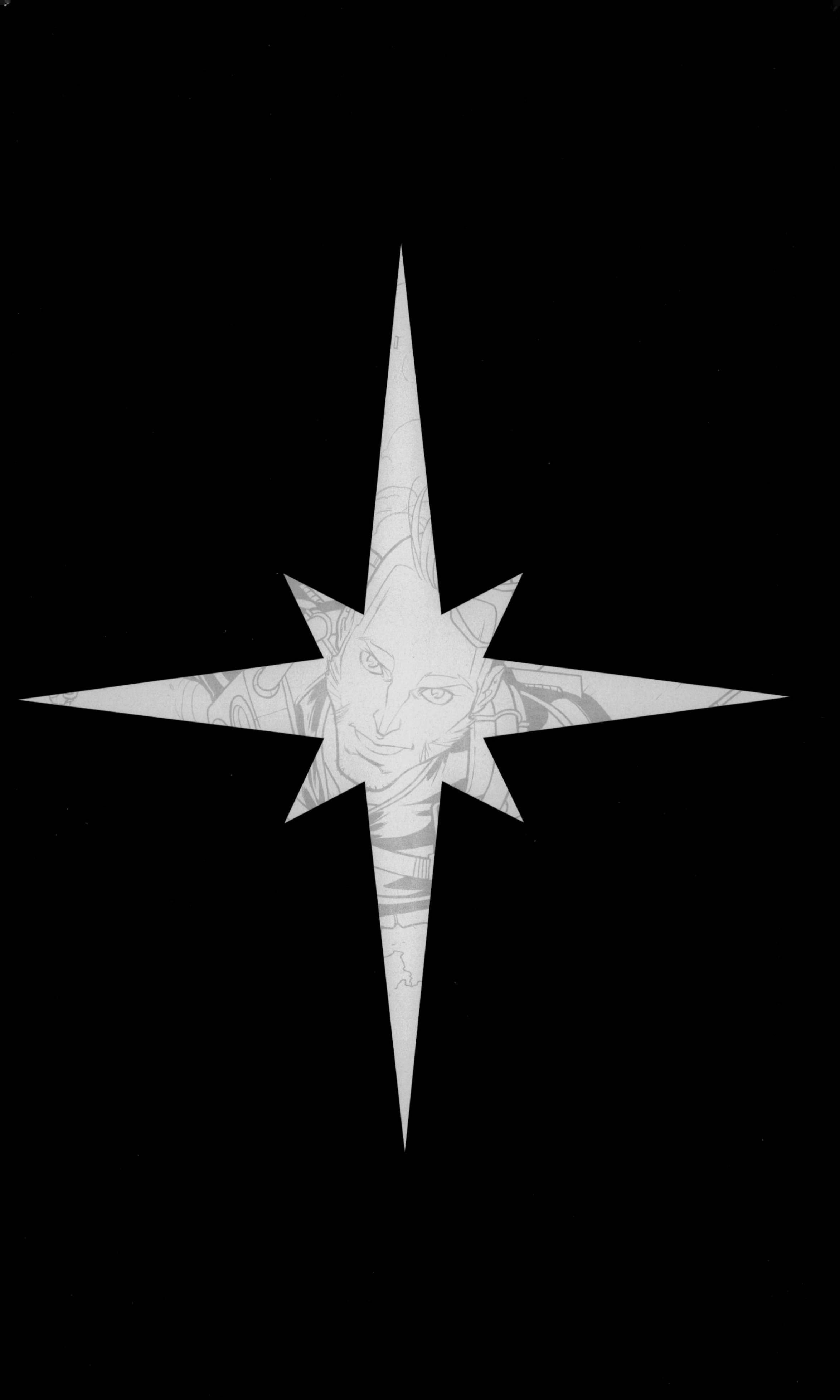

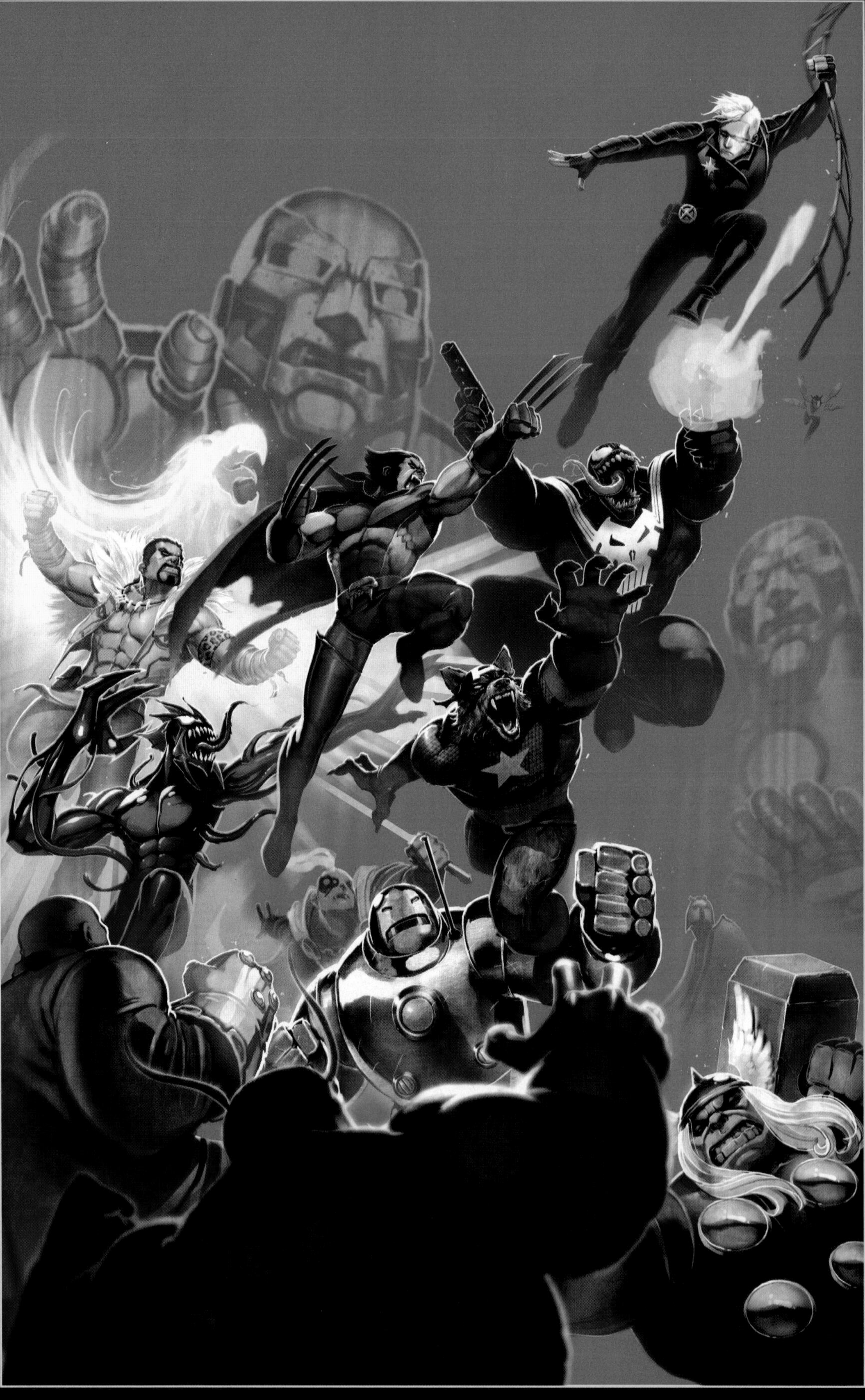

3

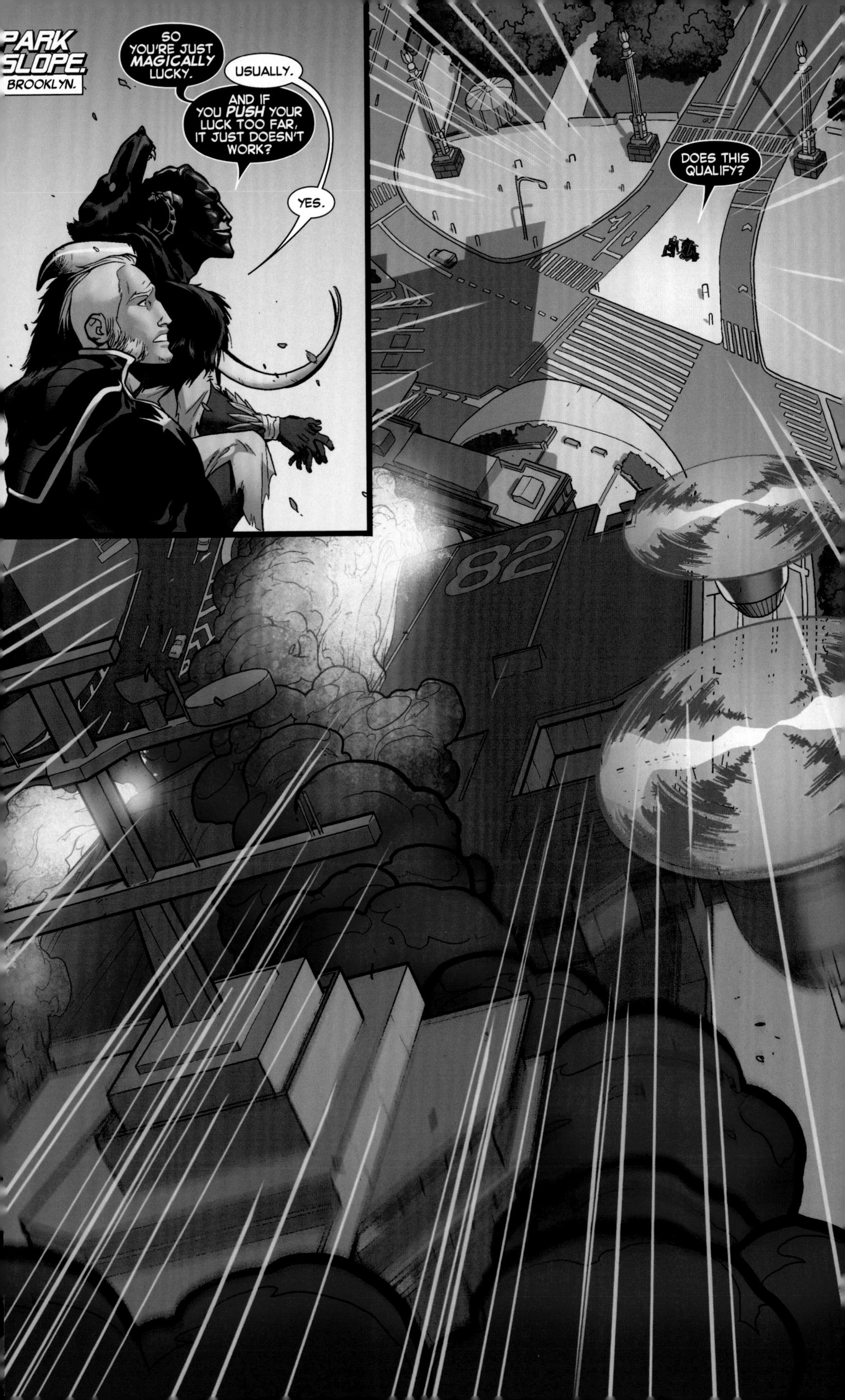
PARK SLOPE. BROOKLYN.
SO YOU'RE JUST MAGICALLY LUCKY.
USUALLY.
AND IF YOU PUSH YOUR LUCK TOO FAR, IT JUST DOESN'T WORK?
YES.
DOES THIS QUALIFY?
82

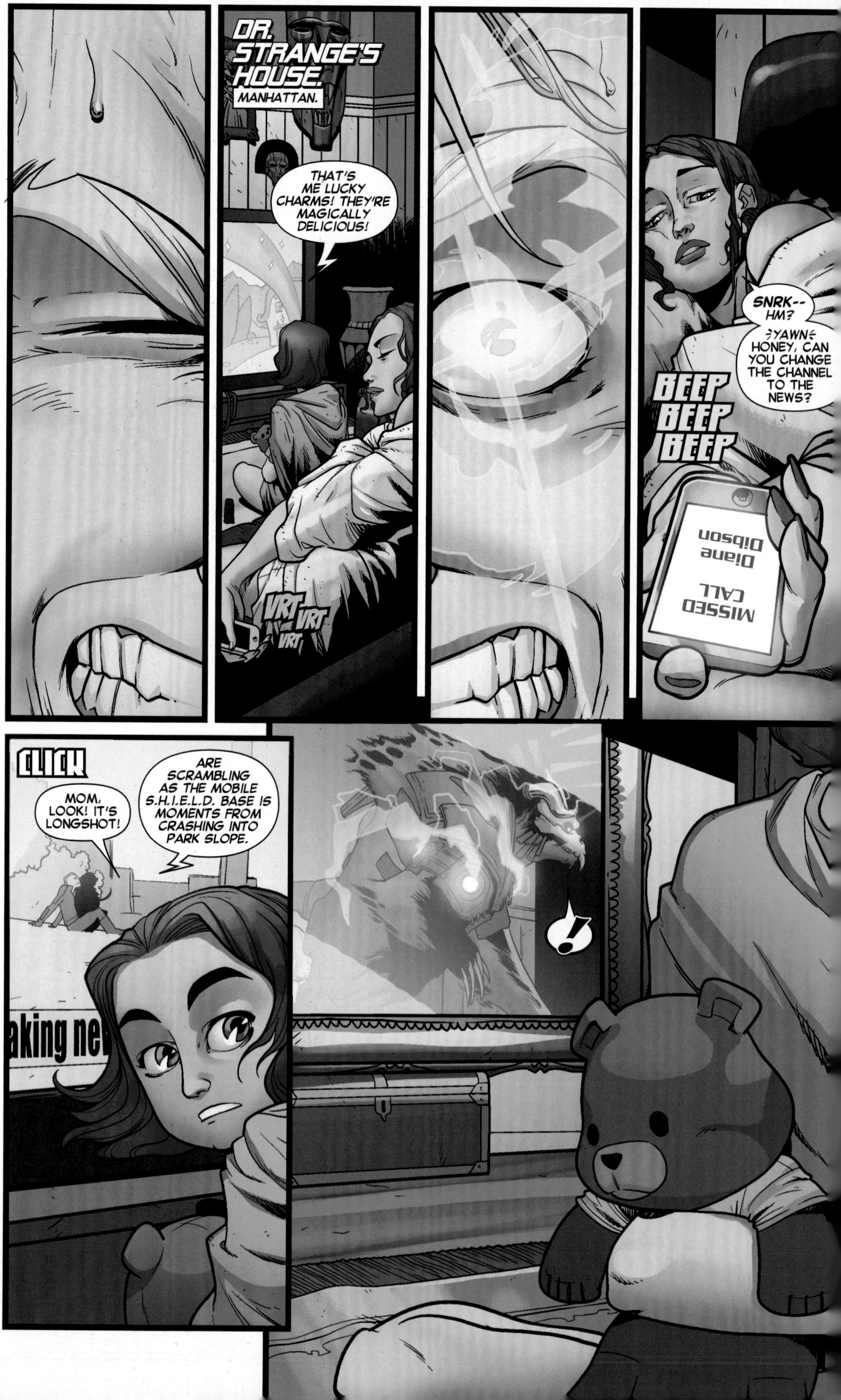
DR. STRANGE'S HOUSE.
MANHATTAN.
THAT'S ME LUCKY CHARMS! THEY'RE MAGICALLY DELICIOUS!
VRT VRT VRT
BEEP BEEP BEEP
SNRK-- HM?
YAWN HONEY, CAN YOU CHANGE THE CHANNEL TO THE NEWS?
MISSED CALL
Diane Dibson
CLICK
MOM, LOOK! IT'S LONGSHOT!
ARE SCRAMBLING AS THE MOBILE S.H.I.E.L.D. BASE IS MOMENTS FROM CRASHING INTO PARK SLOPE.
!

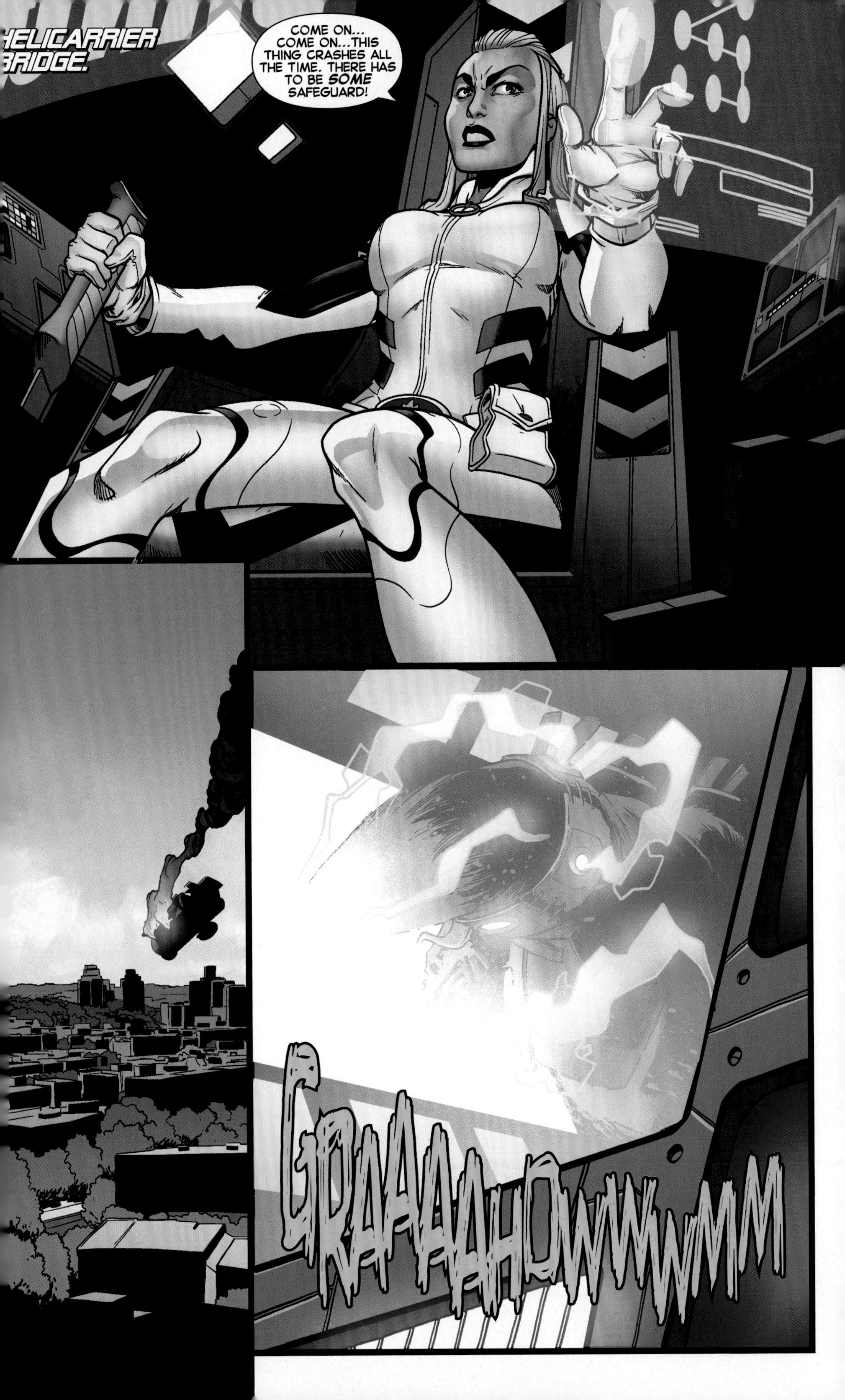
HELICARRIER BRIDGE.
COME ON... COME ON...THIS THING CRASHES ALL THE TIME. THERE HAS TO BE *SOME* SAFEGUARD!
GRAAAAHOWWWWMM

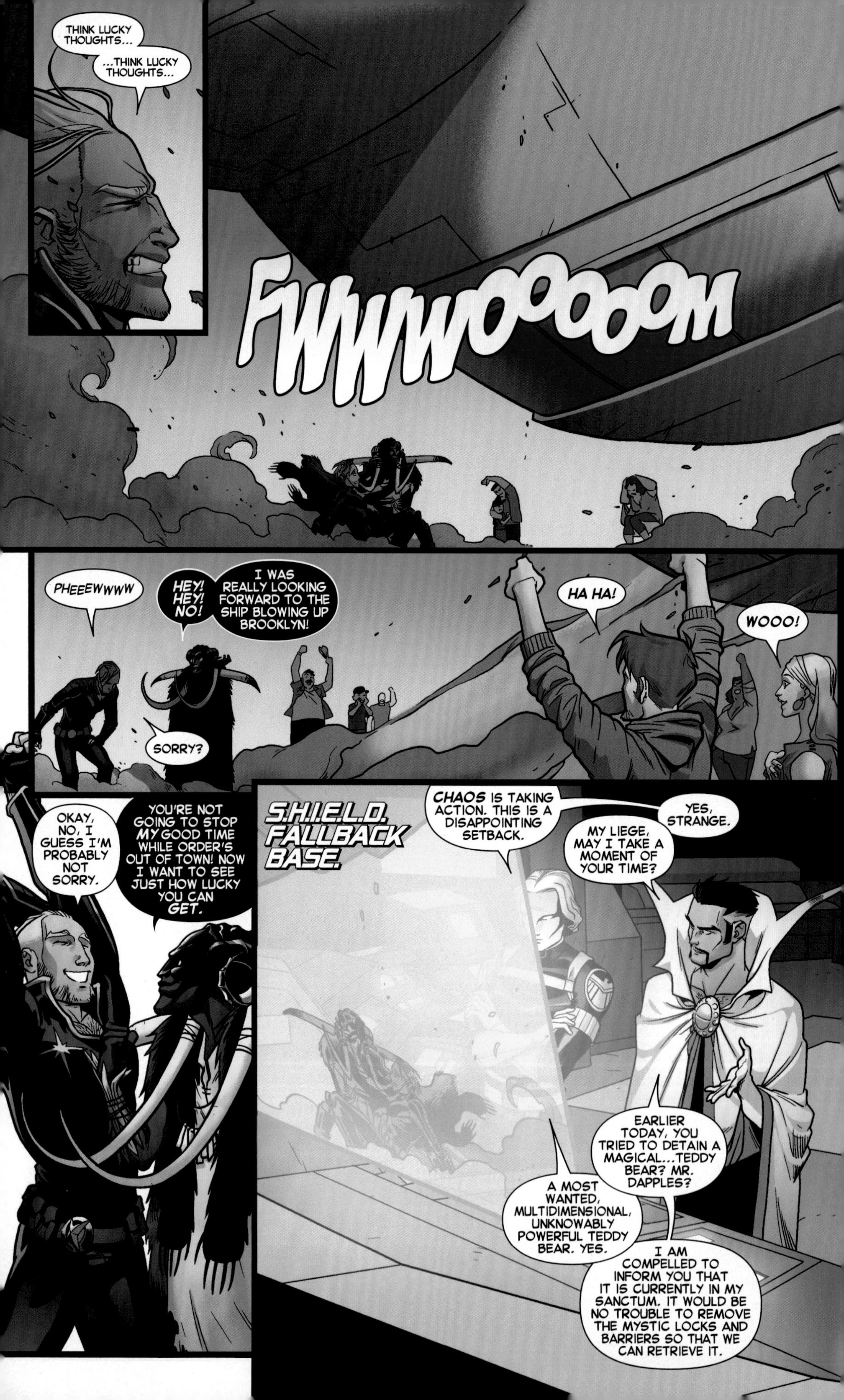
THINK LUCKY THOUGHTS...
...THINK LUCKY THOUGHTS...
FWWWOOOOOM
PHEEEWWWW
HEY! HEY! NO!
I WAS REALLY LOOKING FORWARD TO THE SHIP BLOWING UP BROOKLYN!
SORRY?
HA HA!
WOOO!
OKAY, NO, I GUESS I'M PROBABLY NOT SORRY.
YOU'RE NOT GOING TO STOP MY GOOD TIME WHILE ORDER'S OUT OF TOWN! NOW I WANT TO SEE JUST HOW LUCKY YOU CAN GET.
S.H.I.E.L.D. FALLBACK BASE.
CHAOS IS TAKING ACTION. THIS IS A DISAPPOINTING SETBACK.
YES, STRANGE.
MY LIEGE, MAY I TAKE A MOMENT OF YOUR TIME?
EARLIER TODAY, YOU TRIED TO DETAIN A MAGICAL...TEDDY BEAR? MR. DAPPLES?
A MOST WANTED, MULTIDIMENSIONAL, UNKNOWABLY POWERFUL TEDDY BEAR. YES.
I AM COMPELLED TO INFORM YOU THAT IT IS CURRENTLY IN MY SANCTUM. IT WOULD BE NO TROUBLE TO REMOVE THE MYSTIC LOCKS AND BARRIERS SO THAT WE CAN RETRIEVE IT.

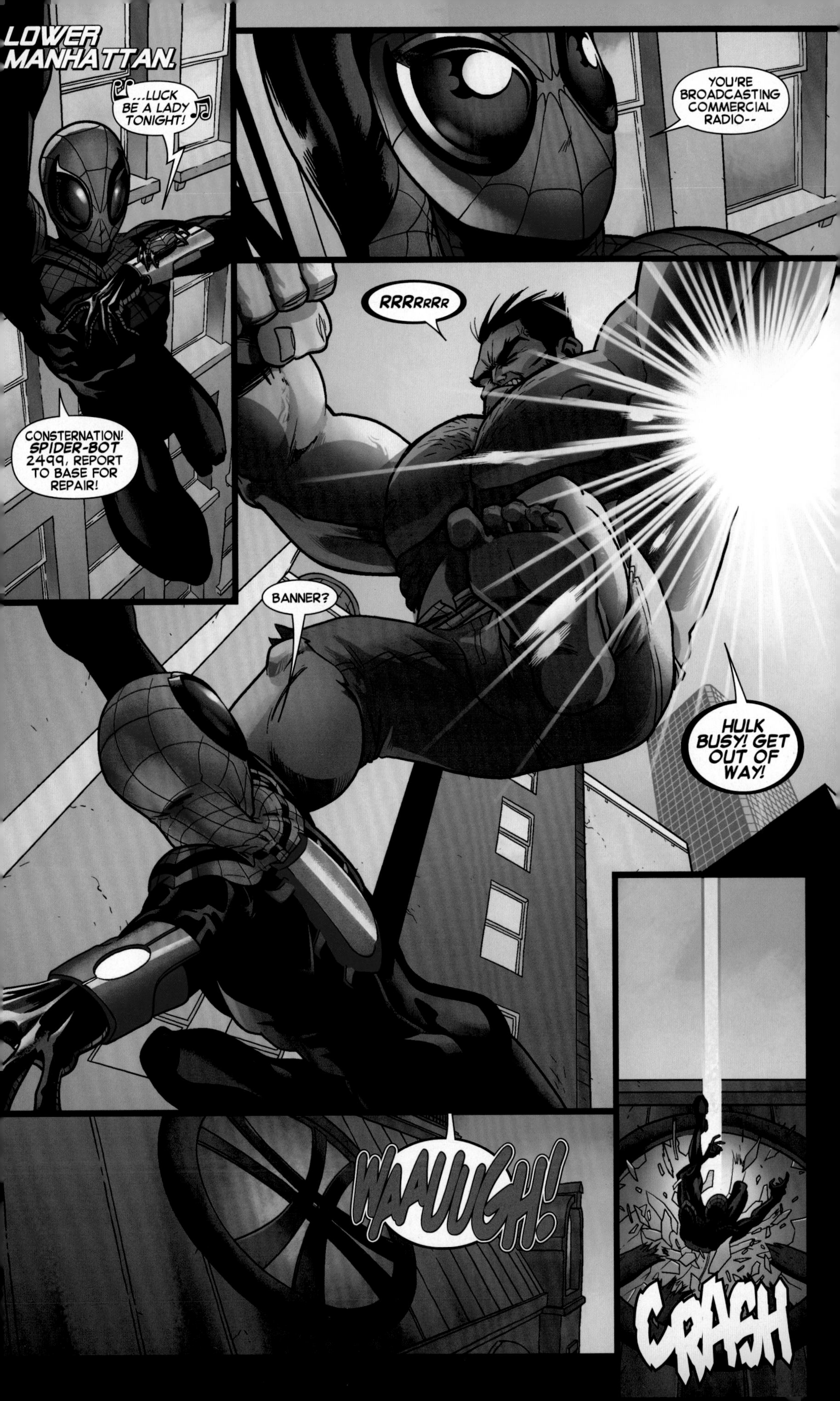
LOWER MANHATTAN.
...LUCK BE A LADY TONIGHT!
CONSTERNATION! SPIDER-BOT 2499, REPORT TO BASE FOR REPAIR!
YOU'RE BROADCASTING COMMERCIAL RADIO--
RRRRRRR
BANNER?
HULK BUSY! GET OUT OF WAY!
WAAUUGH!
CRASH

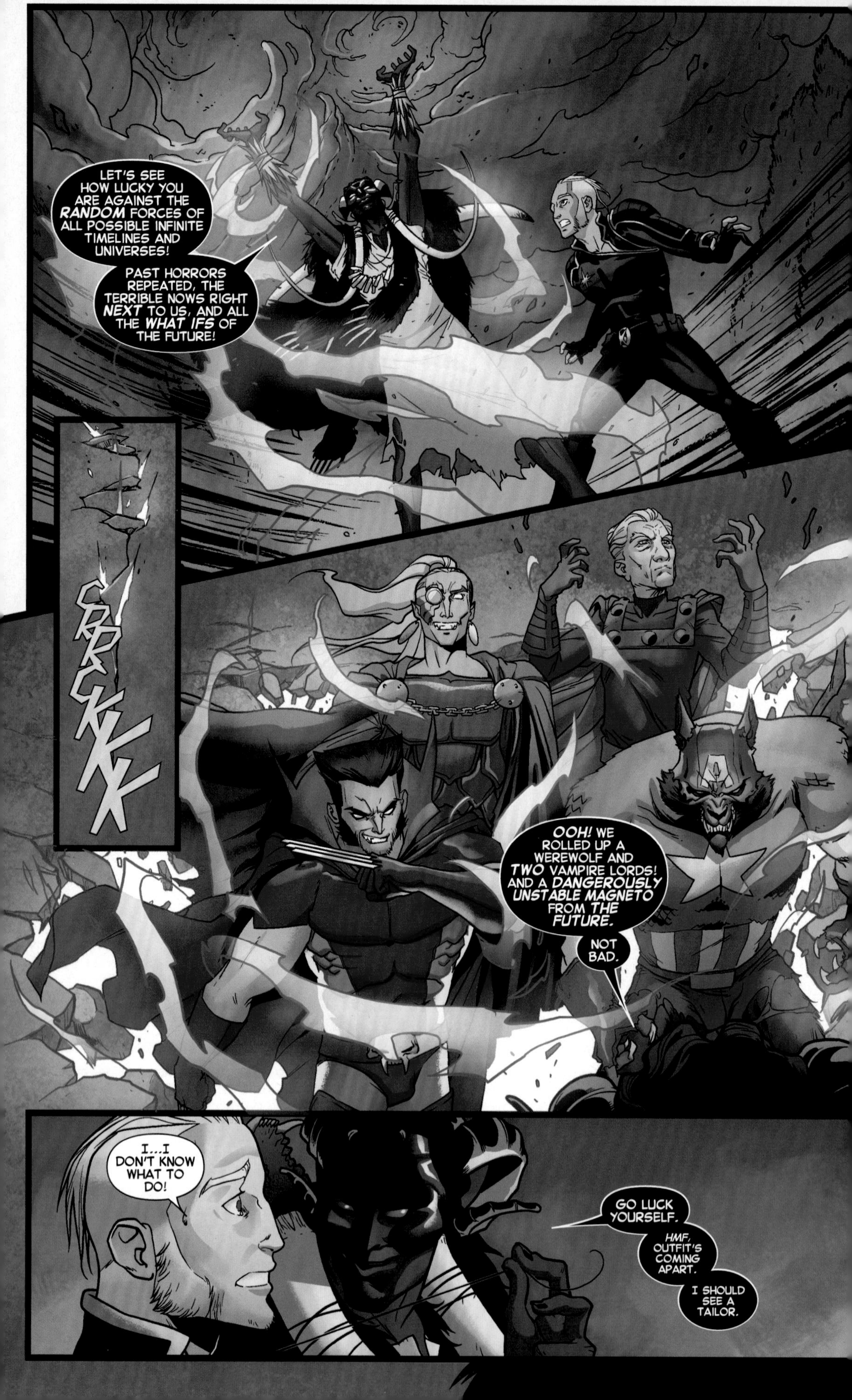

LET'S SEE HOW LUCKY YOU ARE AGAINST THE RANDOM FORCES OF ALL POSSIBLE INFINITE TIMELINES AND UNIVERSES!
PAST HORRORS REPEATED, THE TERRIBLE NOWS RIGHT NEXT TO US, AND ALL THE WHAT IFS OF THE FUTURE!
CRRKKK
OOH! WE ROLLED UP A WEREWOLF AND TWO VAMPIRE LORDS! AND A DANGEROUSLY UNSTABLE MAGNETO FROM THE FUTURE.
NOT BAD.
I...I DON'T KNOW WHAT TO DO!
GO LUCK YOURSELF.
HMF, OUTFIT'S COMING APART.
I SHOULD SEE A TAILOR.

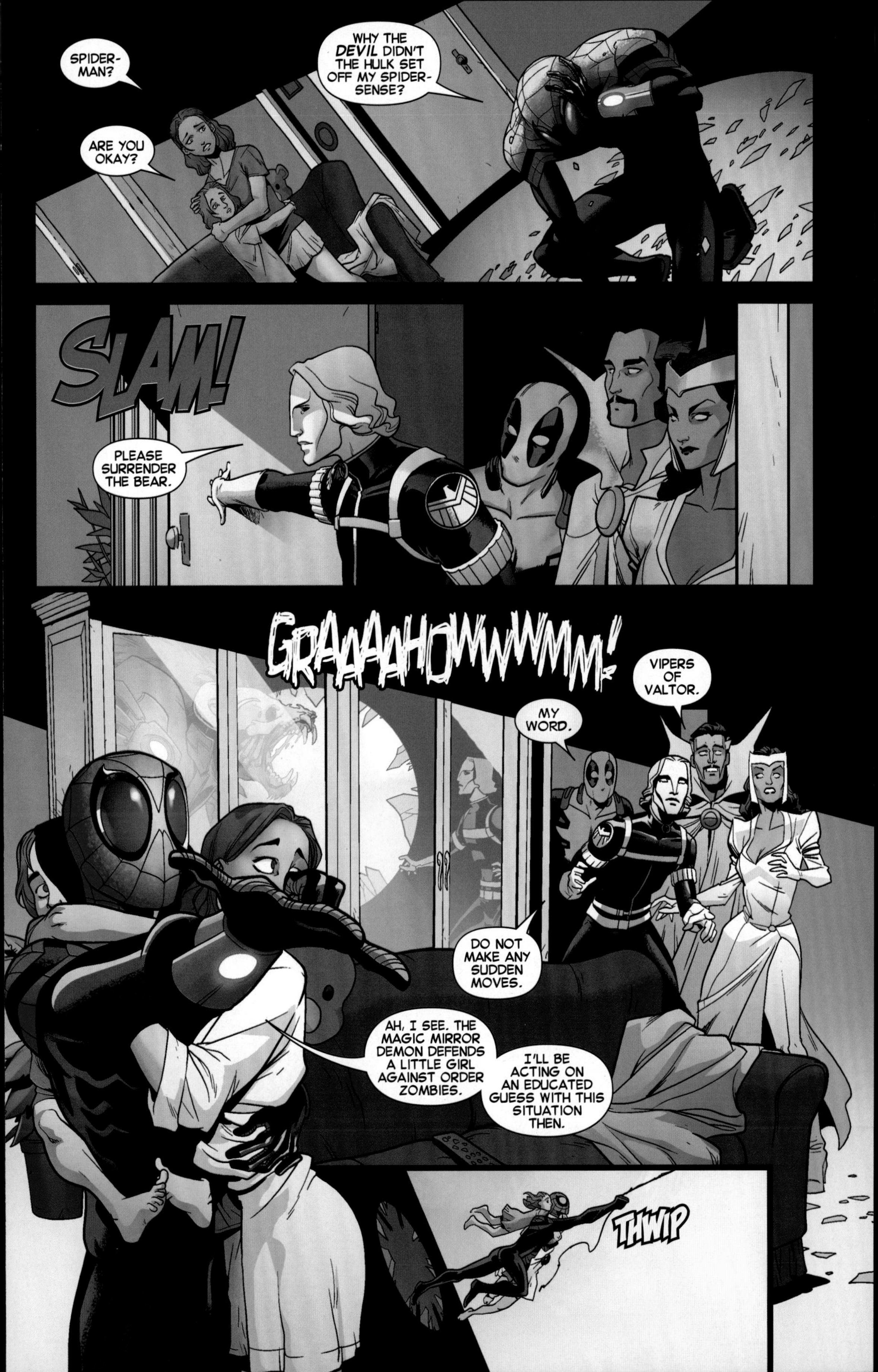
SPIDER-MAN?
WHY THE DEVIL DIDN'T THE HULK SET OFF MY SPIDER-SENSE?
ARE YOU OKAY?
SLAM!
PLEASE SURRENDER THE BEAR.
GRAAAAHOWWWMM!
VIPERS OF VALTOR.
MY WORD.
DO NOT MAKE ANY SUDDEN MOVES.
AH, I SEE. THE MAGIC MIRROR DEMON DEFENDS A LITTLE GIRL AGAINST ORDER ZOMBIES.
I'LL BE ACTING ON AN EDUCATED GUESS WITH THIS SITUATION THEN.
THWIP

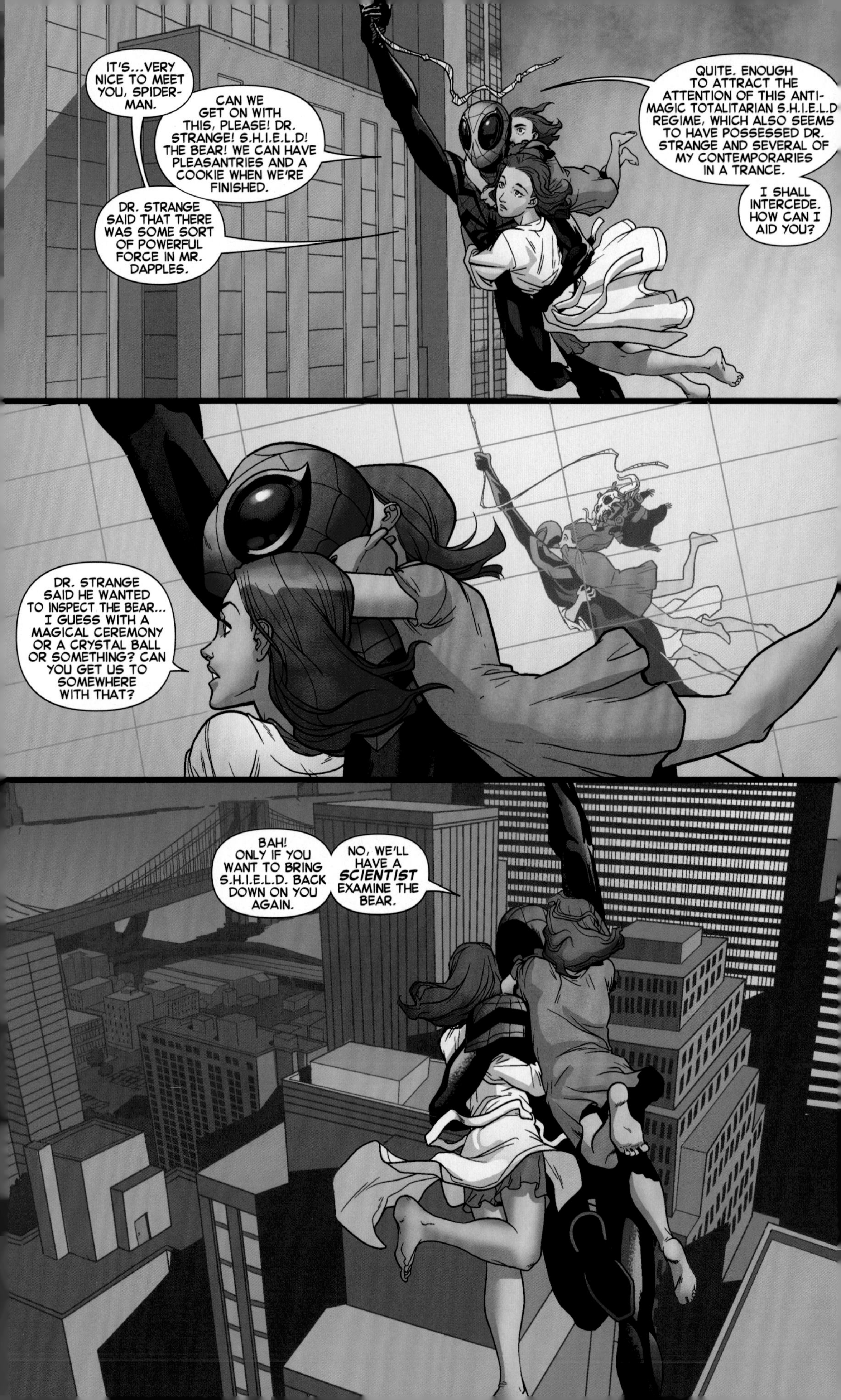
IT'S...VERY NICE TO MEET YOU, SPIDER-MAN.
CAN WE GET ON WITH THIS, PLEASE! DR. STRANGE! S.H.I.E.L.D! THE BEAR! WE CAN HAVE PLEASANTRIES AND A COOKIE WHEN WE'RE FINISHED.
DR. STRANGE SAID THAT THERE WAS SOME SORT OF POWERFUL FORCE IN MR. DAPPLES.
QUITE. ENOUGH TO ATTRACT THE ATTENTION OF THIS ANTI-MAGIC TOTALITARIAN S.H.I.E.L.D REGIME, WHICH ALSO SEEMS TO HAVE POSSESSED DR. STRANGE AND SEVERAL OF MY CONTEMPORARIES IN A TRANCE.
I SHALL INTERCEDE. HOW CAN I AID YOU?
DR. STRANGE SAID HE WANTED TO INSPECT THE BEAR... I GUESS WITH A MAGICAL CEREMONY OR A CRYSTAL BALL OR SOMETHING? CAN YOU GET US TO SOMEWHERE WITH THAT?
BAH! ONLY IF YOU WANT TO BRING S.H.I.E.L.D. BACK DOWN ON YOU AGAIN.
NO, WE'LL HAVE A SCIENTIST EXAMINE THE BEAR.

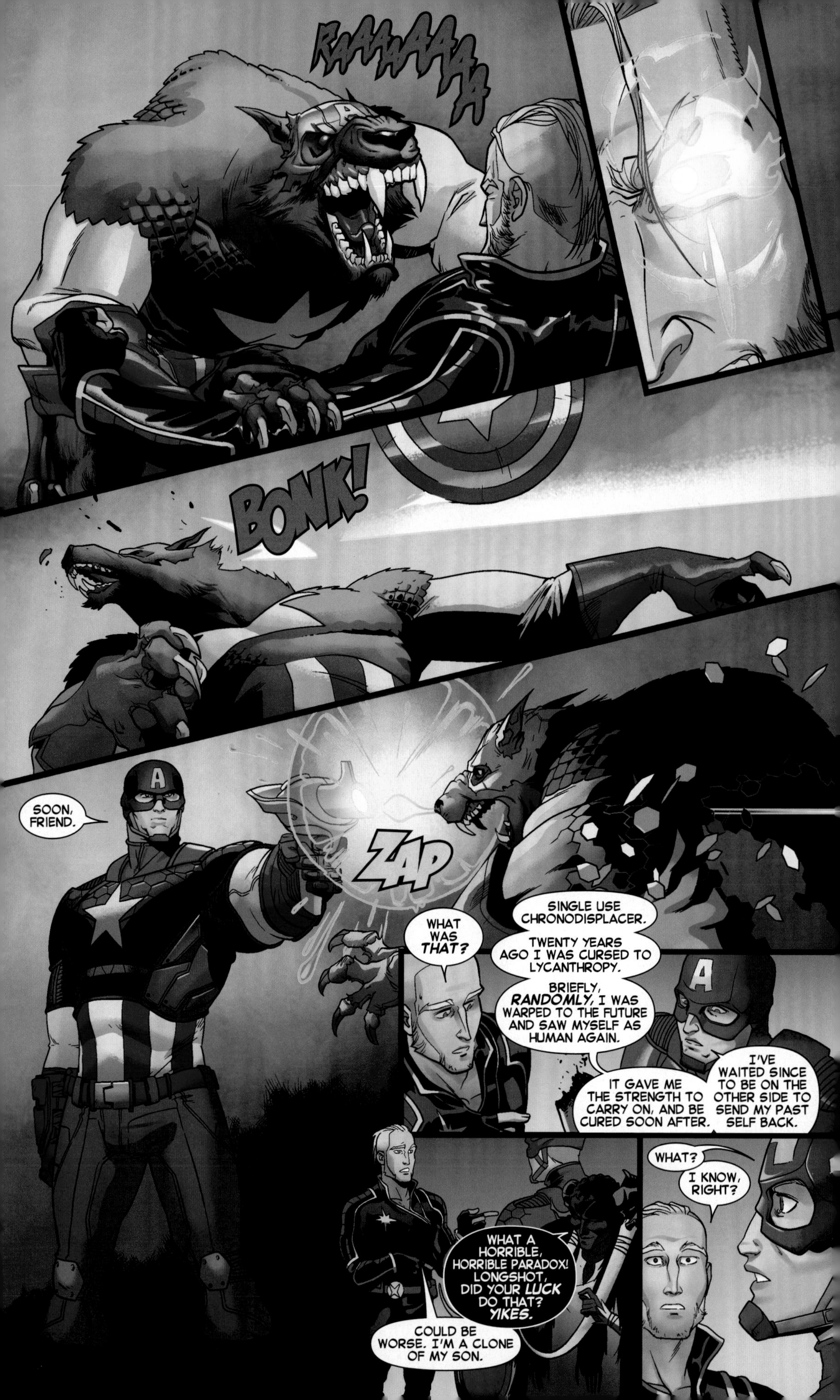
RAAAWAAAAA
BONK!
SOON, FRIEND.
ZAP
WHAT WAS THAT?
SINGLE USE CHRONODISPLACER.
TWENTY YEARS AGO I WAS CURSED TO LYCANTHROPY.
BRIEFLY, RANDOMLY, I WAS WARPED TO THE FUTURE AND SAW MYSELF AS HUMAN AGAIN.
IT GAVE ME THE STRENGTH TO CARRY ON, AND BE CURED SOON AFTER.
I'VE WAITED SINCE TO BE ON THE OTHER SIDE TO SEND MY PAST SELF BACK.
WHAT A HORRIBLE, HORRIBLE PARADOX! LONGSHOT, DID YOUR LUCK DO THAT? YIKES.
COULD BE WORSE. I'M A CLONE OF MY SON.
WHAT?
I KNOW, RIGHT?

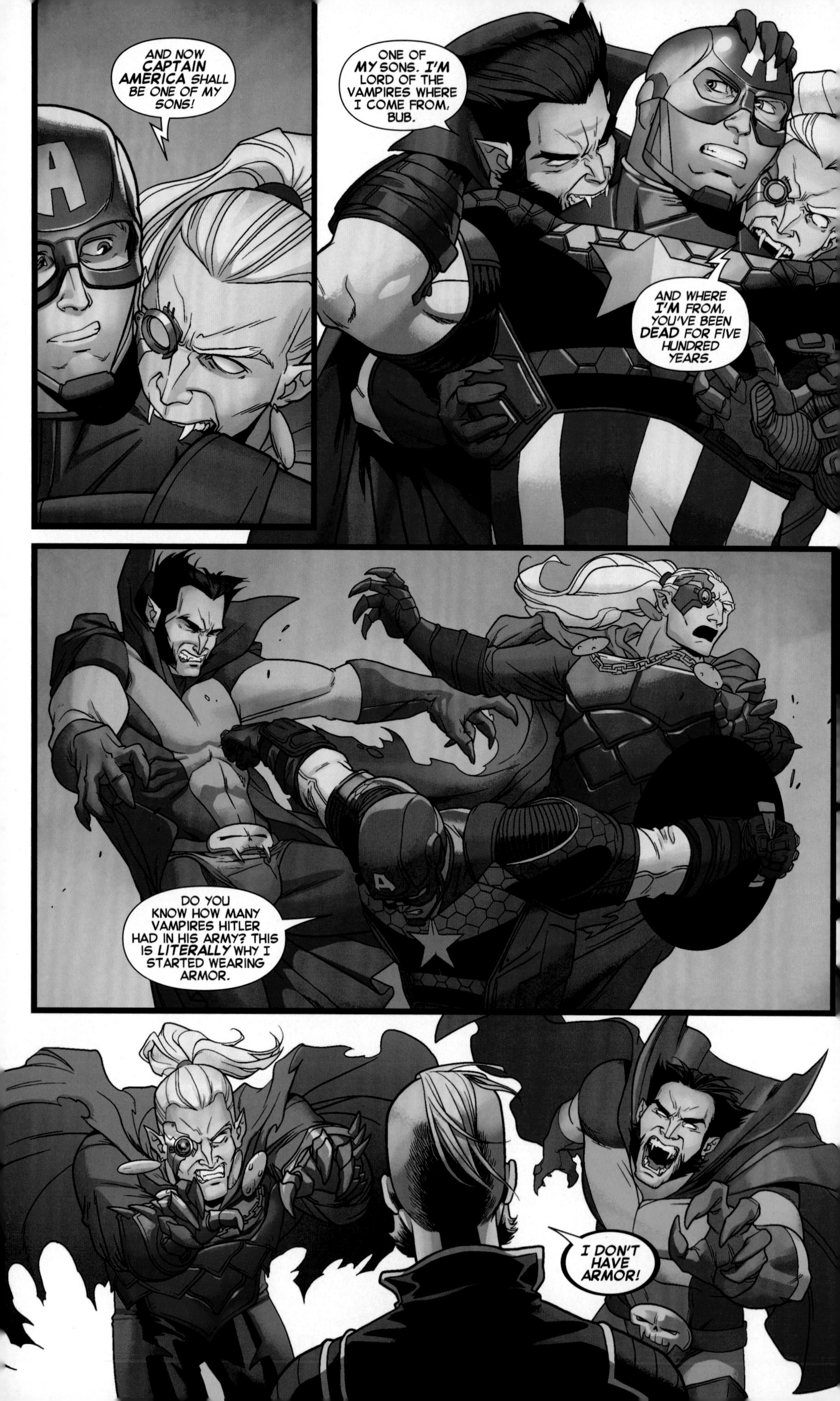
AND NOW CAPTAIN AMERICA SHALL BE ONE OF MY SONS!
ONE OF MY SONS. I'M LORD OF THE VAMPIRES WHERE I COME FROM, BUB.
AND WHERE I'M FROM, YOU'VE BEEN DEAD FOR FIVE HUNDRED YEARS.
DO YOU KNOW HOW MANY VAMPIRES HITLER HAD IN HIS ARMY? THIS IS LITERALLY WHY I STARTED WEARING ARMOR.
I DON'T HAVE ARMOR!

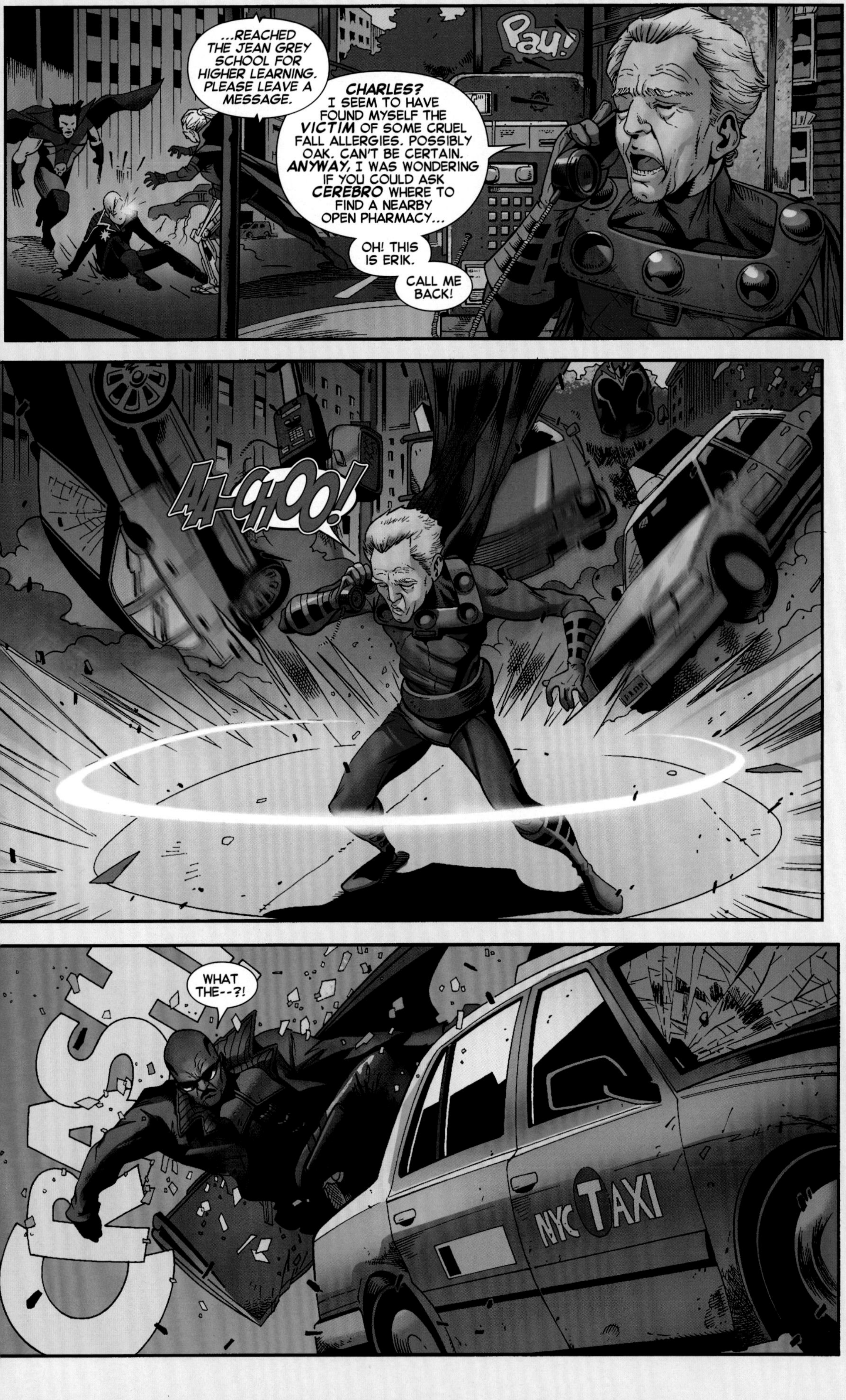

...REACHED THE JEAN GREY SCHOOL FOR HIGHER LEARNING. PLEASE LEAVE A MESSAGE.
Pau!
CHARLES? I SEEM TO HAVE FOUND MYSELF THE VICTIM OF SOME CRUEL FALL ALLERGIES. POSSIBLY OAK. CAN'T BE CERTAIN. ANYWAY, I WAS WONDERING IF YOU COULD ASK CEREBRO WHERE TO FIND A NEARBY OPEN PHARMACY...
OH! THIS IS ERIK.
CALL ME BACK!
AA-CHOO!
WHAT THE--?!
NYC TAXI

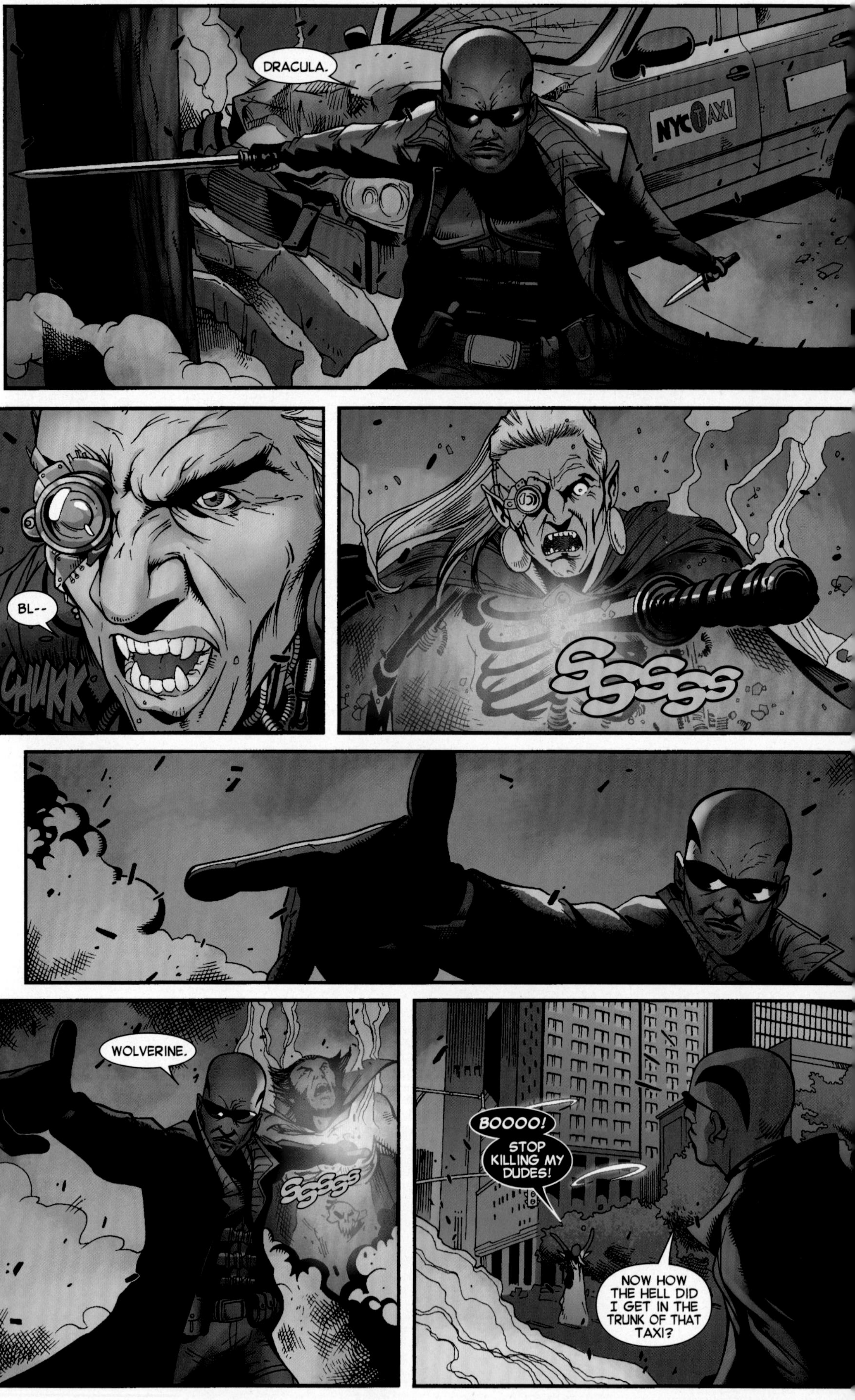
DRACULA.
BL--
CHUKK
SSSSS
WOLVERINE.
SSSSS
BOOOO!
STOP KILLING MY DUDES!
NOW HOW THE HELL DID I GET IN THE TRUNK OF THAT TAXI?

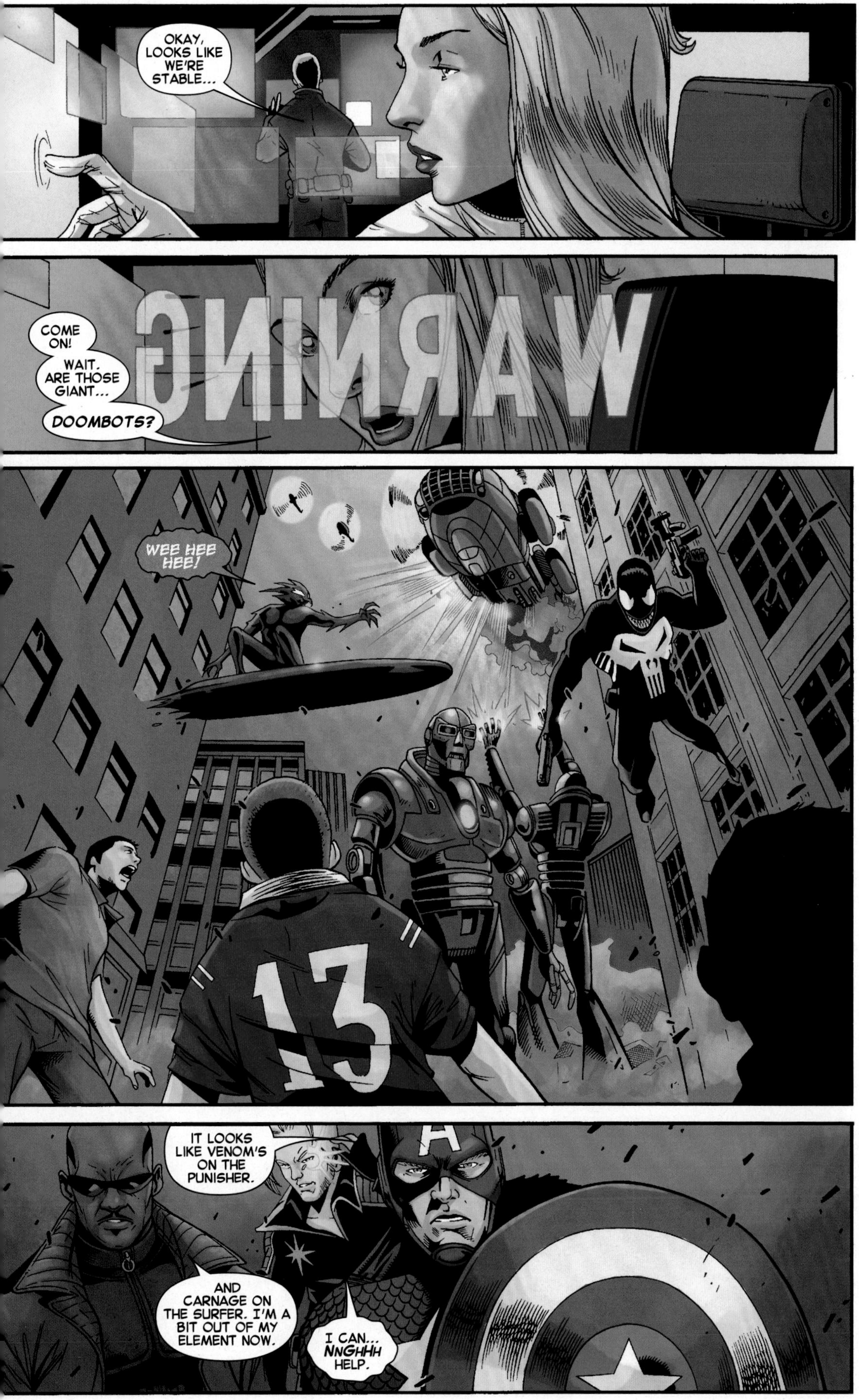
OKAY, LOOKS LIKE WE'RE STABLE...
WARNING
COME ON!
WAIT. ARE THOSE GIANT...
DOOMBOTS?
WEE HEE HEE!
13
IT LOOKS LIKE VENOM'S ON THE PUNISHER.
AND CARNAGE ON THE SURFER. I'M A BIT OUT OF MY ELEMENT NOW.
I CAN... NNGHHH HELP.

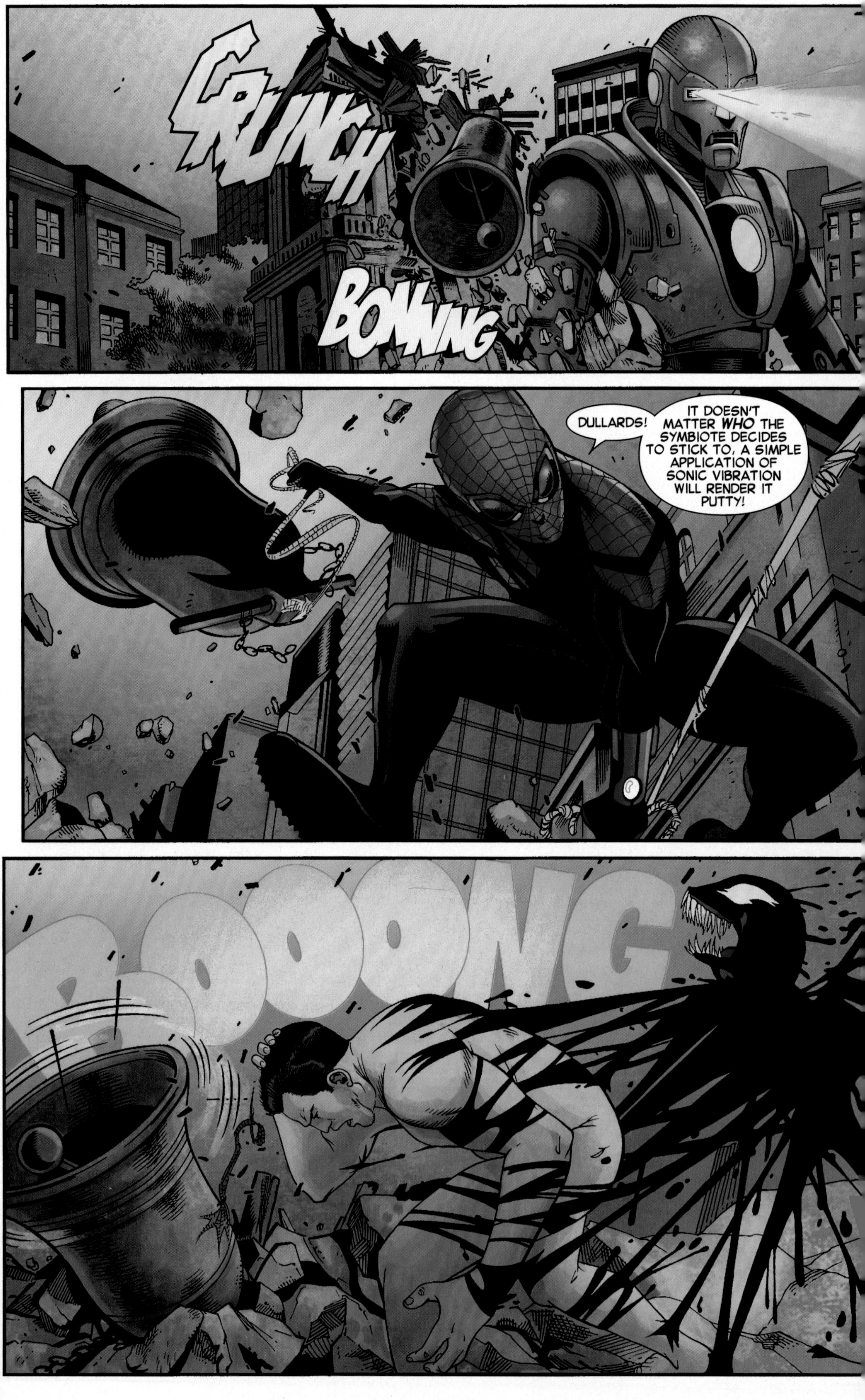
CRUNCH
BONNNG
DULLARDS!
IT DOESN'T MATTER WHO THE SYMBIOTE DECIDES TO STICK TO, A SIMPLE APPLICATION OF SONIC VIBRATION WILL RENDER IT PUTTY!
BOOONG

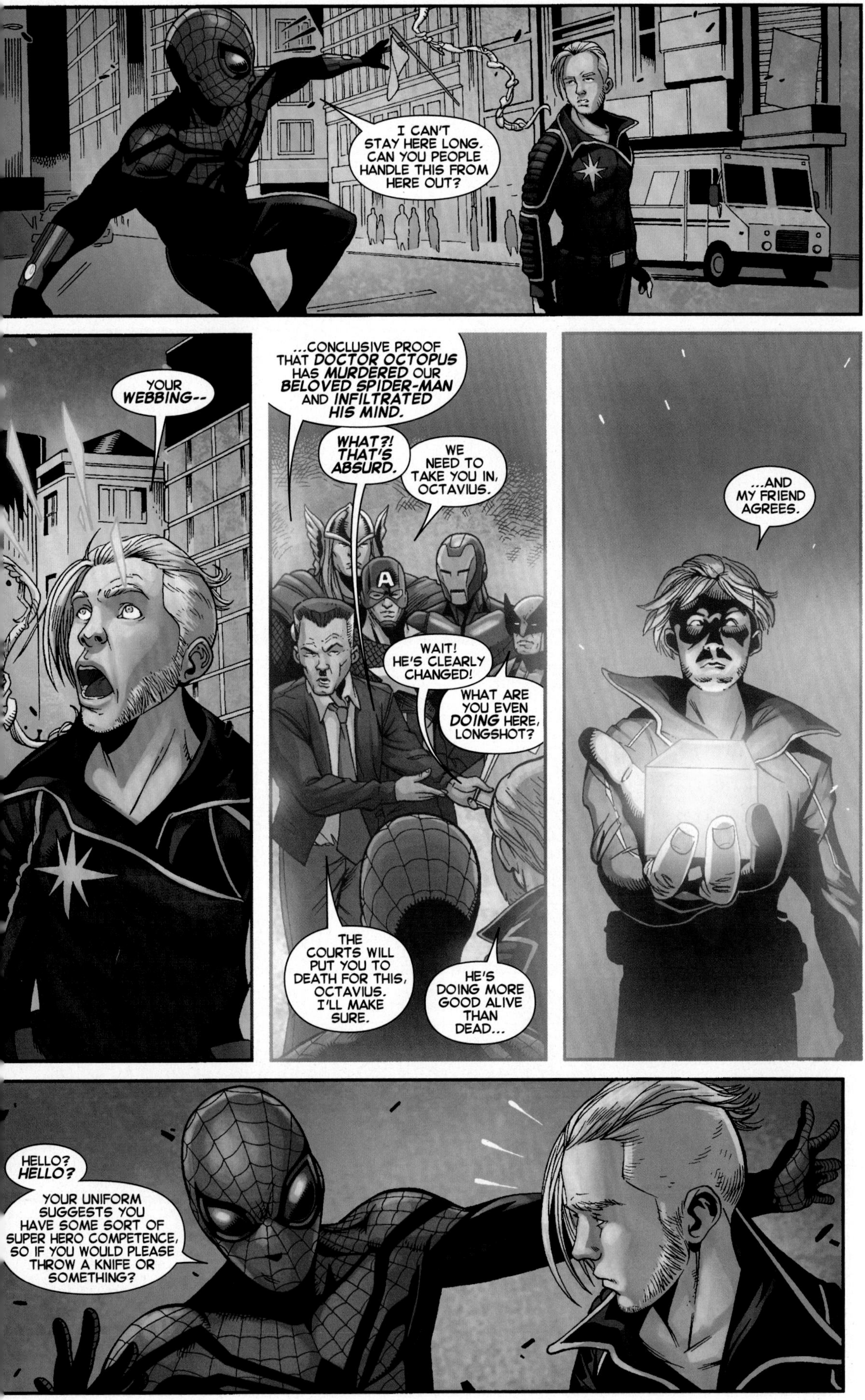
I CAN'T STAY HERE LONG. CAN YOU PEOPLE HANDLE THIS FROM HERE OUT?
YOUR WEBBING--
...CONCLUSIVE PROOF THAT DOCTOR OCTOPUS HAS MURDERED OUR BELOVED SPIDER-MAN AND INFILTRATED HIS MIND.
WHAT?! THAT'S ABSURD.
WE NEED TO TAKE YOU IN, OCTAVIUS.
WAIT! HE'S CLEARLY CHANGED!
WHAT ARE YOU EVEN DOING HERE, LONGSHOT?
THE COURTS WILL PUT YOU TO DEATH FOR THIS, OCTAVIUS. I'LL MAKE SURE.
HE'S DOING MORE GOOD ALIVE THAN DEAD...
...AND MY FRIEND AGREES.
HELLO? HELLO?
YOUR UNIFORM SUGGESTS YOU HAVE SOME SORT OF SUPER HERO COMPETENCE, SO IF YOU WOULD PLEASE THROW A KNIFE OR SOMETHING?

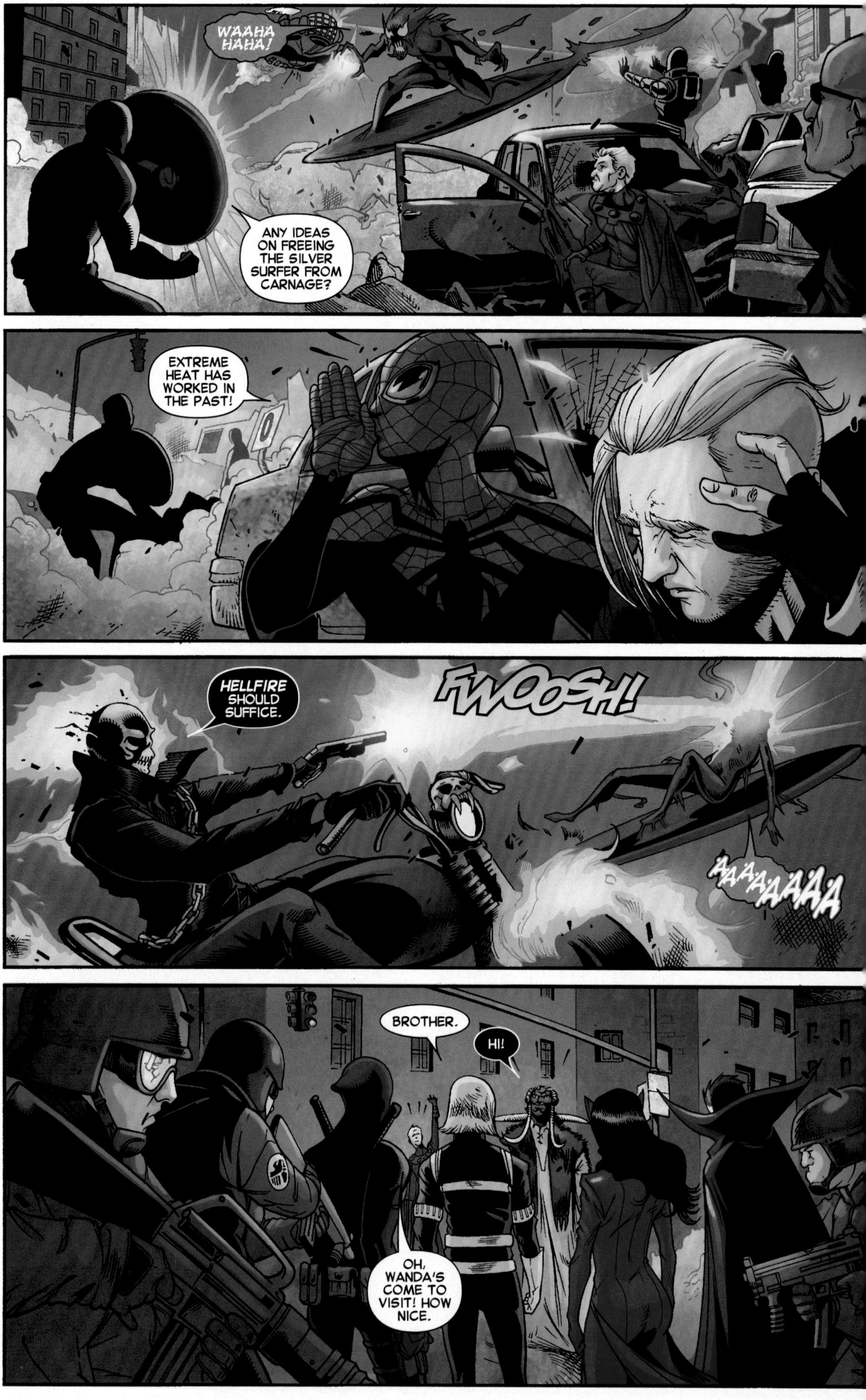
WAAHA HAHA!
ANY IDEAS ON FREEING THE SILVER SURFER FROM CARNAGE?
EXTREME HEAT HAS WORKED IN THE PAST!
HELLFIRE SHOULD SUFFICE.
FWOOSH!
AAAAAAAA
BROTHER.
HI!
OH, WANDA'S COME TO VISIT! HOW NICE.

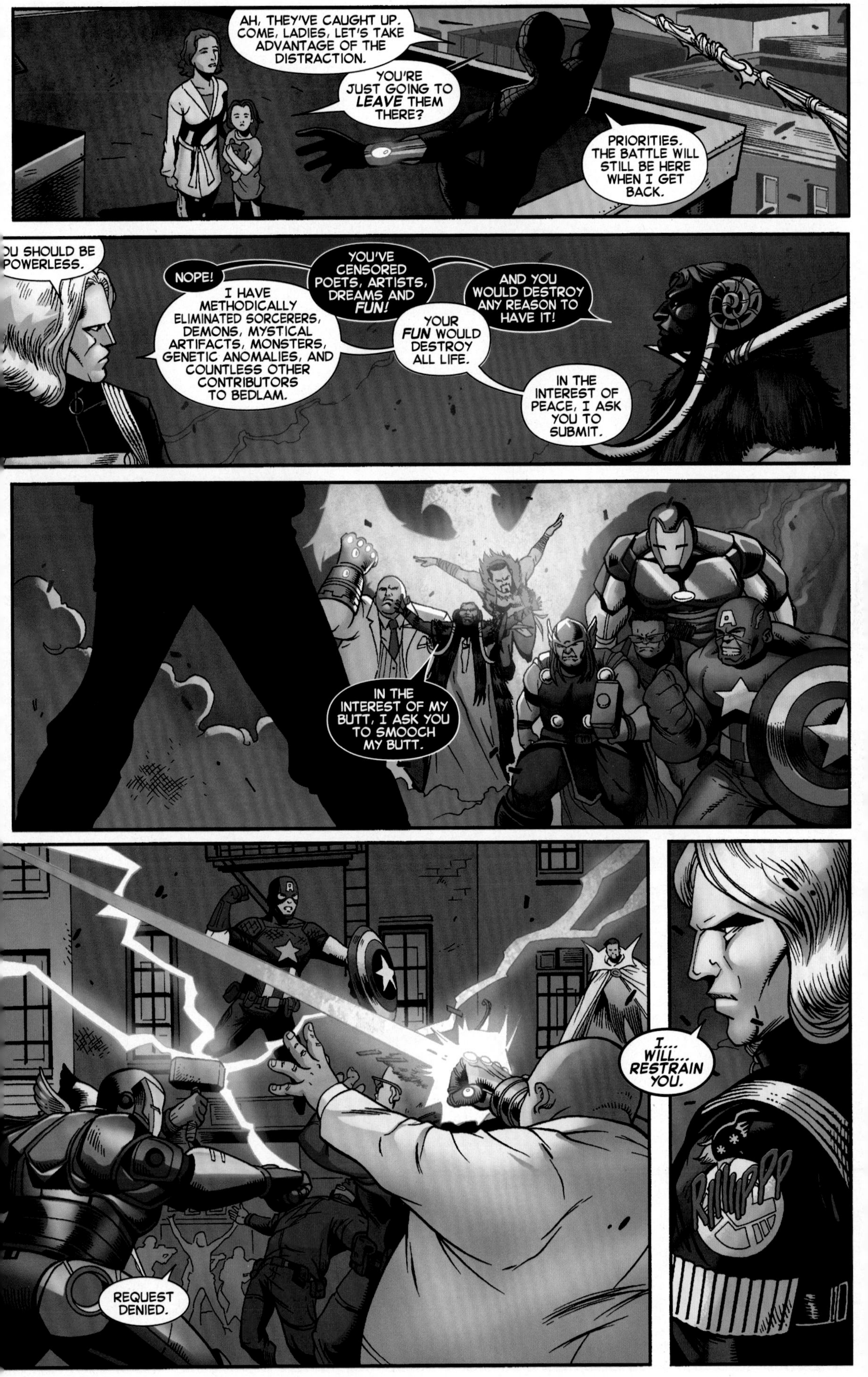
AH, THEY'VE CAUGHT UP. COME, LADIES, LET'S TAKE ADVANTAGE OF THE DISTRACTION.
YOU'RE JUST GOING TO LEAVE THEM THERE?
PRIORITIES. THE BATTLE WILL STILL BE HERE WHEN I GET BACK.
OU SHOULD BE POWERLESS.
NOPE!
I HAVE METHODICALLY ELIMINATED SORCERERS, DEMONS, MYSTICAL ARTIFACTS, MONSTERS, GENETIC ANOMALIES, AND COUNTLESS OTHER CONTRIBUTORS TO BEDLAM.
YOU'VE CENSORED POETS, ARTISTS, DREAMS AND FUN!
YOUR FUN WOULD DESTROY ALL LIFE.
AND YOU WOULD DESTROY ANY REASON TO HAVE IT!
IN THE INTEREST OF PEACE, I ASK YOU TO SUBMIT.
IN THE INTEREST OF MY BUTT, I ASK YOU TO SMOOCH MY BUTT.
REQUEST DENIED.
I... WILL... RESTRAIN YOU.
RHIIPPP

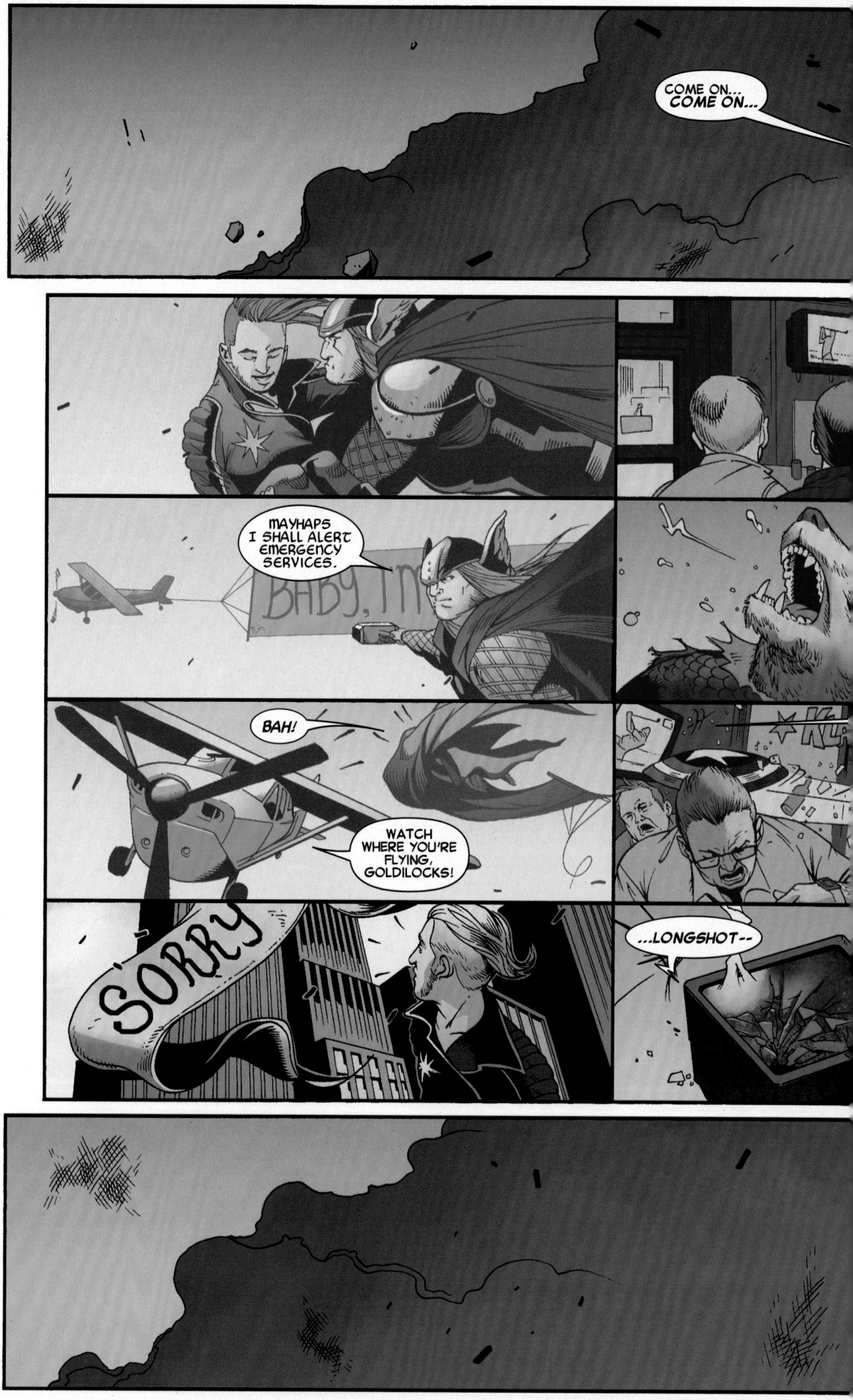
COME ON...
COME ON...
MAYHAPS I SHALL ALERT EMERGENCY SERVICES.
BAH!
WATCH WHERE YOU'RE FLYING, GOLDILOCKS!
SORRY
...LONGSHOT--

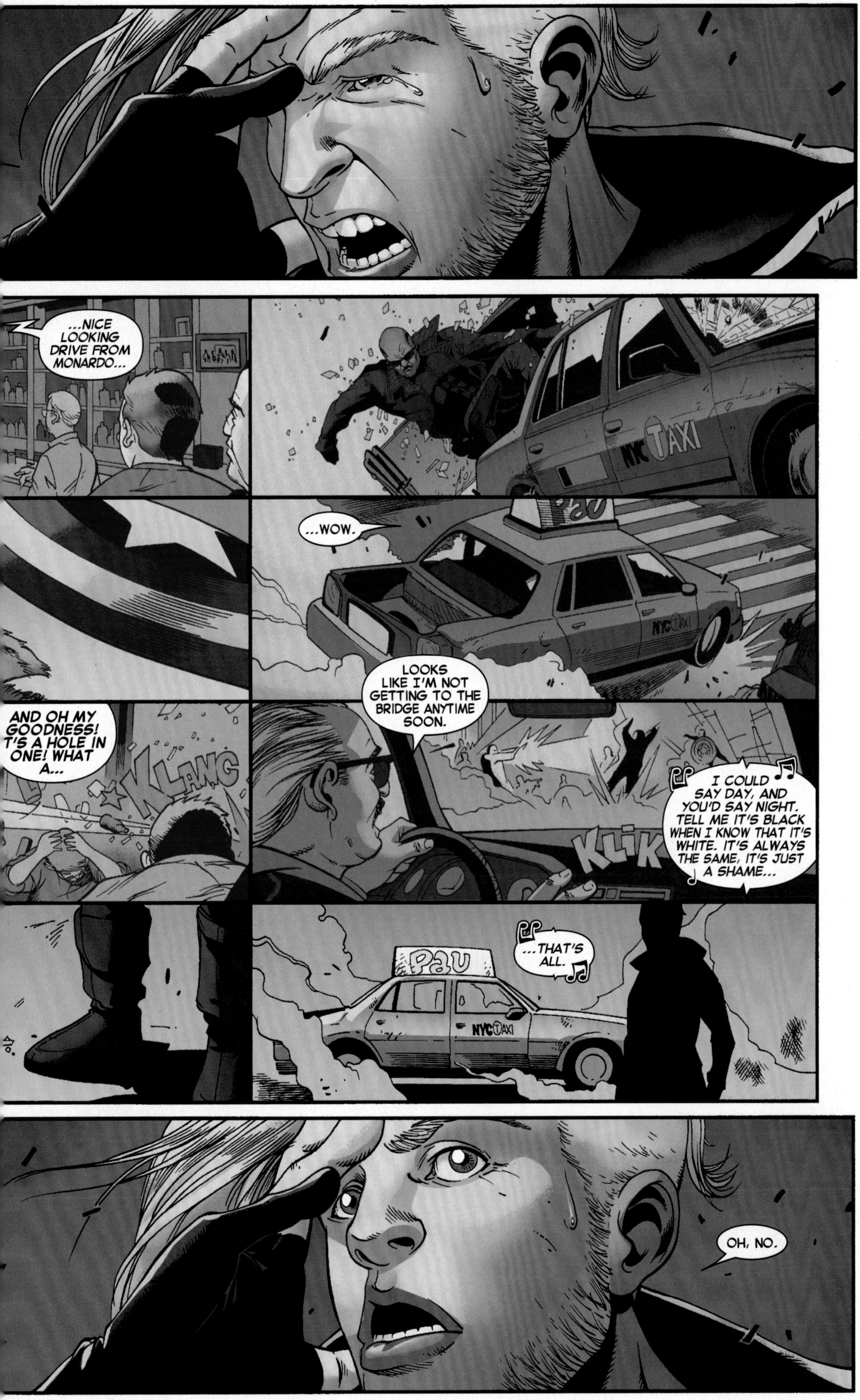
...NICE LOOKING DRIVE FROM MONARDO...
NYC TAXI
...WOW.
NYC TAXI
LOOKS LIKE I'M NOT GETTING TO THE BRIDGE ANYTIME SOON.
AND OH MY GOODNESS! IT'S A HOLE IN ONE! WHAT A...
KLLANG
I COULD SAY DAY, AND YOU'D SAY NIGHT. TELL ME IT'S BLACK WHEN I KNOW THAT IT'S WHITE. IT'S ALWAYS THE SAME, IT'S JUST A SHAME...
KLIK
...THAT'S ALL.
PAU
NYC TAXI
OH, NO.

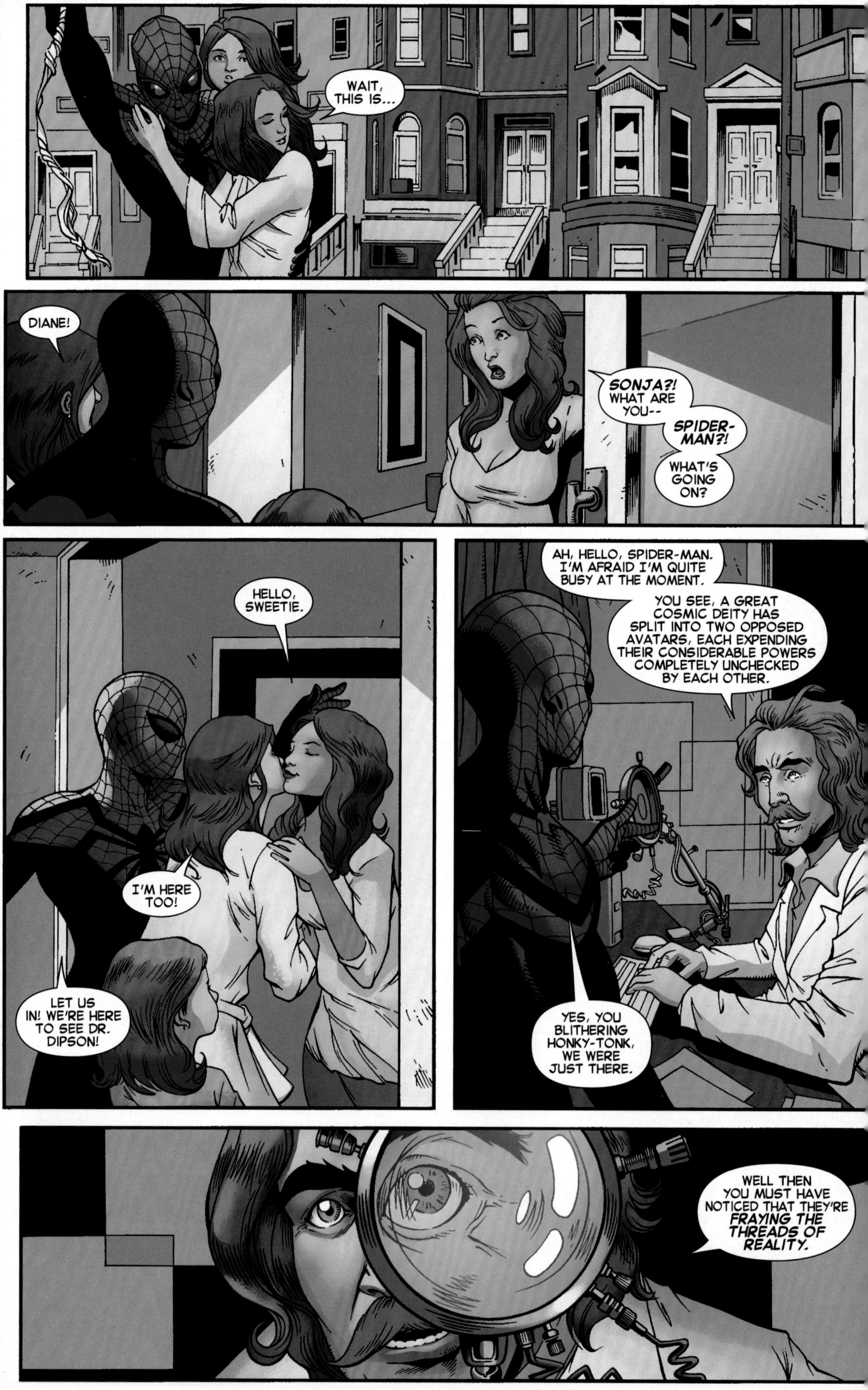
WAIT, THIS IS...
DIANE!
SONJA?! WHAT ARE YOU--
SPIDER-MAN?!
WHAT'S GOING ON?
HELLO, SWEETIE.
I'M HERE TOO!
LET US IN! WE'RE HERE TO SEE DR. DIPSON!
AH, HELLO, SPIDER-MAN. I'M AFRAID I'M QUITE BUSY AT THE MOMENT.
YOU SEE, A GREAT COSMIC DEITY HAS SPLIT INTO TWO OPPOSED AVATARS, EACH EXPENDING THEIR CONSIDERABLE POWERS COMPLETELY UNCHECKED BY EACH OTHER.
YES, YOU BLITHERING HONKY-TONK, WE WERE JUST THERE.
WELL THEN YOU MUST HAVE NOTICED THAT THEY'RE FRAYING THE THREADS OF REALITY.

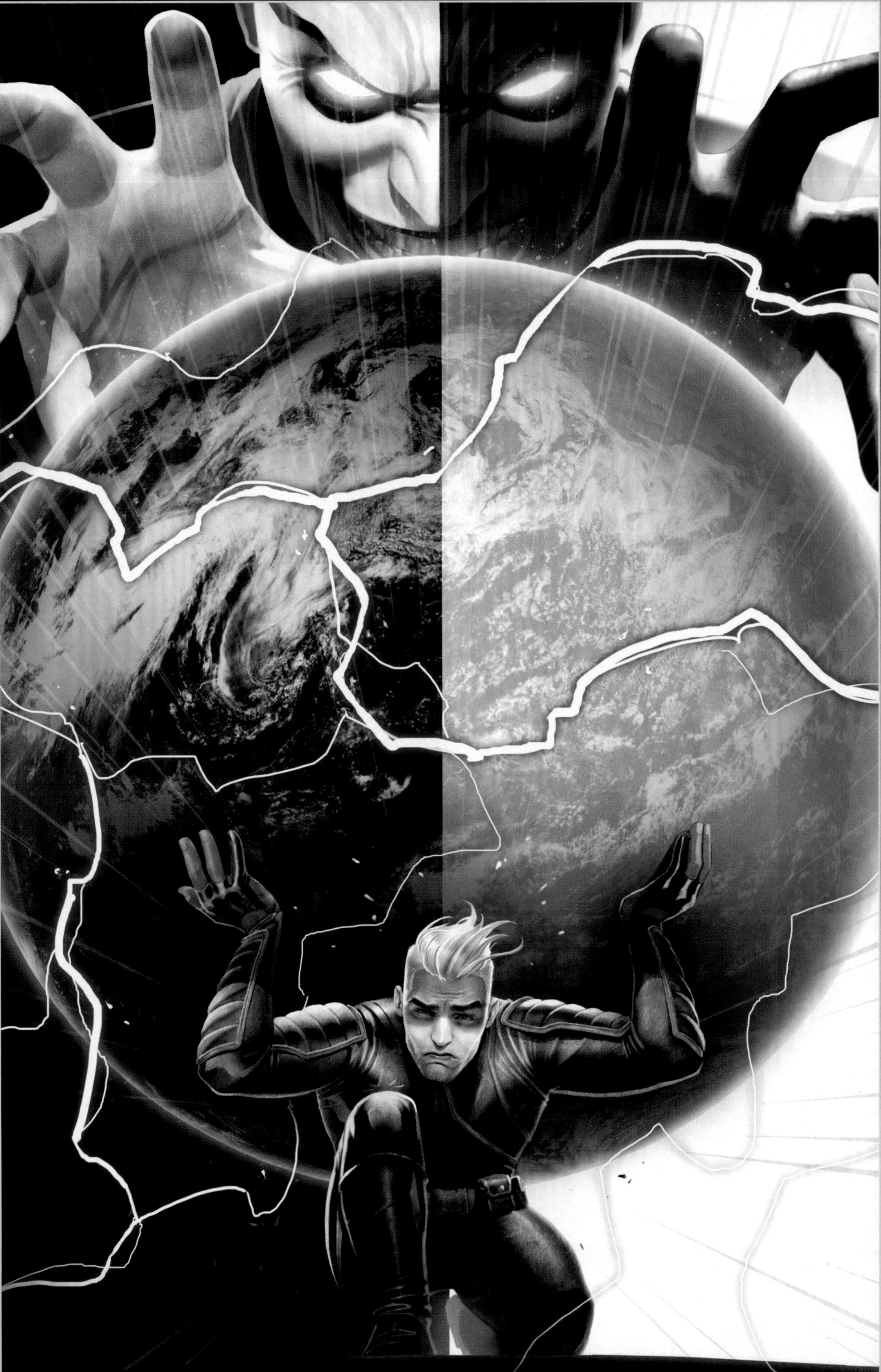

4

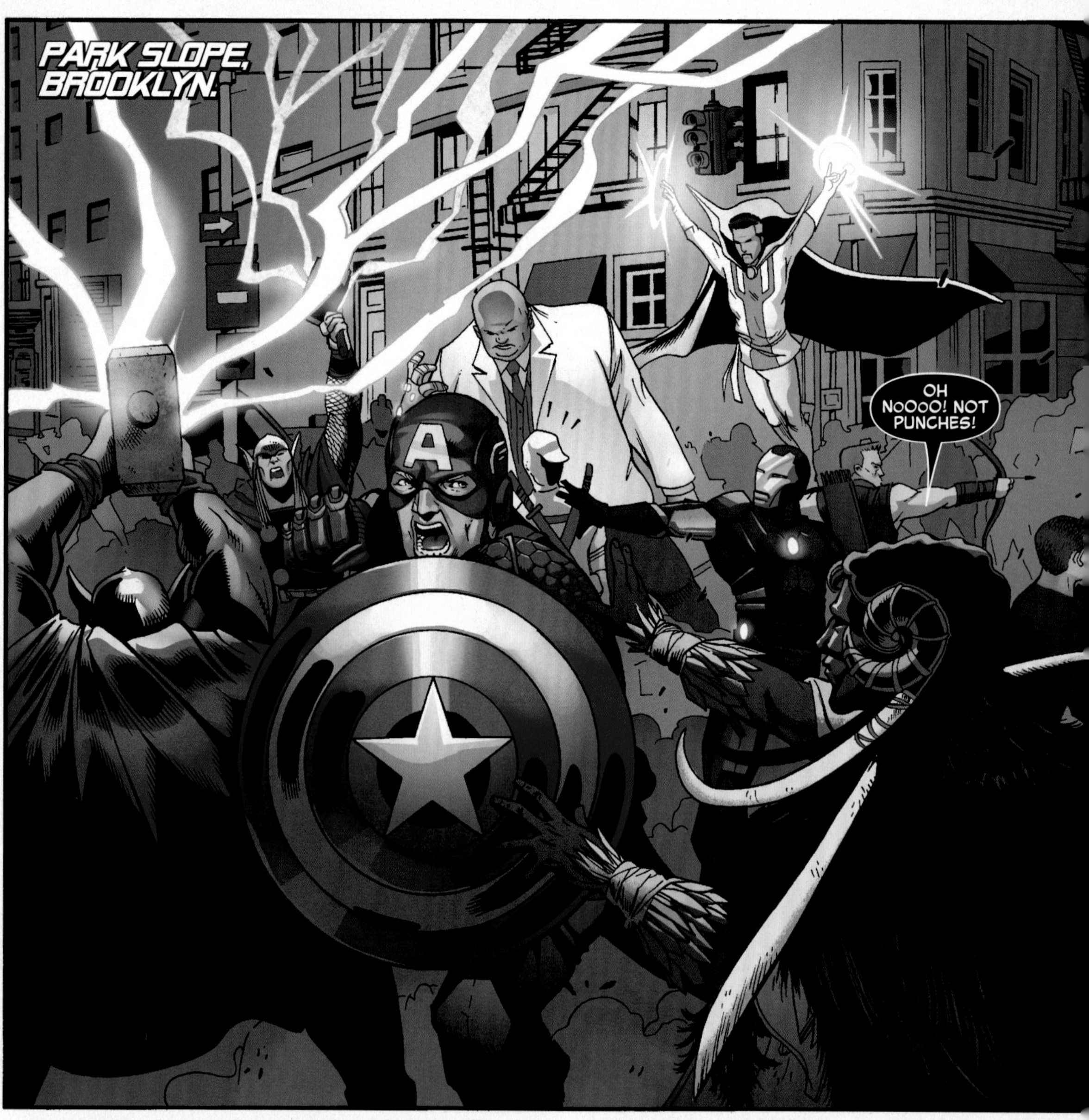
PARK SLOPE, BROOKLYN.
OH NOOOO! NOT PUNCHES!

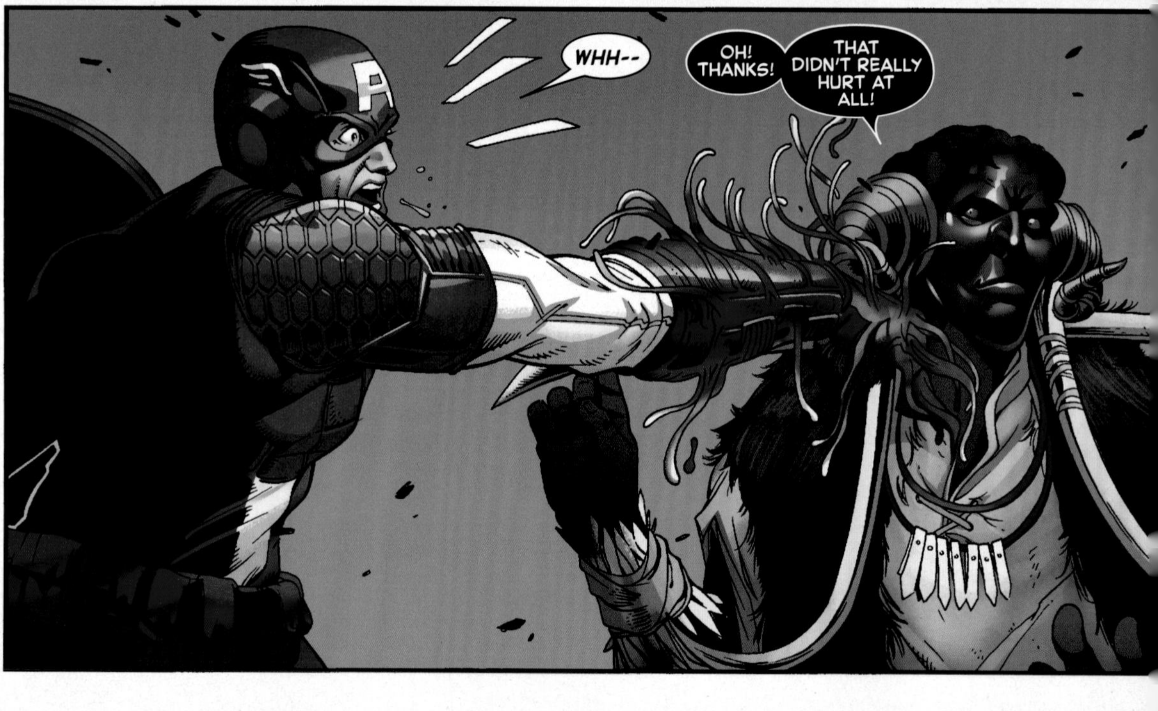
WHH--
OH! THANKS!
THAT DIDN'T REALLY HURT AT ALL!

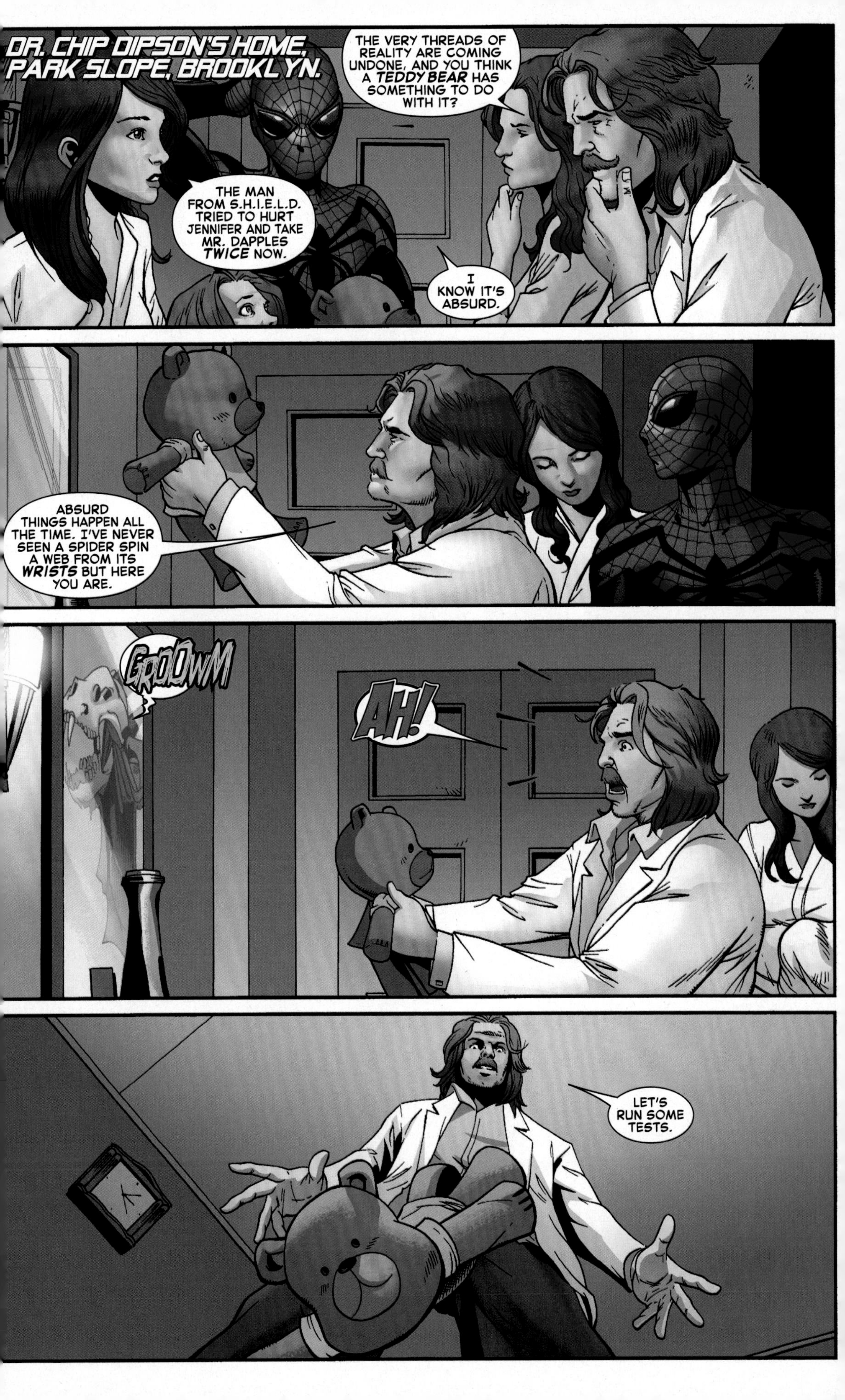
DR. CHIP DIPSON'S HOME, PARK SLOPE, BROOKLYN.
THE VERY THREADS OF REALITY ARE COMING UNDONE, AND YOU THINK A TEDDY BEAR HAS SOMETHING TO DO WITH IT?
THE MAN FROM S.H.I.E.L.D. TRIED TO HURT JENNIFER AND TAKE MR. DAPPLES TWICE NOW.
I KNOW IT'S ABSURD.
ABSURD THINGS HAPPEN ALL THE TIME. I'VE NEVER SEEN A SPIDER SPIN A WEB FROM ITS WRISTS BUT HERE YOU ARE.
GROOWM
AH!
LET'S RUN SOME TESTS.

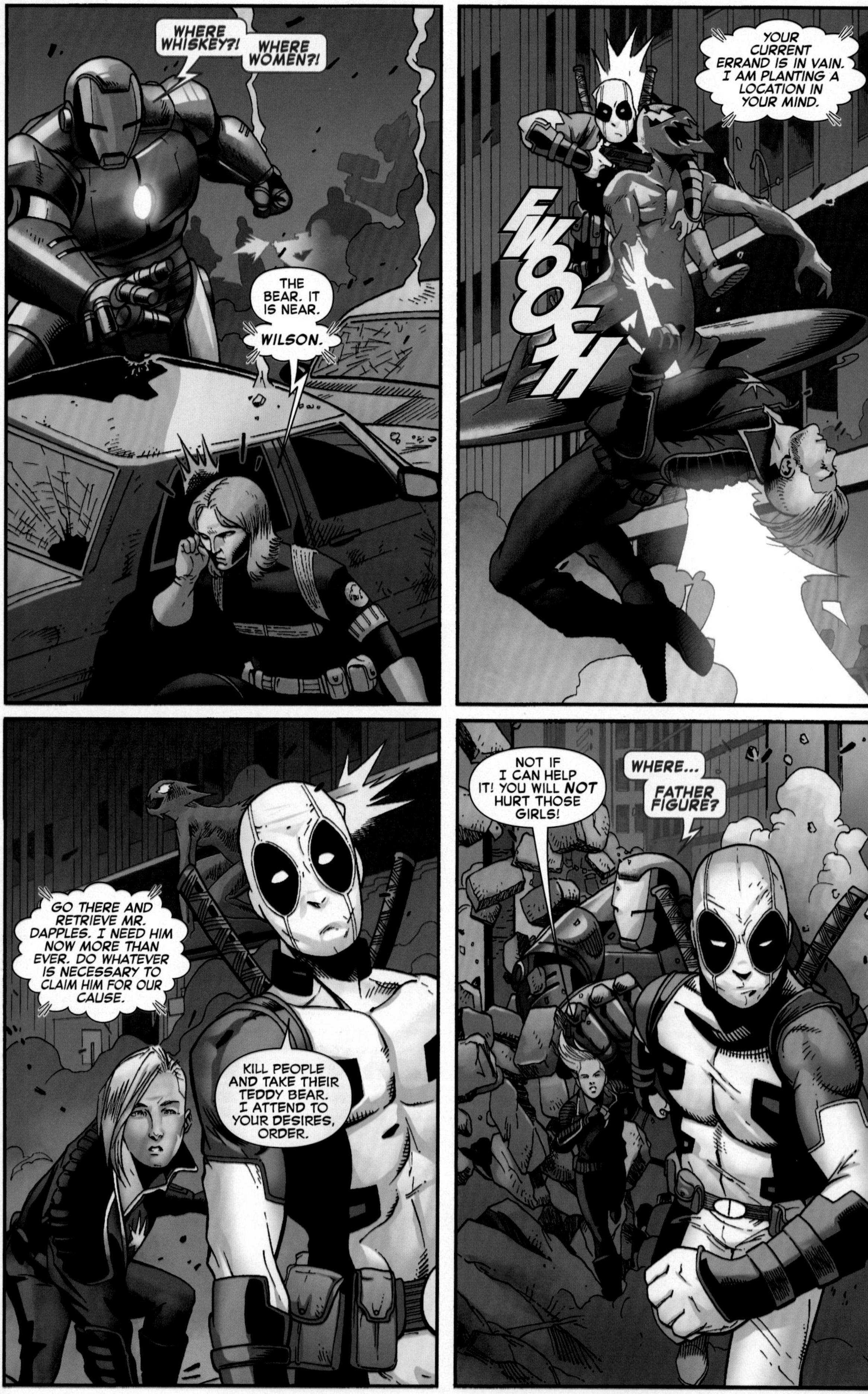
WHERE WHISKEY?!
WHERE WOMEN?!
THE BEAR. IT IS NEAR.
WILSON.
YOUR CURRENT ERRAND IS IN VAIN. I AM PLANTING A LOCATION IN YOUR MIND.
FWOOOH
GO THERE AND RETRIEVE MR. DAPPLES. I NEED HIM NOW MORE THAN EVER. DO WHATEVER IS NECESSARY TO CLAIM HIM FOR OUR CAUSE.
KILL PEOPLE AND TAKE THEIR TEDDY BEAR. I ATTEND TO YOUR DESIRES, ORDER.
NOT IF I CAN HELP IT! YOU WILL NOT HURT THOSE GIRLS!
WHERE... FATHER FIGURE?

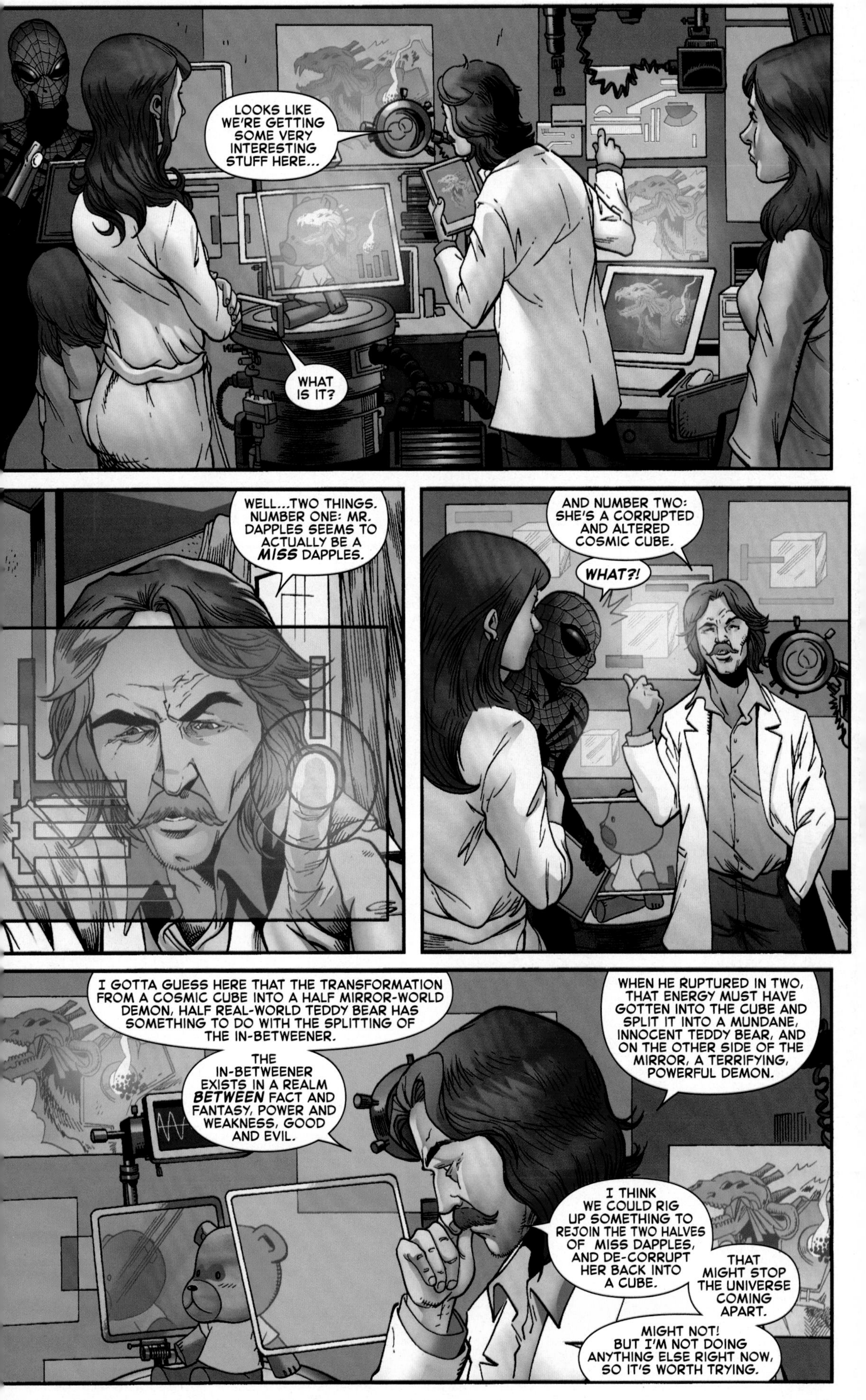

LOOKS LIKE WE'RE GETTING SOME VERY INTERESTING STUFF HERE...
WHAT IS IT?
WELL...TWO THINGS. NUMBER ONE: MR. DAPPLES SEEMS TO ACTUALLY BE A *MISS* DAPPLES.
AND NUMBER TWO: SHE'S A CORRUPTED AND ALTERED COSMIC CUBE.
WHAT?!
I GOTTA GUESS HERE THAT THE TRANSFORMATION FROM A COSMIC CUBE INTO A HALF MIRROR-WORLD DEMON, HALF REAL-WORLD TEDDY BEAR HAS SOMETHING TO DO WITH THE SPLITTING OF THE IN-BETWEENER.
THE IN-BETWEENER EXISTS IN A REALM *BETWEEN* FACT AND FANTASY, POWER AND WEAKNESS, GOOD AND EVIL.
WHEN HE RUPTURED IN TWO, THAT ENERGY MUST HAVE GOTTEN INTO THE CUBE AND SPLIT IT INTO A MUNDANE, INNOCENT TEDDY BEAR, AND ON THE OTHER SIDE OF THE MIRROR, A TERRIFYING, POWERFUL DEMON.
I THINK WE COULD RIG UP SOMETHING TO REJOIN THE TWO HALVES OF MISS DAPPLES, AND DE-CORRUPT HER BACK INTO A CUBE.
THAT MIGHT STOP THE UNIVERSE COMING APART.
MIGHT NOT! BUT I'M NOT DOING ANYTHING ELSE RIGHT NOW, SO IT'S WORTH TRYING.

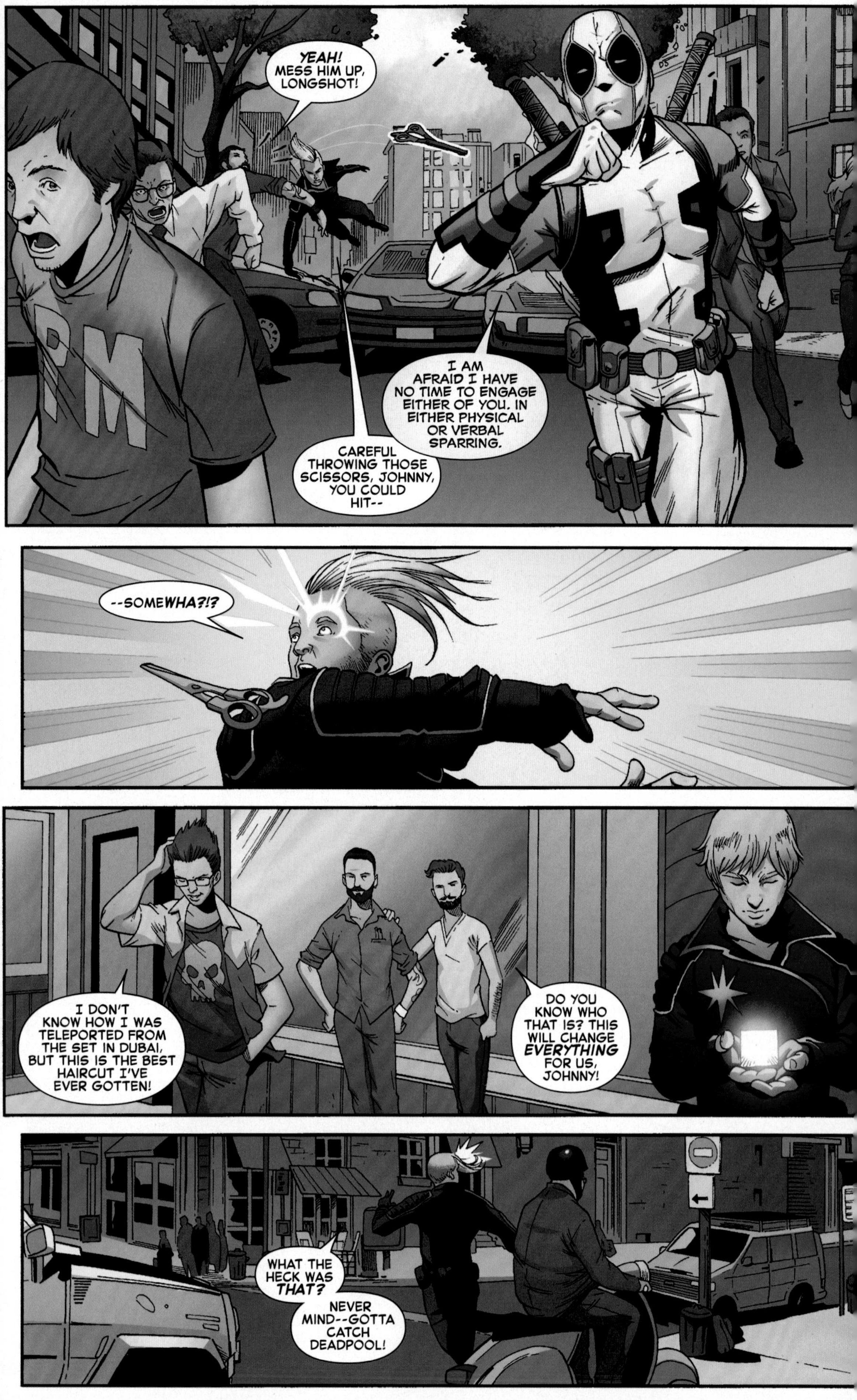

YEAH! MESS HIM UP, LONGSHOT!
I AM AFRAID I HAVE NO TIME TO ENGAGE EITHER OF YOU. IN EITHER PHYSICAL OR VERBAL SPARRING.
CAREFUL THROWING THOSE SCISSORS, JOHNNY, YOU COULD HIT--
--SOMEWHA?!?
I DON'T KNOW HOW I WAS TELEPORTED FROM THE SET IN DUBAI, BUT THIS IS THE BEST HAIRCUT I'VE EVER GOTTEN!
DO YOU KNOW WHO THAT IS? THIS WILL CHANGE EVERYTHING FOR US, JOHNNY!
WHAT THE HECK WAS THAT?
NEVER MIND--GOTTA CATCH DEADPOOL!

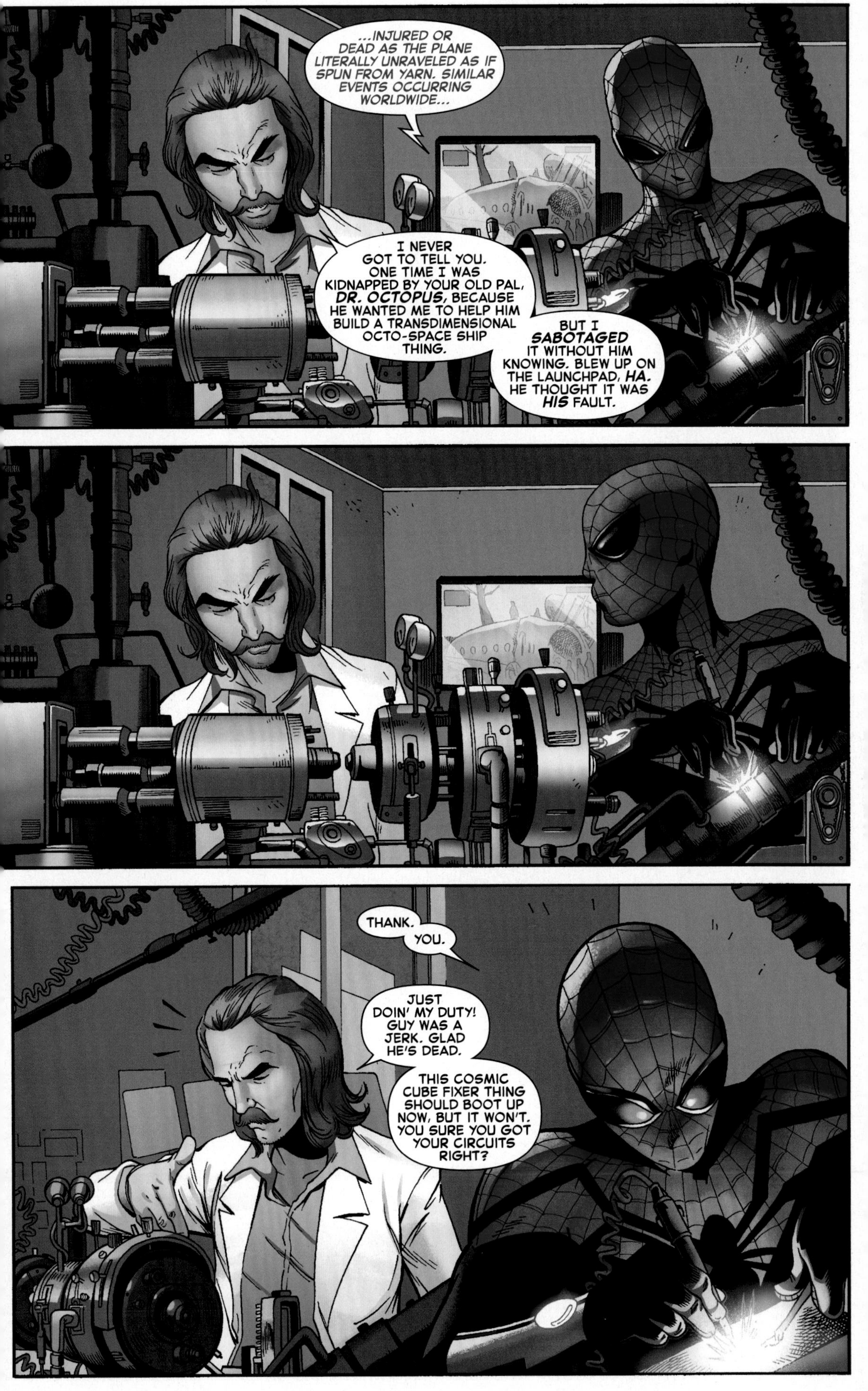
...INJURED OR DEAD AS THE PLANE LITERALLY UNRAVELED AS IF SPUN FROM YARN. SIMILAR EVENTS OCCURRING WORLDWIDE...
I NEVER GOT TO TELL YOU. ONE TIME I WAS KIDNAPPED BY YOUR OLD PAL, DR. OCTOPUS, BECAUSE HE WANTED ME TO HELP HIM BUILD A TRANSDIMENSIONAL OCTO-SPACE SHIP THING.
BUT I SABOTAGED IT WITHOUT HIM KNOWING. BLEW UP ON THE LAUNCHPAD, HA. HE THOUGHT IT WAS HIS FAULT.
THANK. YOU.
JUST DOIN' MY DUTY! GUY WAS A JERK. GLAD HE'S DEAD.
THIS COSMIC CUBE FIXER THING SHOULD BOOT UP NOW, BUT IT WON'T. YOU SURE YOU GOT YOUR CIRCUITS RIGHT?

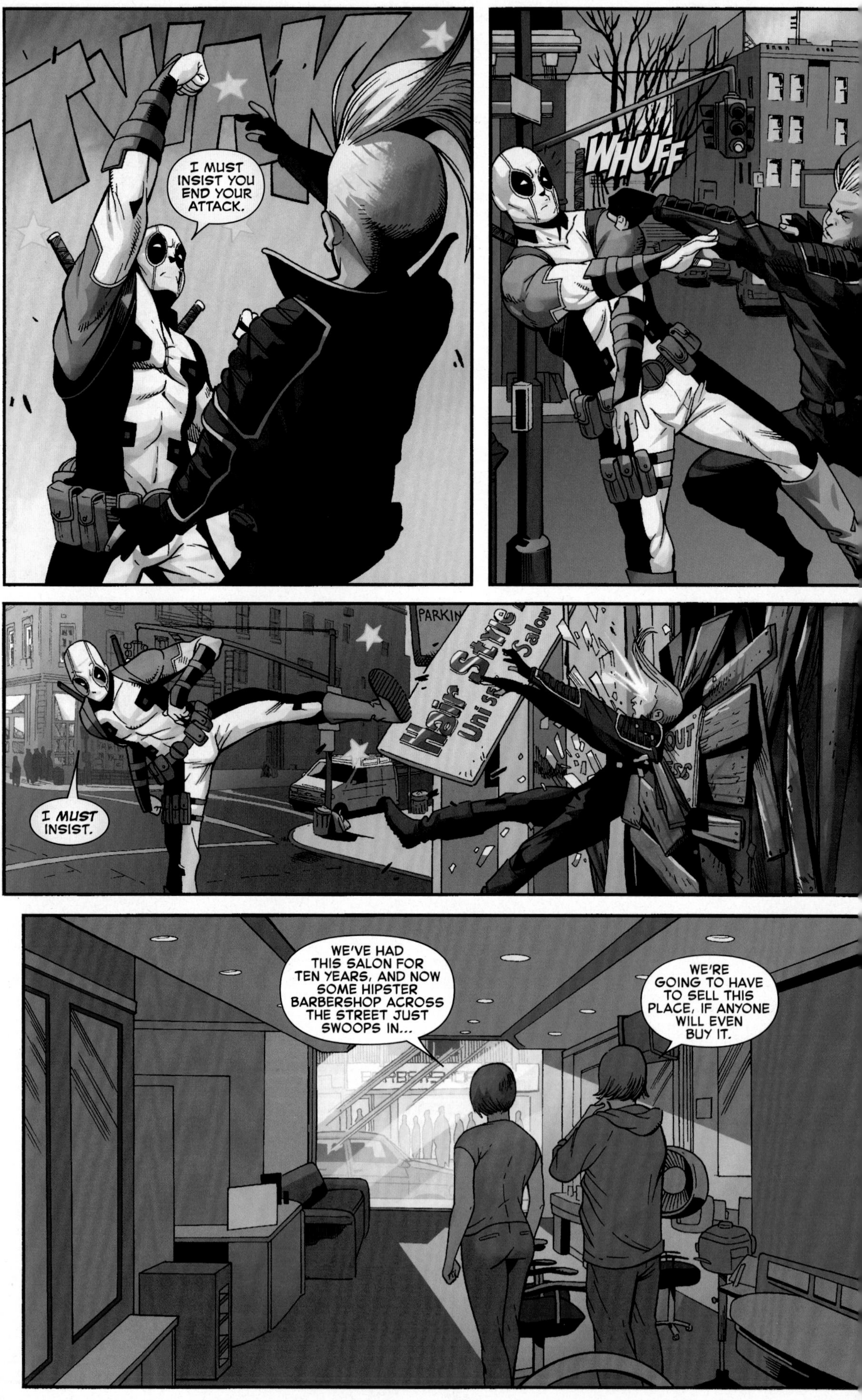
I MUST INSIST YOU END YOUR ATTACK.
WHUFF
I MUST INSIST.
WE'VE HAD THIS SALON FOR TEN YEARS, AND NOW SOME HIPSTER BARBERSHOP ACROSS THE STREET JUST SWOOPS IN...
WE'RE GOING TO HAVE TO SELL THIS PLACE, IF ANYONE WILL EVEN BUY IT.

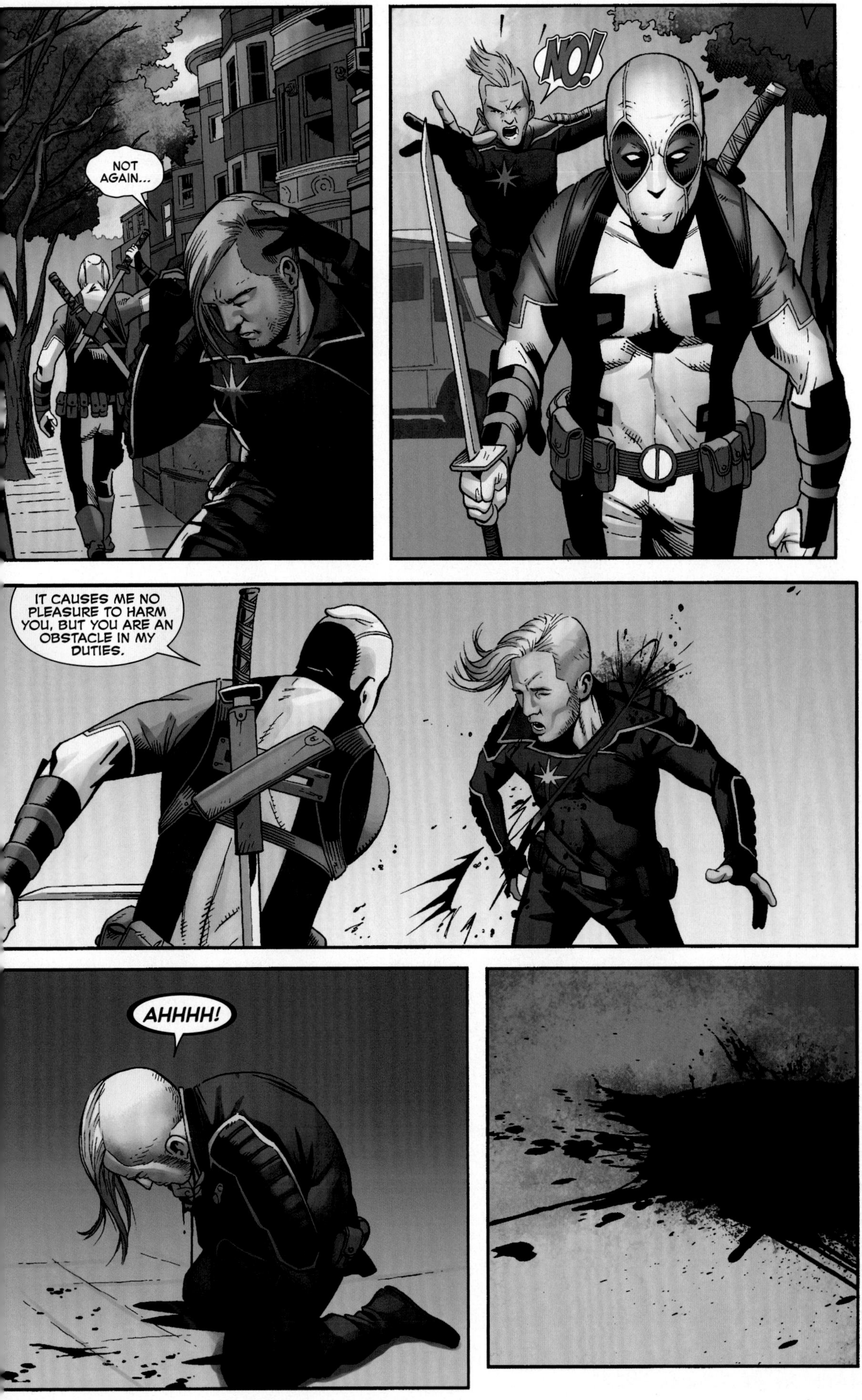
NOT AGAIN...
NO!
IT CAUSES ME NO PLEASURE TO HARM YOU, BUT YOU ARE AN OBSTACLE IN MY DUTIES.
AHHHH!

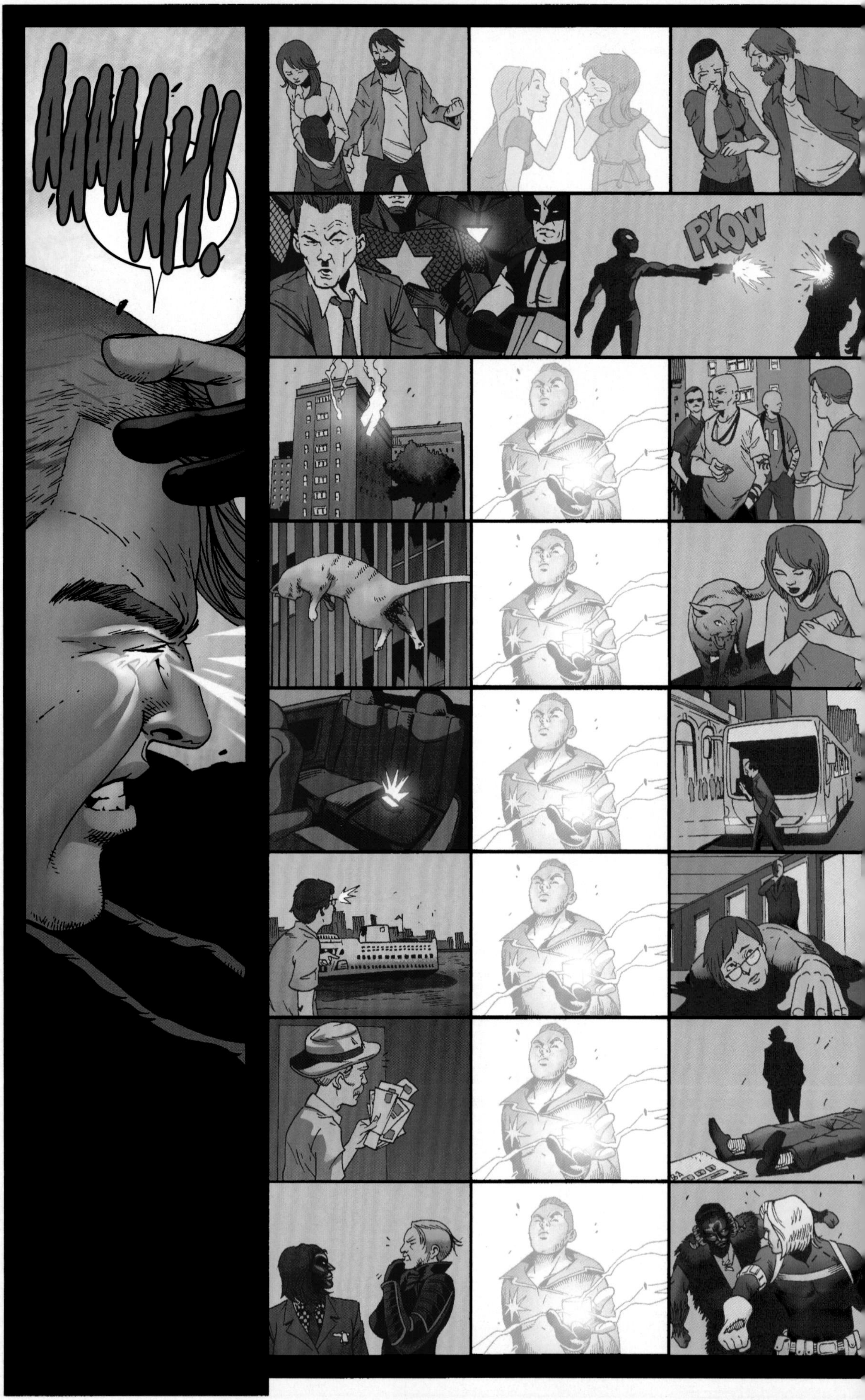
AAAAAH!!
PKOW

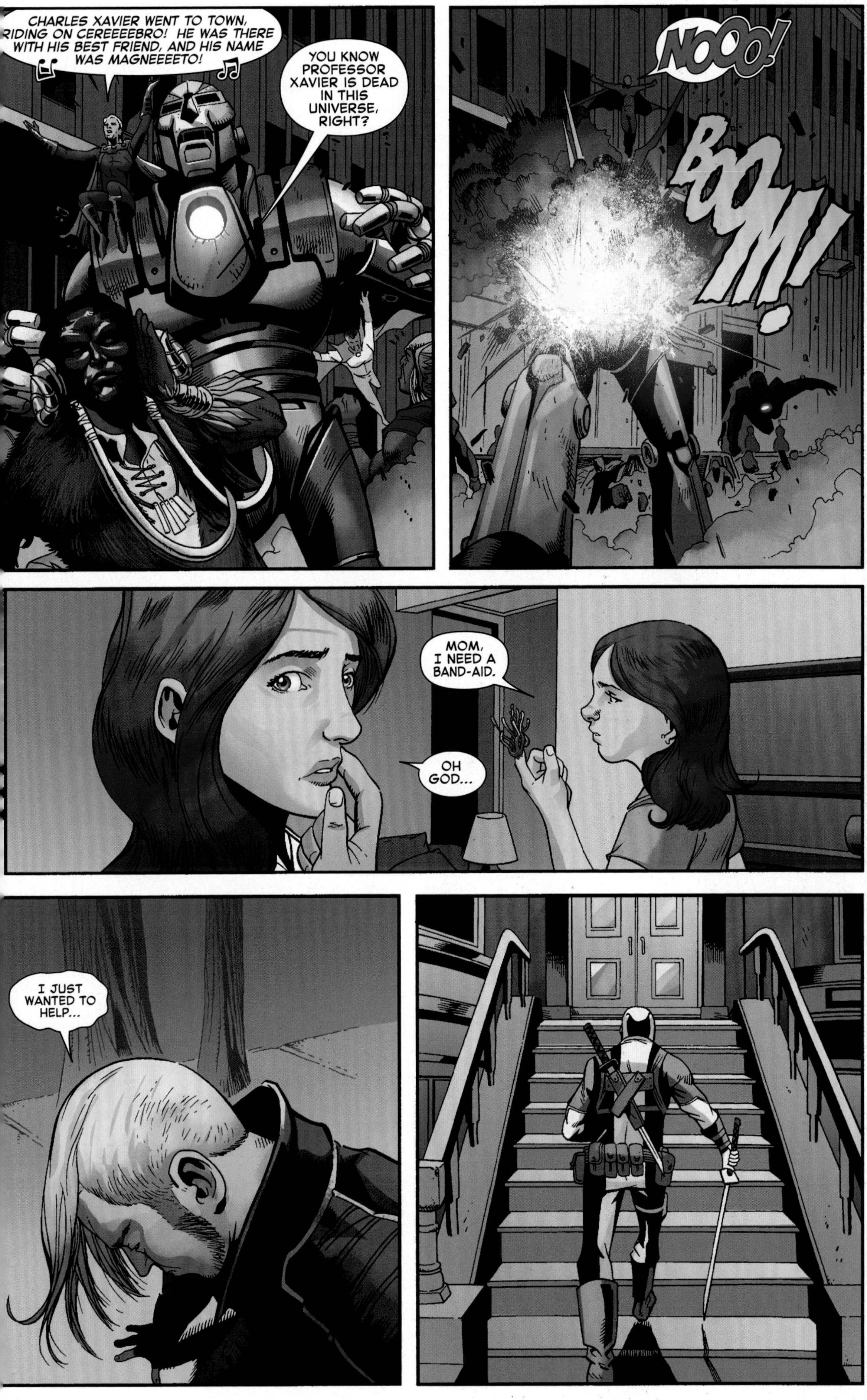
CHARLES XAVIER WENT TO TOWN, RIDING ON CEREEEEBRO! HE WAS THERE WITH HIS BEST FRIEND, AND HIS NAME WAS MAGNEEEETO!
YOU KNOW PROFESSOR XAVIER IS DEAD IN THIS UNIVERSE, RIGHT?
NOOO!
BOOM!
MOM, I NEED A BAND-AID.
OH GOD...
I JUST WANTED TO HELP...

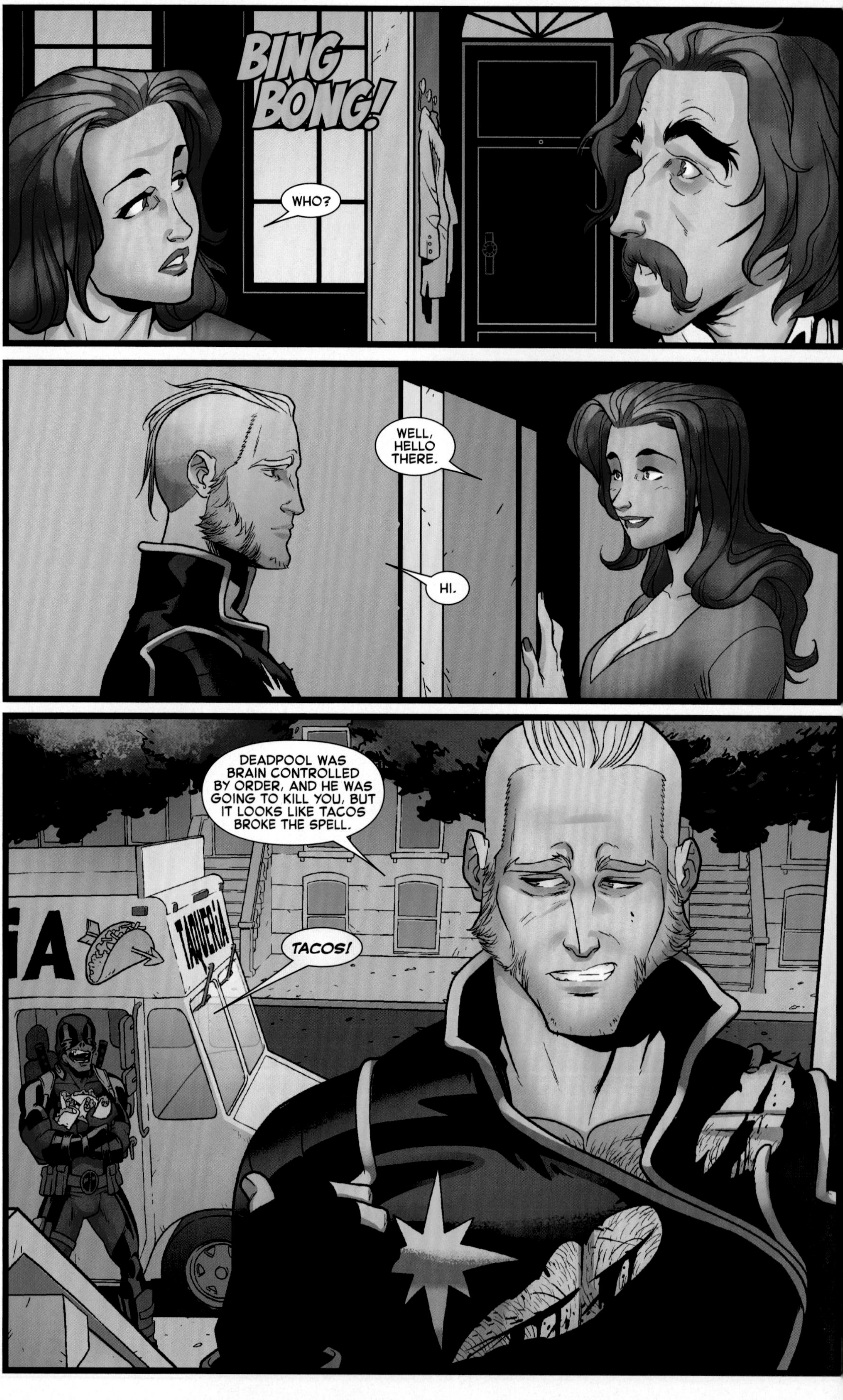
BING BONG!
WHO?
WELL, HELLO THERE.
HI.
DEADPOOL WAS BRAIN CONTROLLED BY ORDER, AND HE WAS GOING TO KILL YOU, BUT IT LOOKS LIKE TACOS BROKE THE SPELL.
TAQUERIA
TACOS!

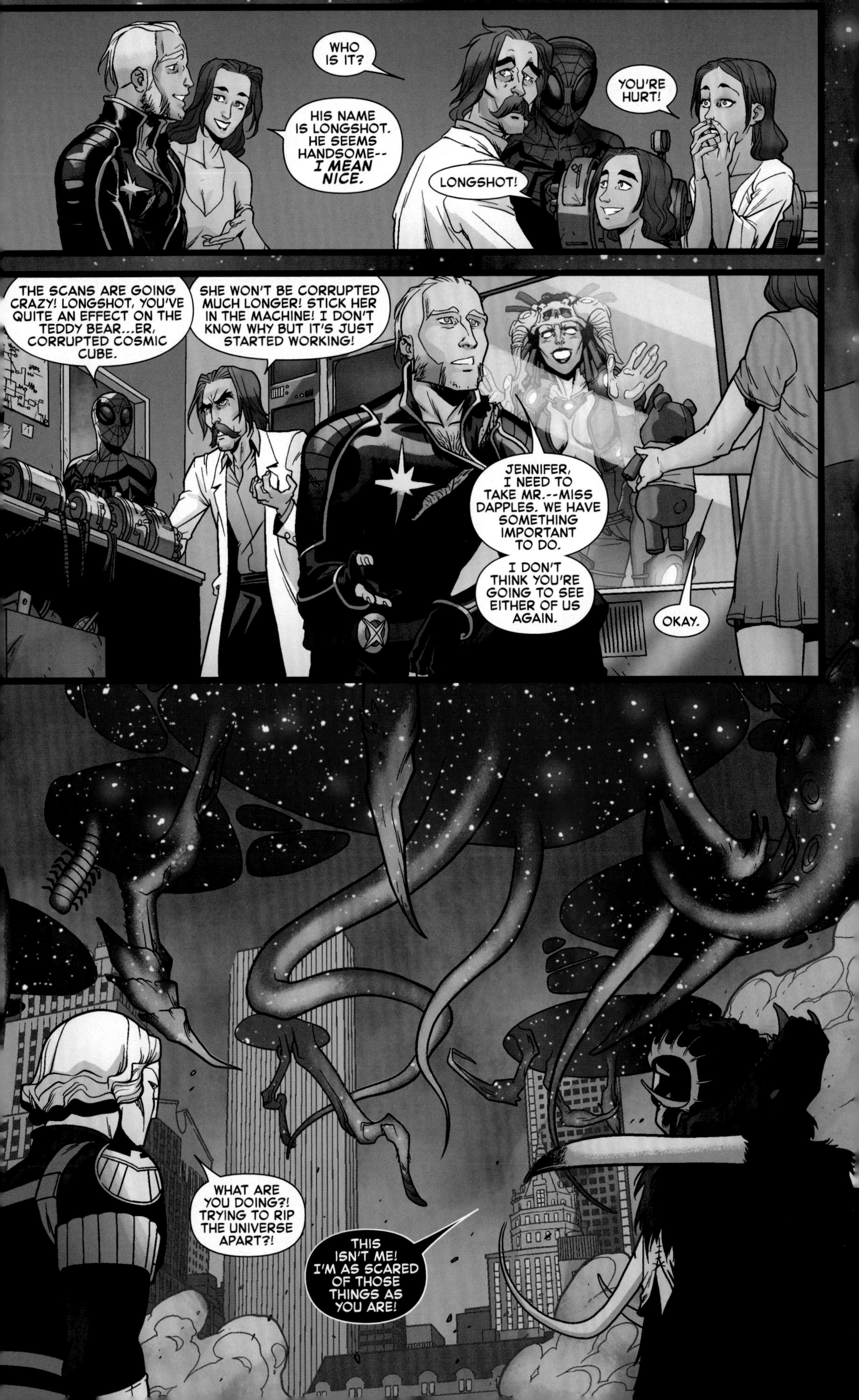
WHO IS IT?
HIS NAME IS LONGSHOT. HE SEEMS HANDSOME-- *I MEAN NICE.*
YOU'RE HURT!
LONGSHOT!
THE SCANS ARE GOING CRAZY! LONGSHOT, YOU'VE QUITE AN EFFECT ON THE TEDDY BEAR...ER, CORRUPTED COSMIC CUBE.
SHE WON'T BE CORRUPTED MUCH LONGER! STICK HER IN THE MACHINE! I DON'T KNOW WHY BUT IT'S JUST STARTED WORKING!
JENNIFER, I NEED TO TAKE MR.--MISS DAPPLES. WE HAVE SOMETHING IMPORTANT TO DO.
I DON'T THINK YOU'RE GOING TO SEE EITHER OF US AGAIN.
OKAY.
WHAT ARE YOU DOING?! TRYING TO RIP THE UNIVERSE APART?!
THIS ISN'T ME! I'M AS SCARED OF THOSE THINGS AS YOU ARE!

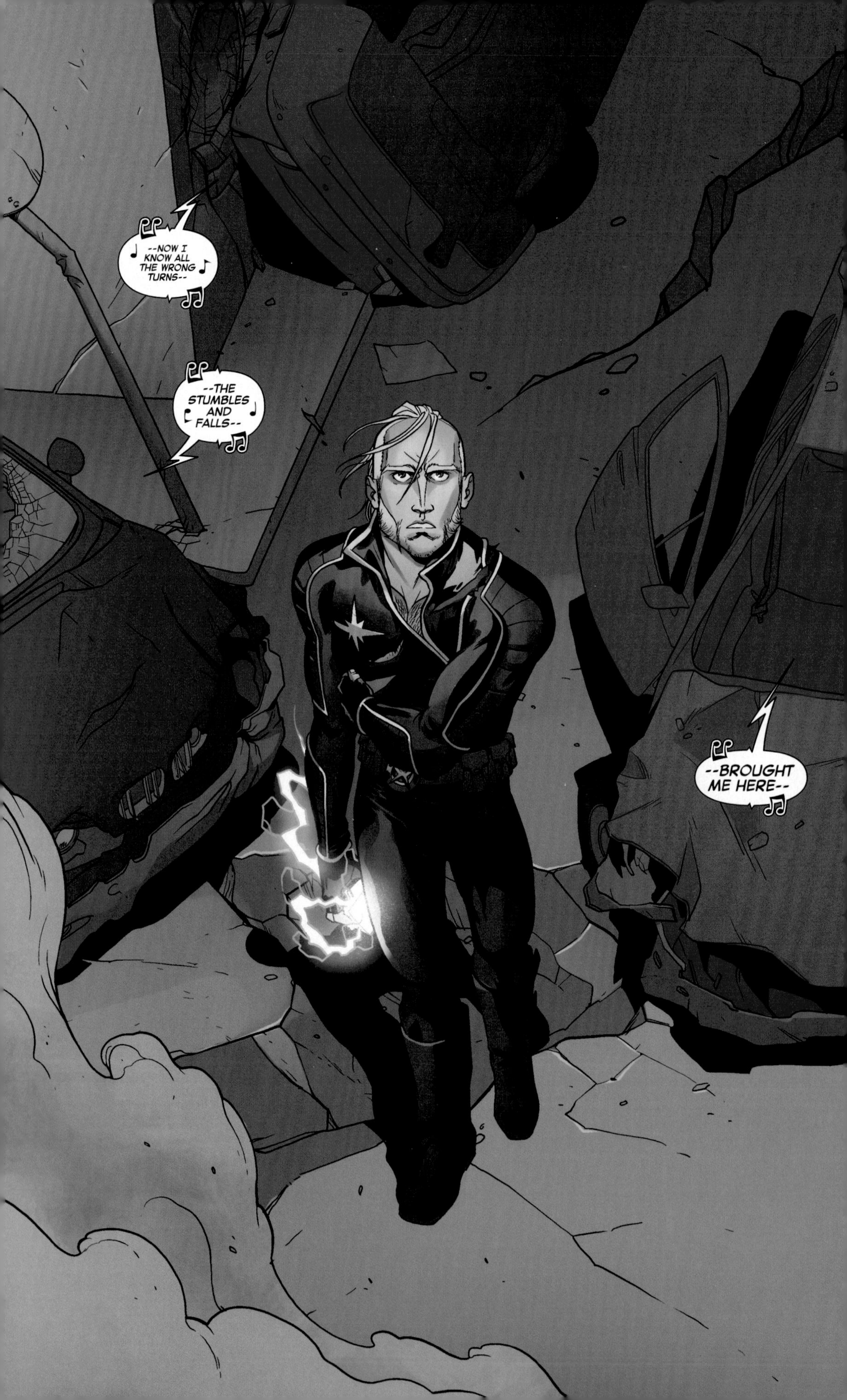
--NOW I KNOW ALL THE WRONG TURNS--
--THE STUMBLES AND FALLS--
--BROUGHT ME HERE--

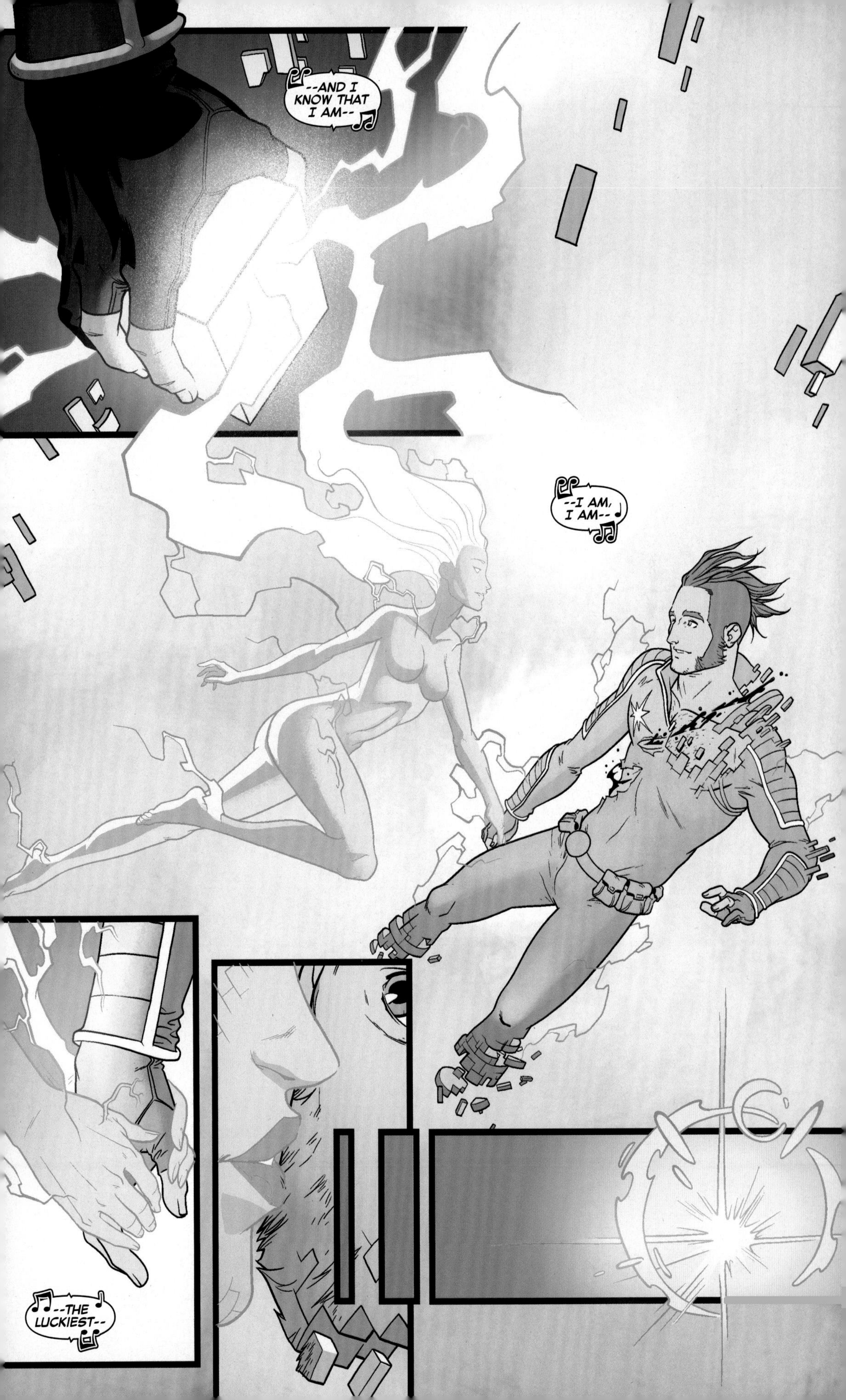
--AND I KNOW THAT I AM--
--I AM, I AM--
--THE LUCKIEST--

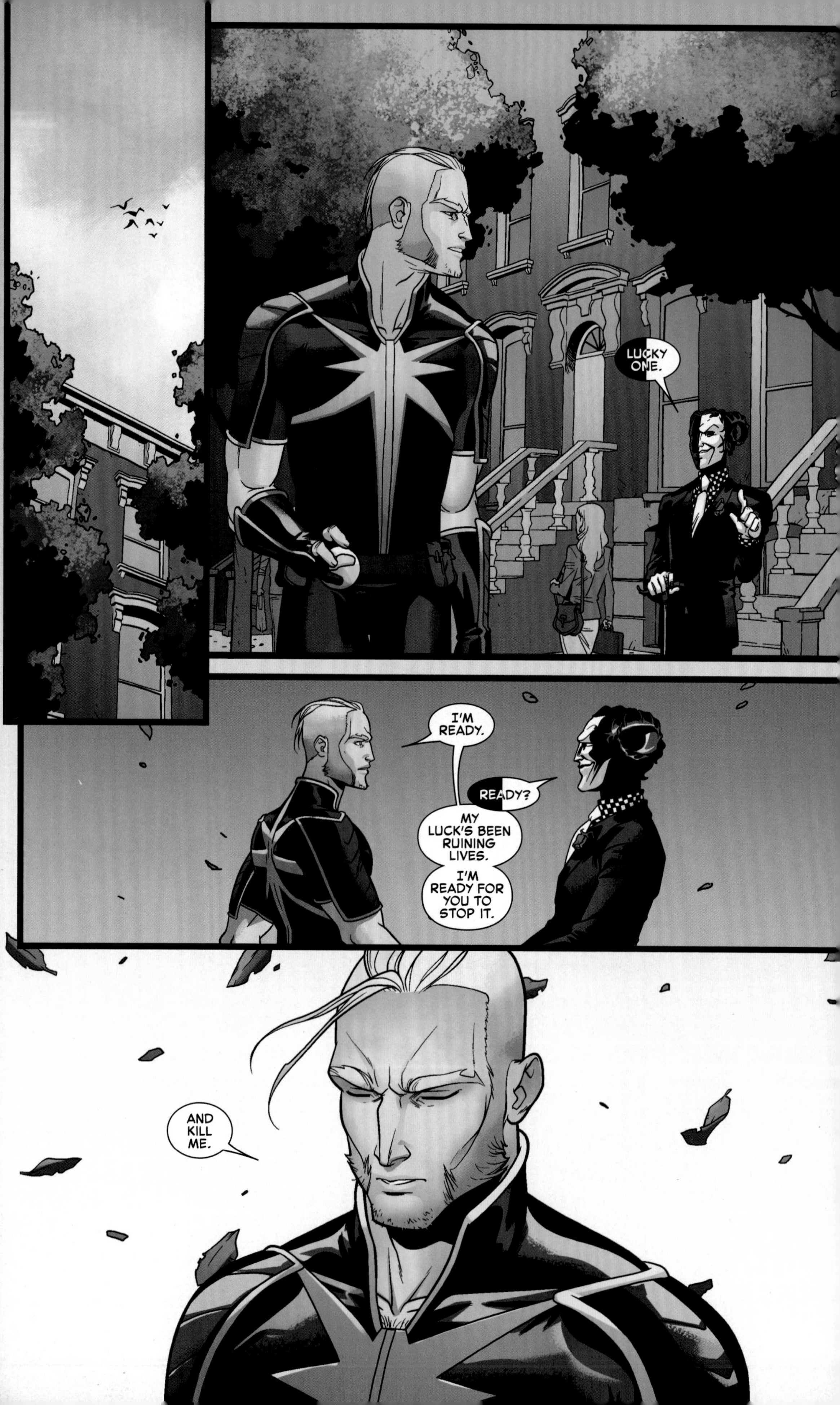
LUCKY ONE.
I'M READY.
READY?
MY LUCK'S BEEN RUINING LIVES.
I'M READY FOR YOU TO STOP IT.
AND KILL ME.

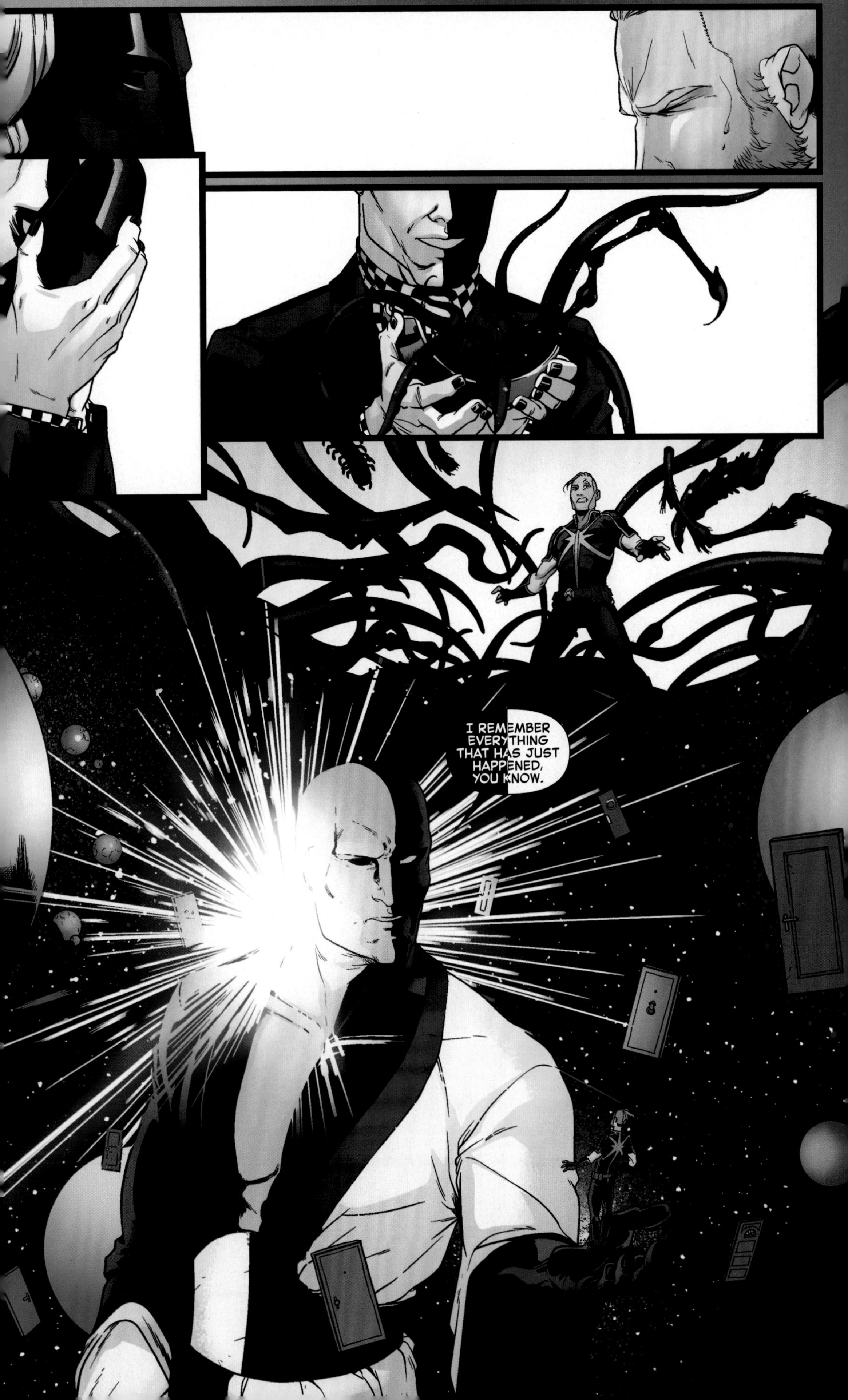
I REMEMBER EVERYTHING THAT HAS JUST HAPPENED, YOU KNOW.

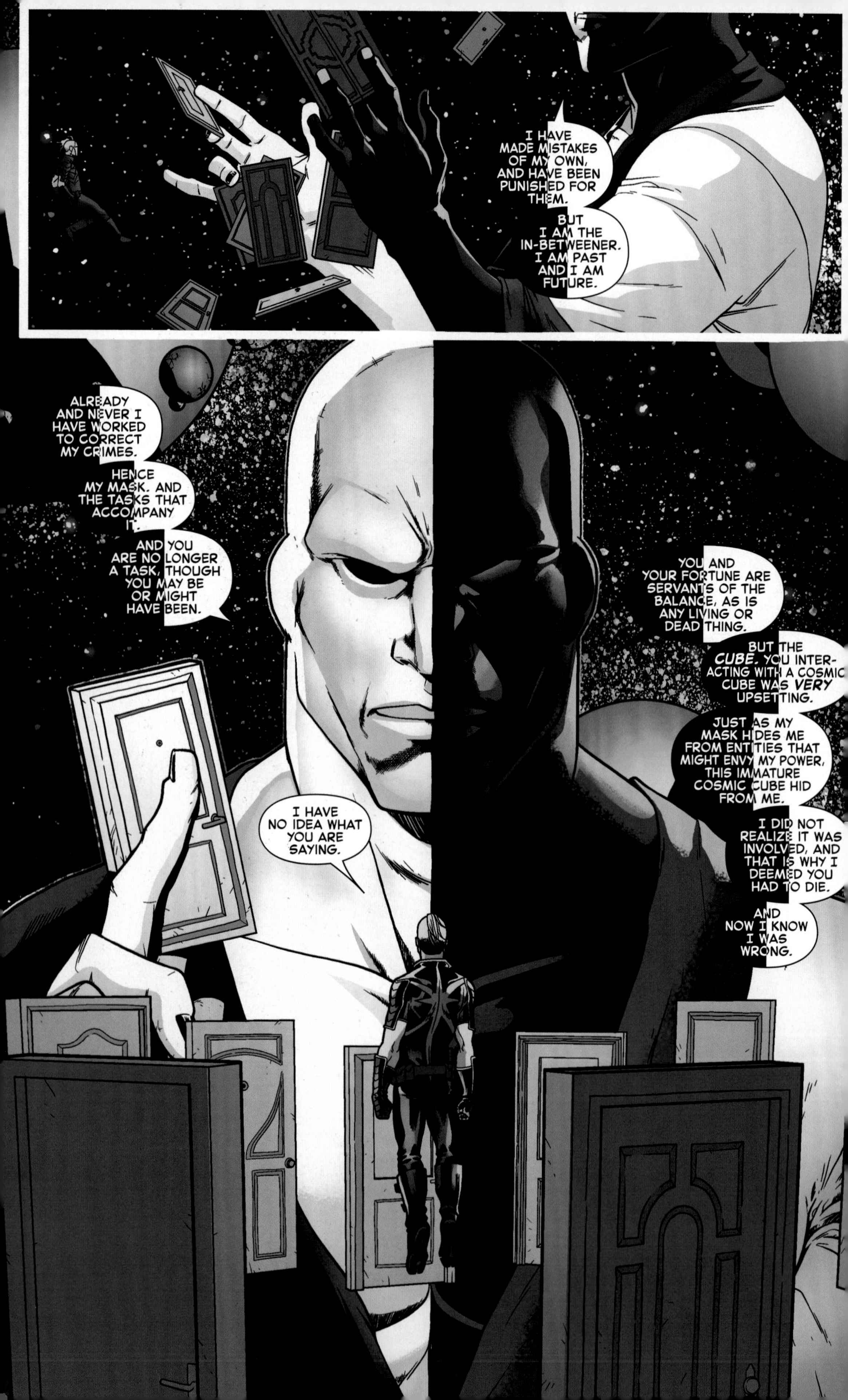
I HAVE MADE MISTAKES OF MY OWN, AND HAVE BEEN PUNISHED FOR THEM.
BUT I AM THE IN-BETWEENER. I AM PAST AND I AM FUTURE.
ALREADY AND NEVER I HAVE WORKED TO CORRECT MY CRIMES.
HENCE MY MASK. AND THE TASKS THAT ACCOMPANY IT.
AND YOU ARE NO LONGER A TASK, THOUGH YOU MAY BE OR MIGHT HAVE BEEN.
YOU AND YOUR FORTUNE ARE SERVANTS OF THE BALANCE, AS IS ANY LIVING OR DEAD THING.
BUT THE CUBE. YOU INTERACTING WITH A COSMIC CUBE WAS VERY UPSETTING.
JUST AS MY MASK HIDES ME FROM ENTITIES THAT MIGHT ENVY MY POWER, THIS IMMATURE COSMIC CUBE HID FROM ME.
I DID NOT REALIZE IT WAS INVOLVED, AND THAT IS WHY I DEEMED YOU HAD TO DIE.
AND NOW I KNOW I WAS WRONG.
I HAVE NO IDEA WHAT YOU ARE SAYING.

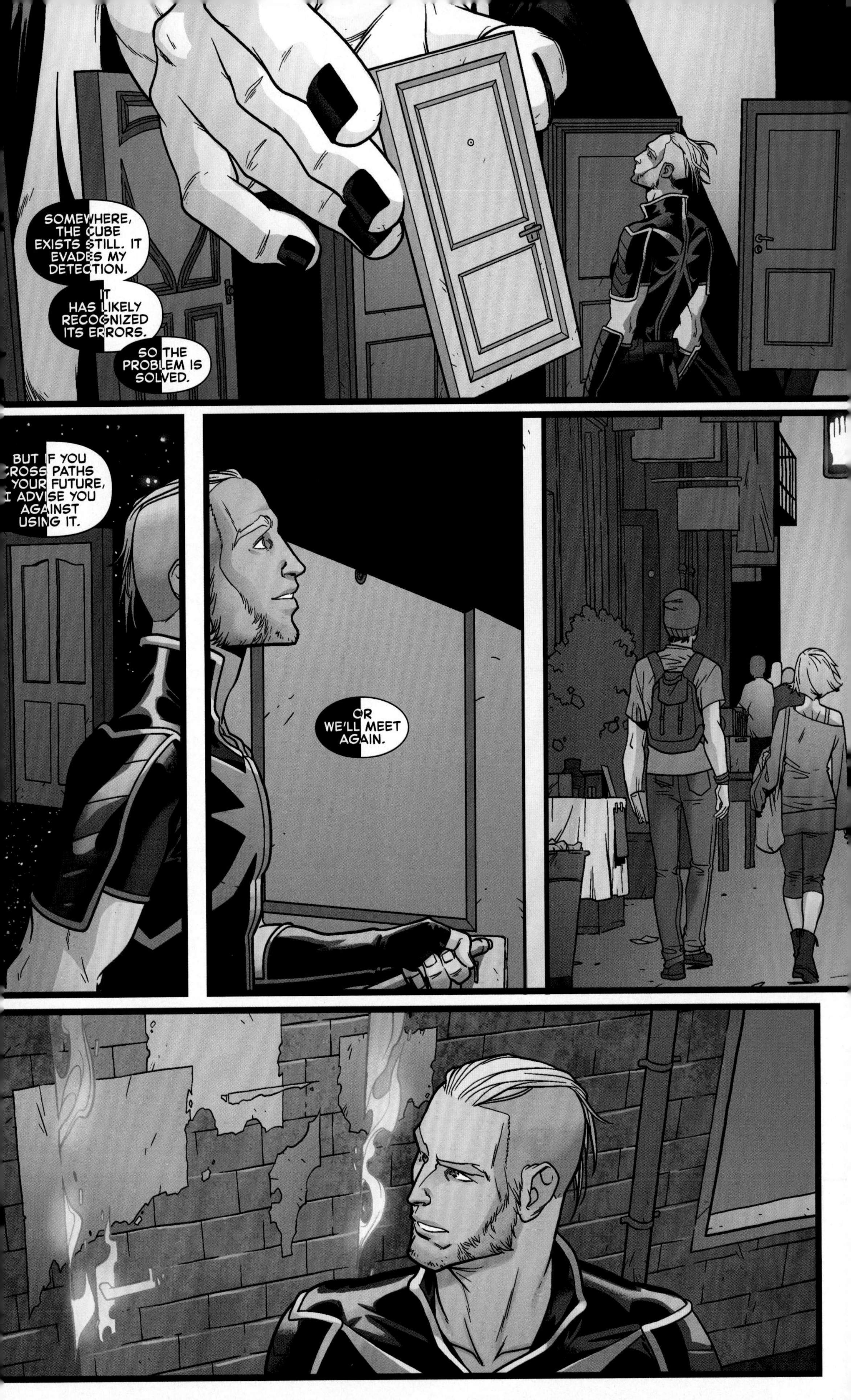
SOMEWHERE, THE CUBE EXISTS STILL. IT EVADES MY DETECTION.
IT HAS LIKELY RECOGNIZED ITS ERRORS.
SO THE PROBLEM IS SOLVED.
BUT IF YOU CROSS PATHS YOUR FUTURE, I ADVISE YOU AGAINST USING IT.
OR WE'LL MEET AGAIN.

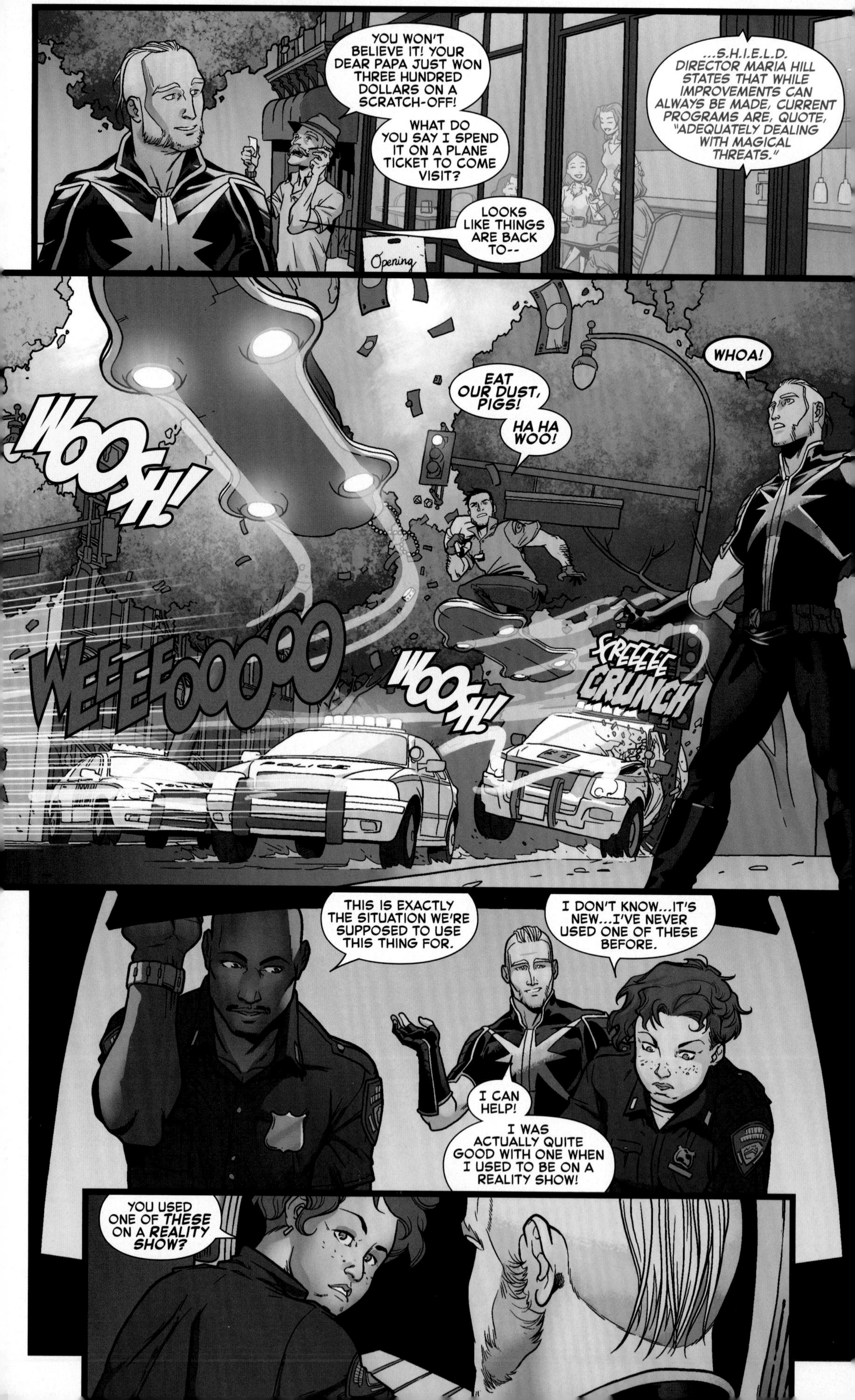
YOU WON'T BELIEVE IT! YOUR DEAR PAPA JUST WON THREE HUNDRED DOLLARS ON A SCRATCH-OFF!
WHAT DO YOU SAY I SPEND IT ON A PLANE TICKET TO COME VISIT?
Opening
LOOKS LIKE THINGS ARE BACK TO--
...S.H.I.E.L.D. DIRECTOR MARIA HILL STATES THAT WHILE IMPROVEMENTS CAN ALWAYS BE MADE, CURRENT PROGRAMS ARE, QUOTE, "ADEQUATELY DEALING WITH MAGICAL THREATS."
WOOSH!
EAT OUR DUST, PIGS!
HA HA WOO!
WHOA!
WEEEEOOOOO
WOOSH!
SCREEEE CRUNCH
POLICE
THIS IS EXACTLY THE SITUATION WE'RE SUPPOSED TO USE THIS THING FOR.
I DON'T KNOW...IT'S NEW...I'VE NEVER USED ONE OF THESE BEFORE.
I CAN HELP!
I WAS ACTUALLY QUITE GOOD WITH ONE WHEN I USED TO BE ON A REALITY SHOW!
YOU USED ONE OF THESE ON A REALITY SHOW?

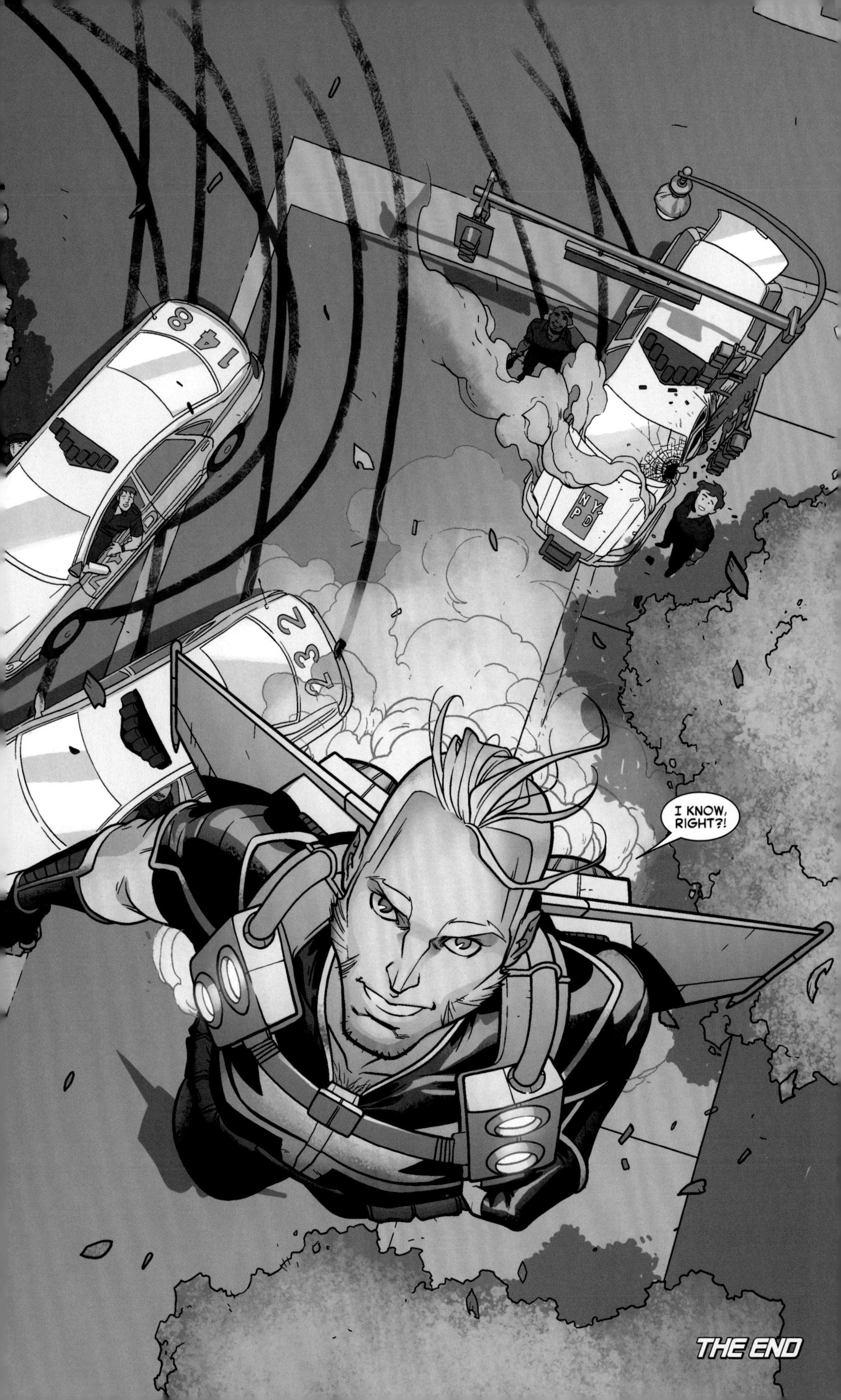
148
NYPD
232
I KNOW, RIGHT?!
THE END

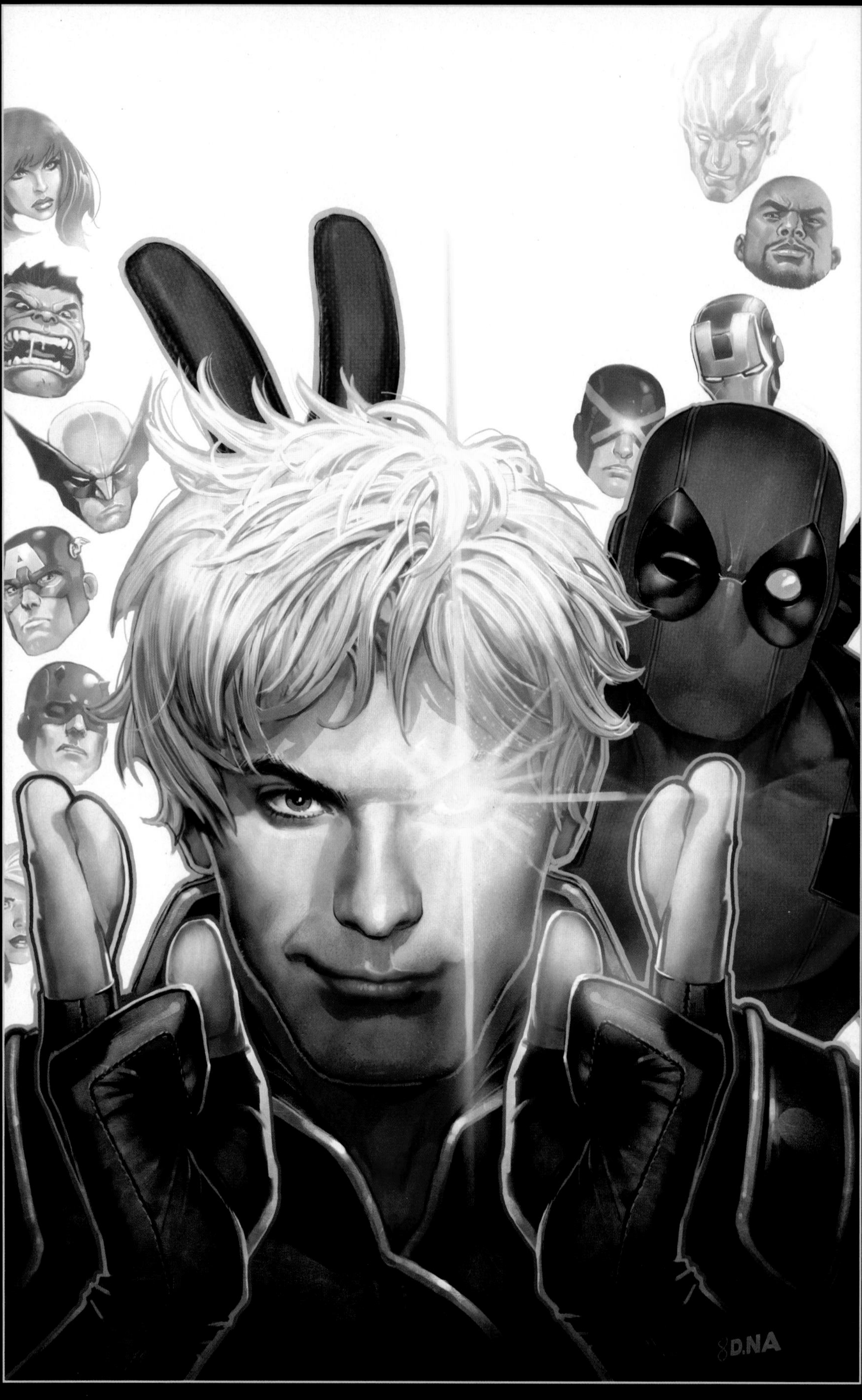
D.NA

#1 DEADPOOL VARIANT BY DAVID NAKAYAMA

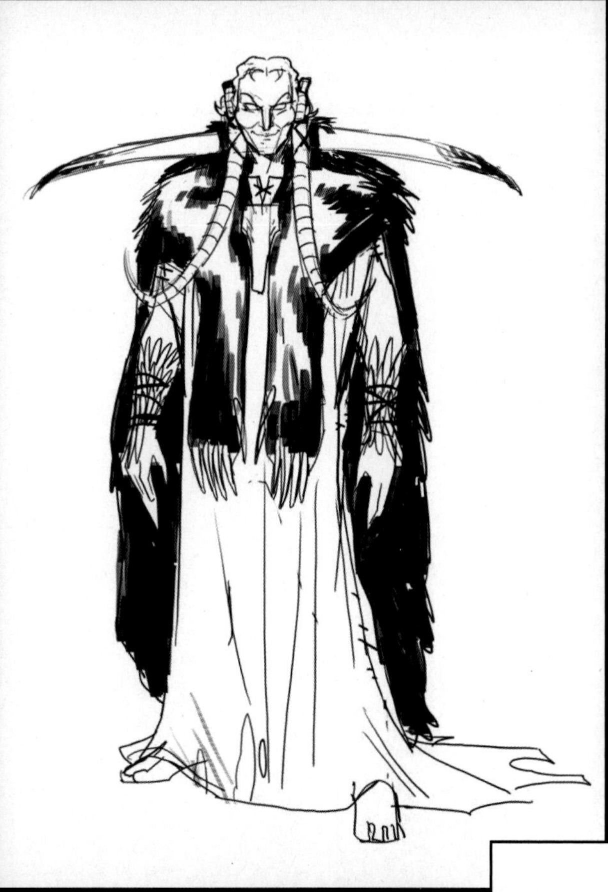

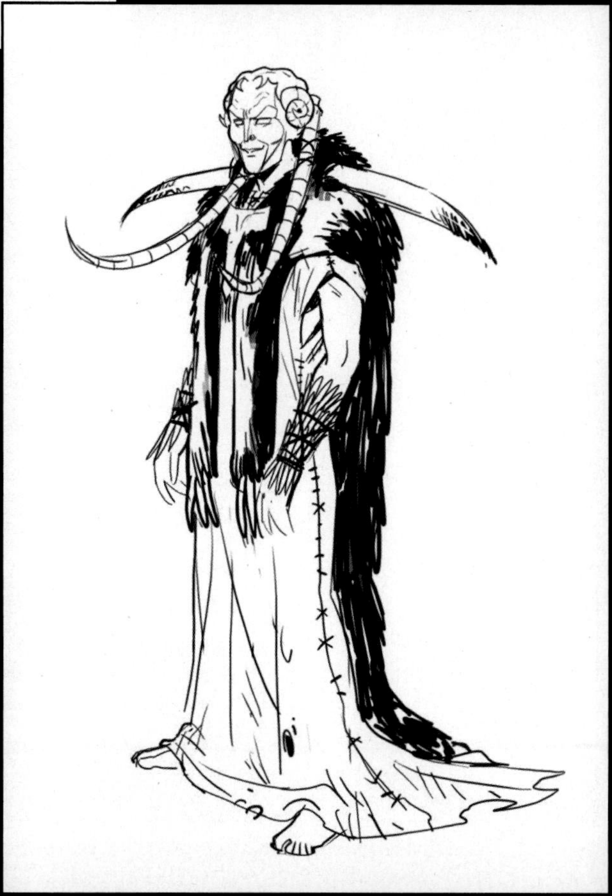

CHAOS CHARACTER DESIGNS BY JACOPO CAMAGNI

A. ORIGINAL

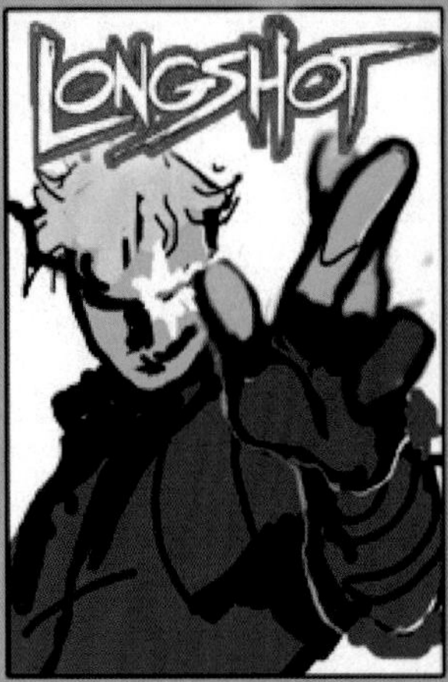
LONGSHOT

A2. w/ HEADS

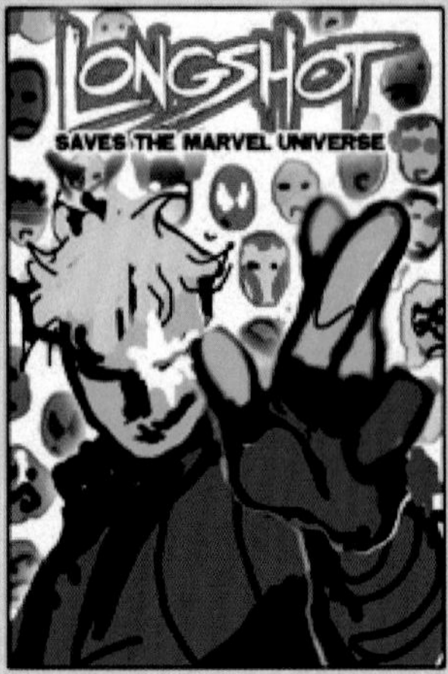
LONGSHOT
SAVES THE MARVEL UNIVERSE

A3. w/ BODIES

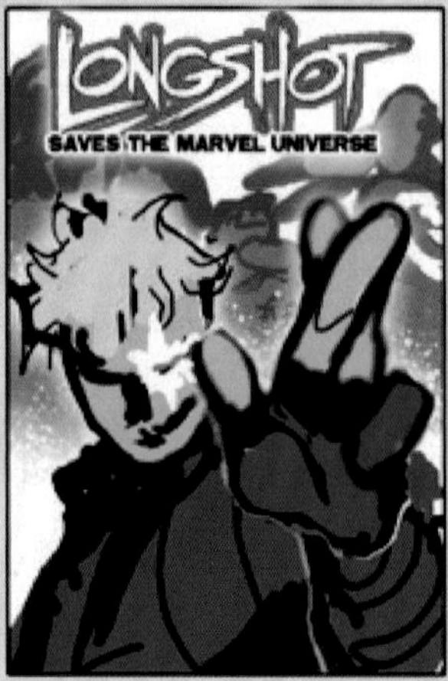
LONGSHOT
SAVES THE MARVEL UNIVERSE

H. ORIGINAL

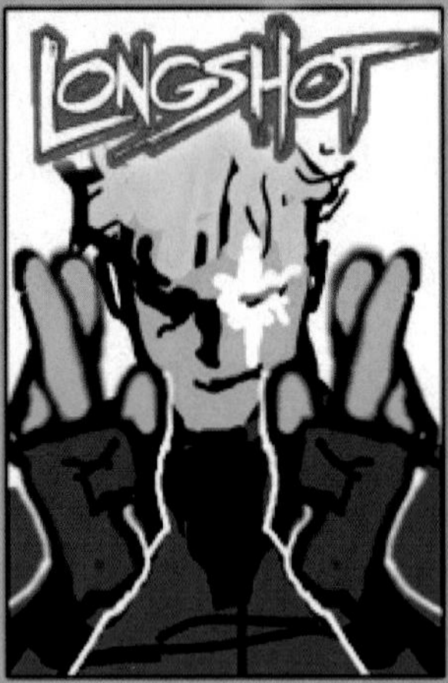
LONGSHOT

H2. w/ HEADS

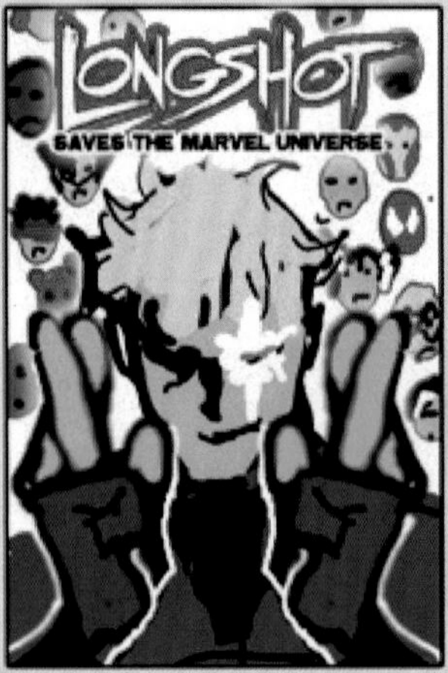
LONGSHOT
SAVES THE MARVEL UNIVERSE

H3. w/ BODIES

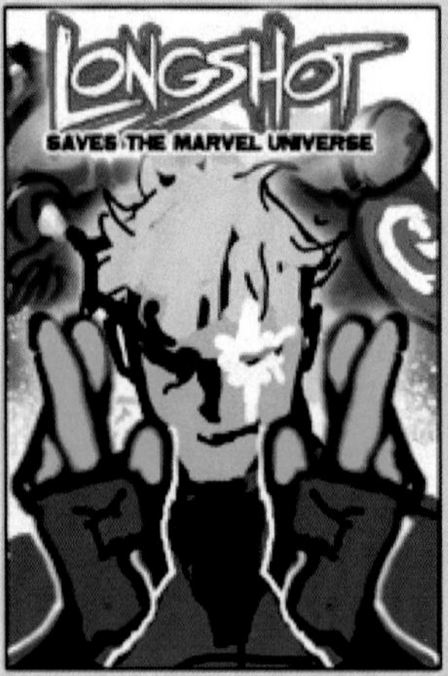
LONGSHOT
SAVES THE MARVEL UNIVERSE

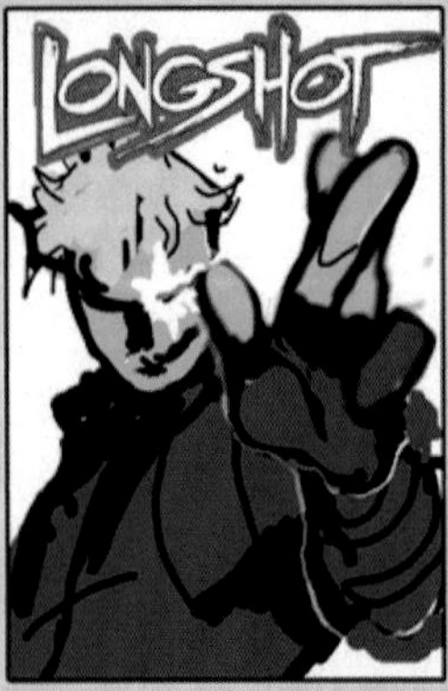
LONGSHOT

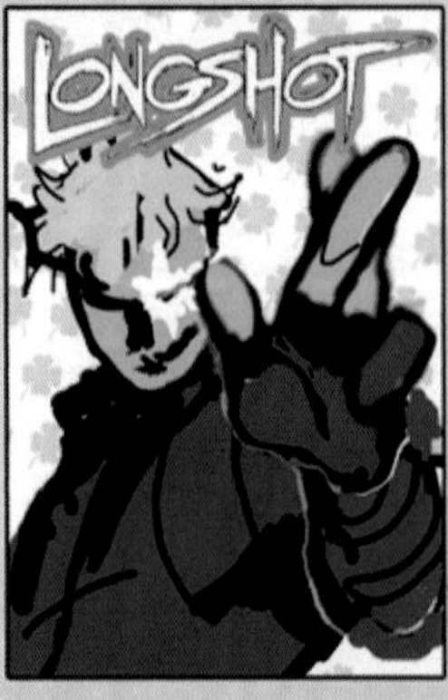
LONGSHOT

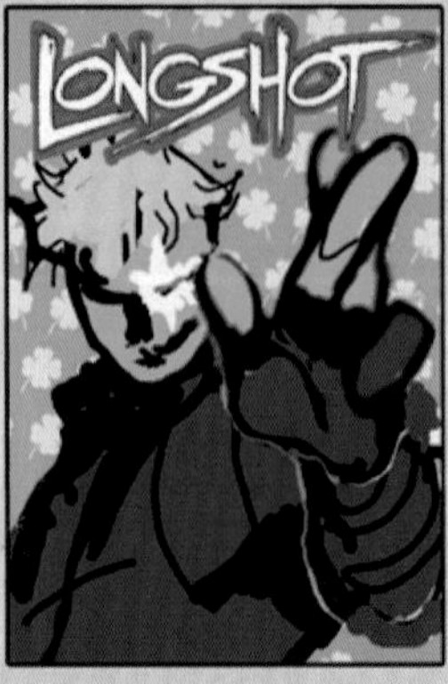
LONGSHOT

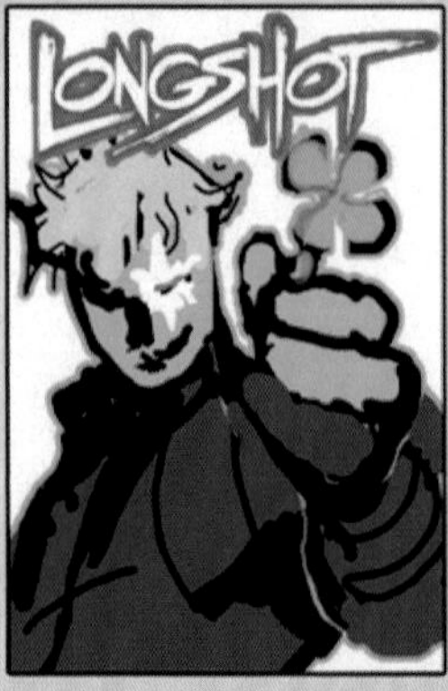
LONGSHOT

A. STANDING

B. ACTION

C. PIMPIN' w/dazzler

D. PIMPIN' w/ frame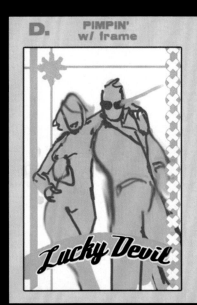

Lucky Devil

E. PIMPIN' w/ dazzler & scarlet witch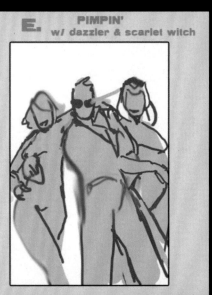

#2 COVER SKETCHES BY DAVID NAKAYAMA

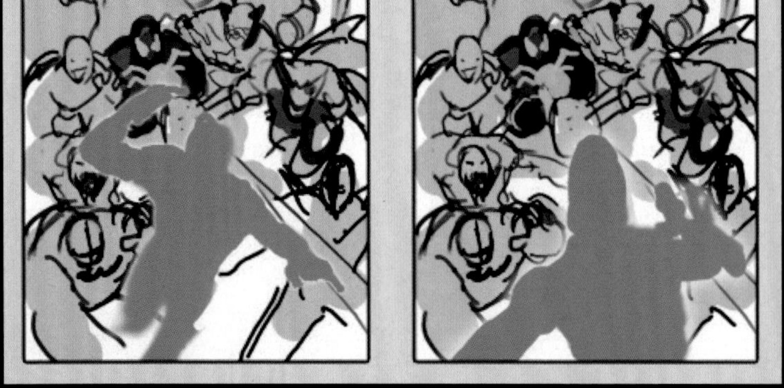

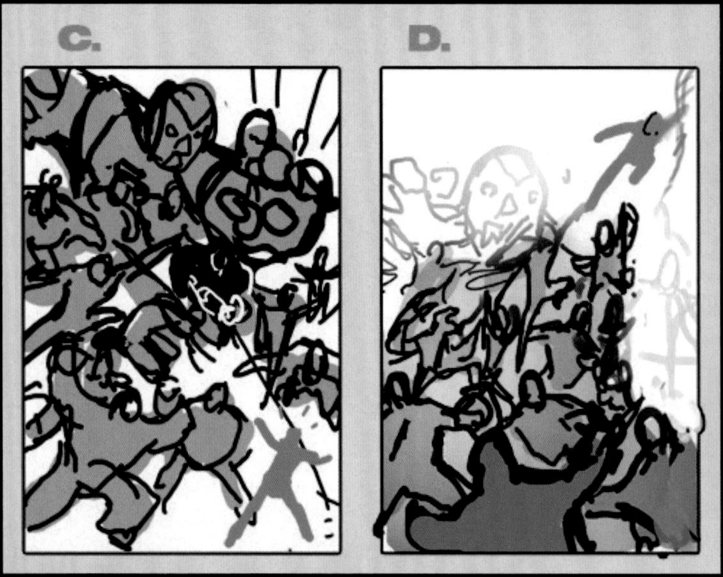
C.
D.

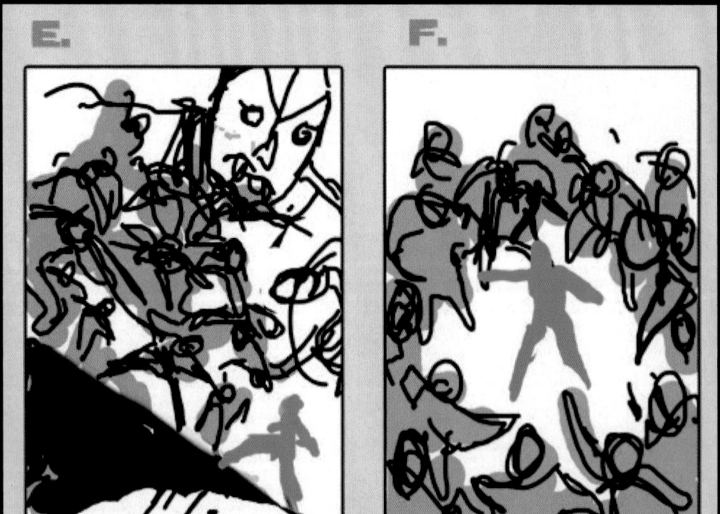
E.
F.

#3 COVER SKETCHES BY DAVID NAKAYAMA

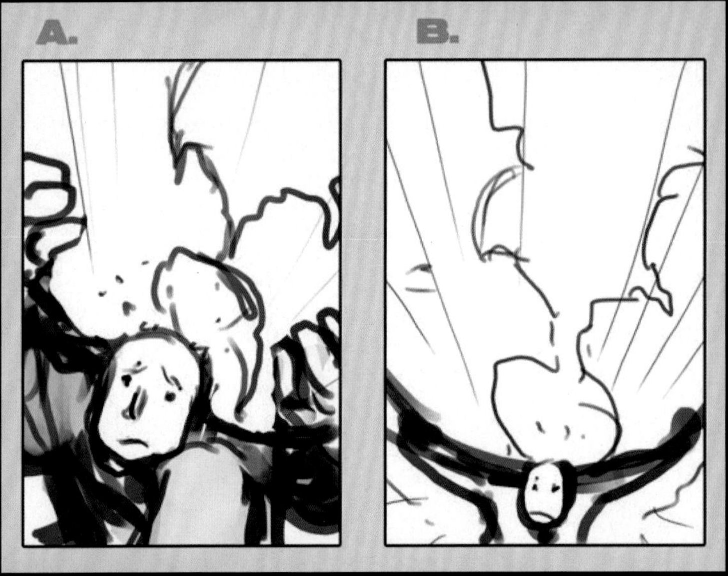
A.
B.

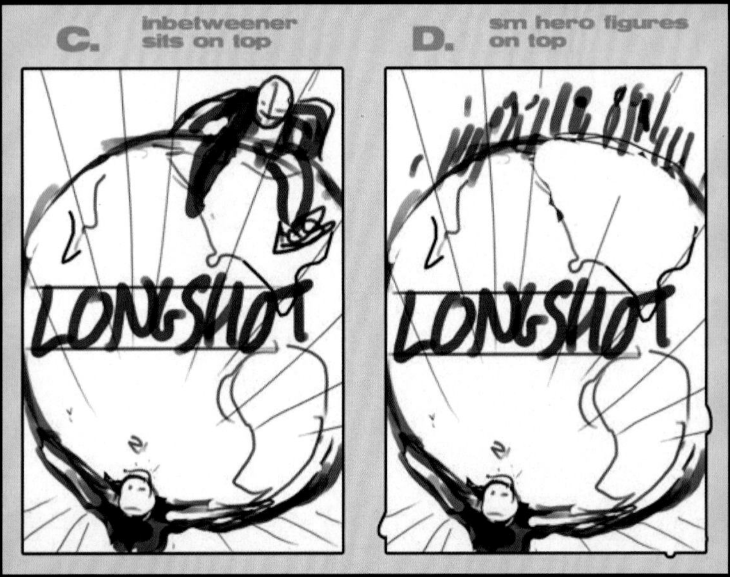
C.
inbetweener sits on top
LONGSHOT
D.
sm hero figures on top
LONGSHOT

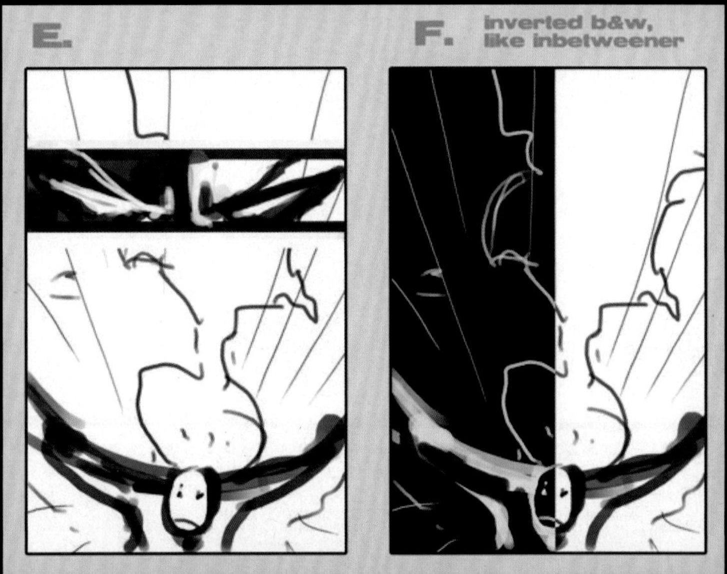
E.
F.
inverted b&w, like inbetweener

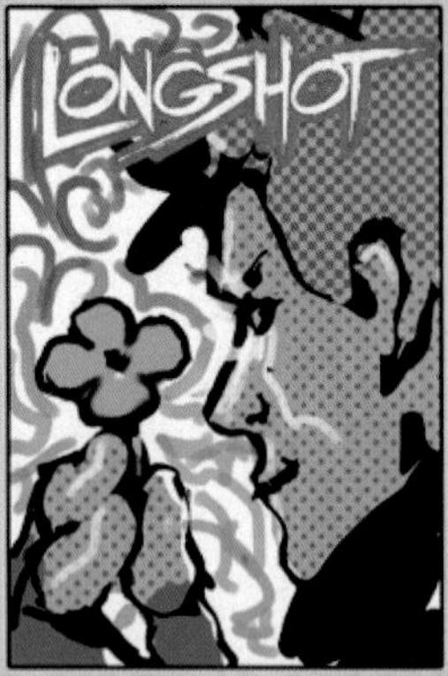
LONGSHOT

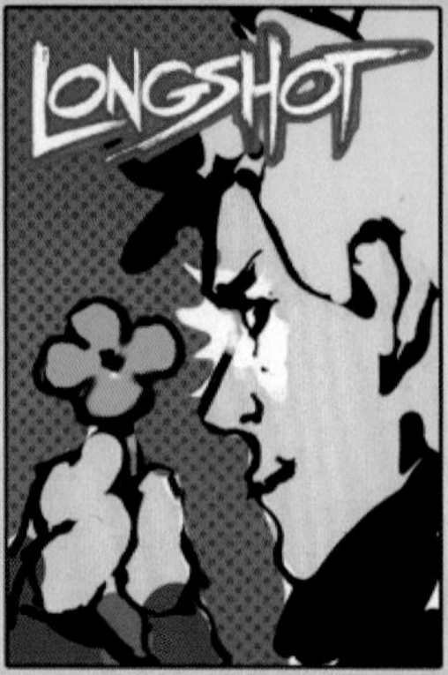
LONGSHOT

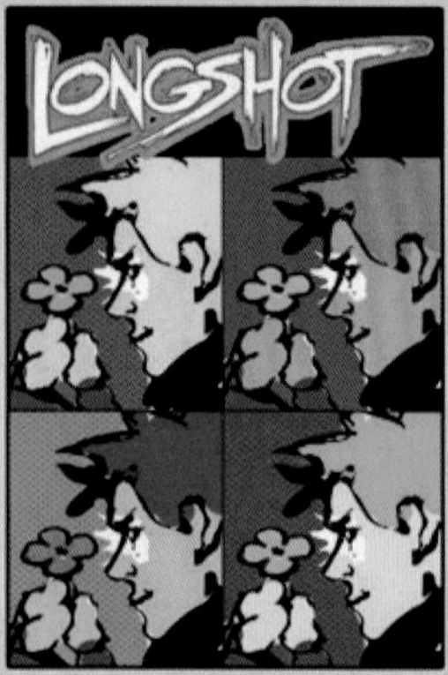
LONGSHOT

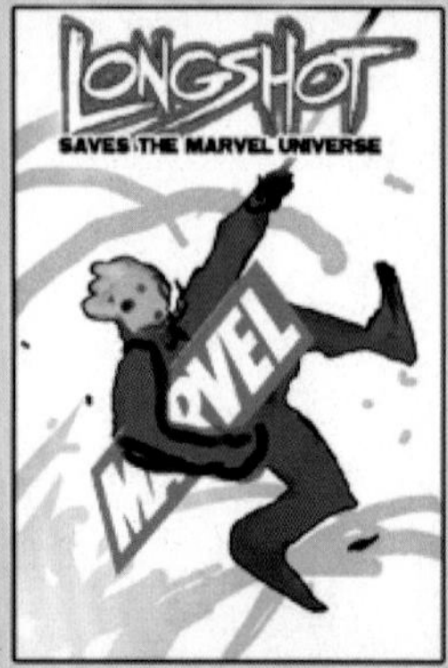
LONGSHOT
SAVES THE MARVEL UNIVERSE
MARVEL

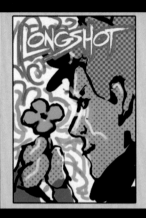

I. 'LUCKY CHARMS' stars

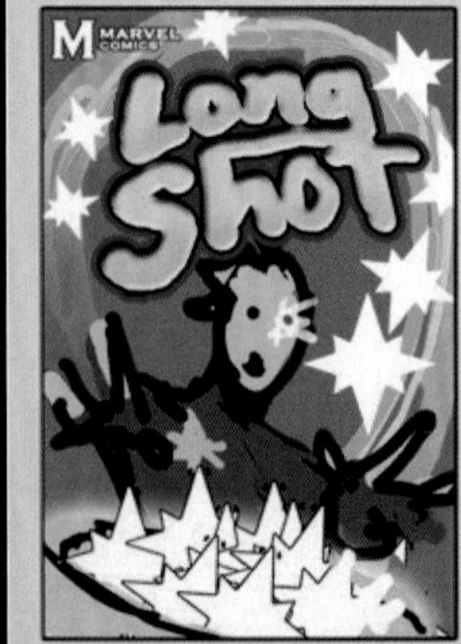
M MARVEL COMICS
Long Shot

J. 'LUCKY CHARMS' clovers

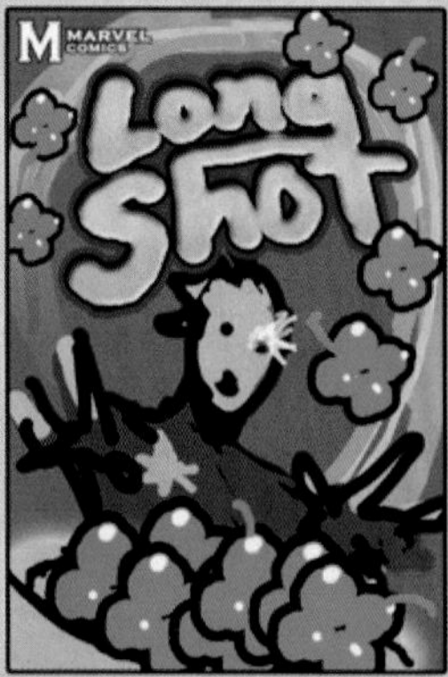
M MARVEL COMICS
Long Shot

K. 'VEGAS MOTIFs'

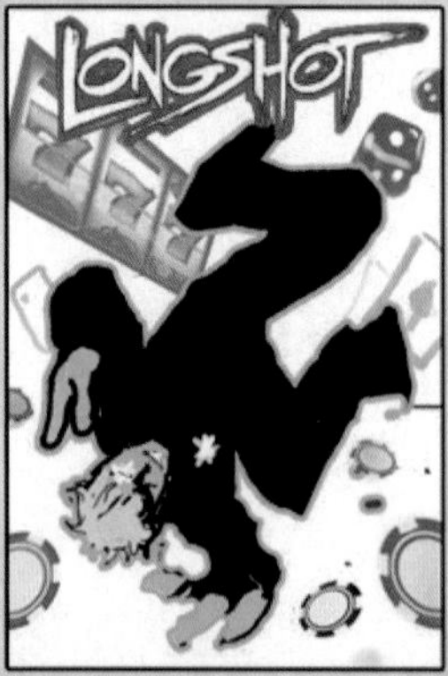
LONGSHOT

L. 'TRADITIONAL'

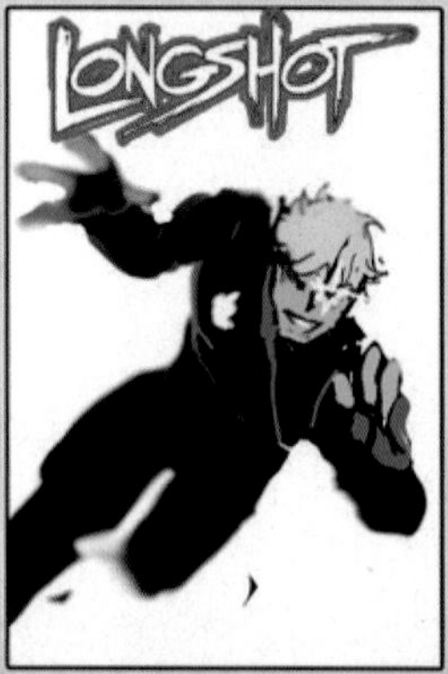
LONGSHOT

M. 'LONG ODDS'

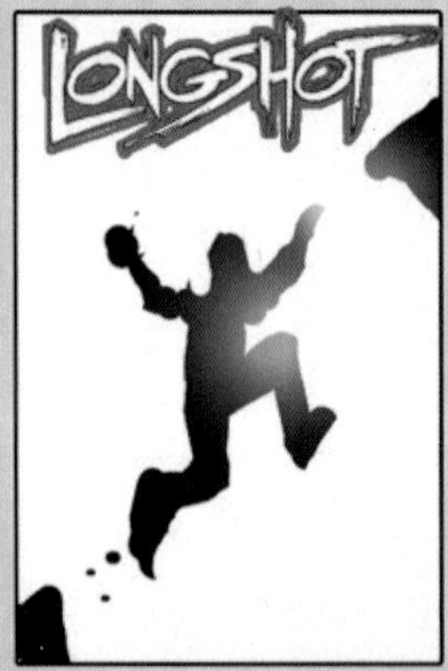
LONGSHOT

N. 'SUICIDE KING'

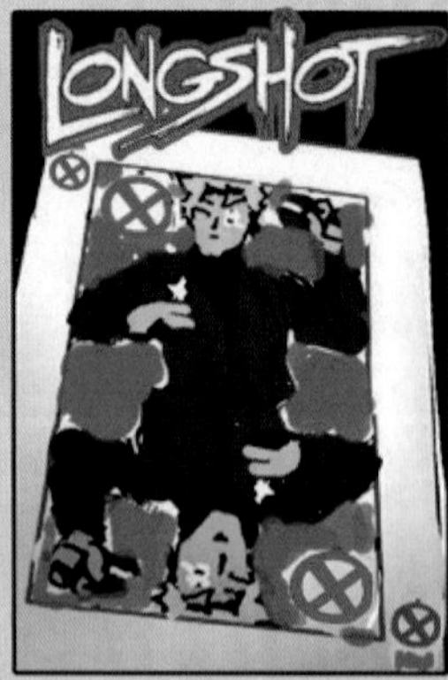
LONGSHOT

O. 'CARD RAIN'

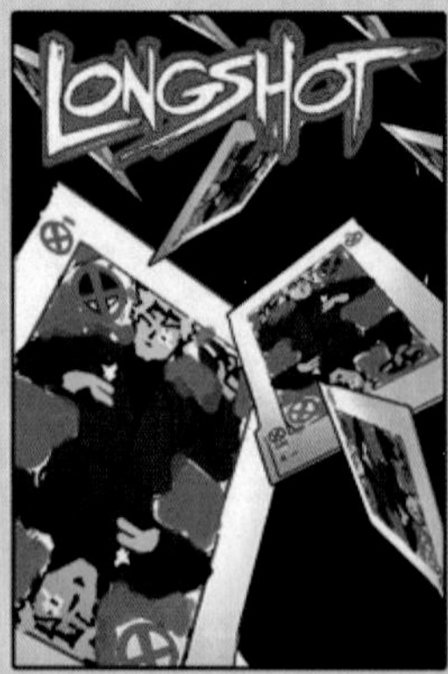
LONGSHOT

P. 'BLACKJACK'

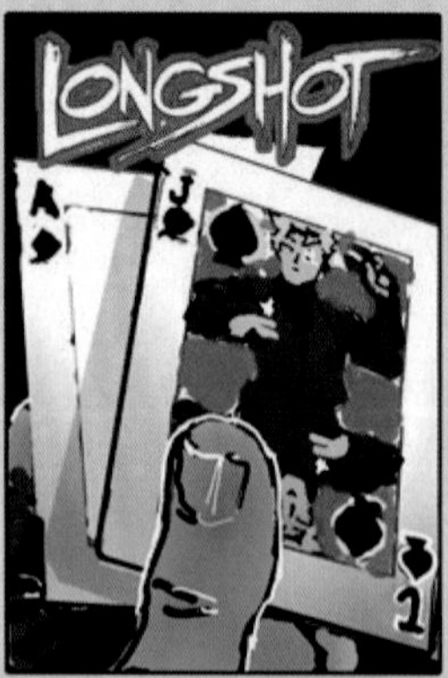
LONGSHOT